Coordinated Portfolio Investment Survey Guide

Second Edition

INTERNATIONAL MONETARY FUND

2002

Cataloging-in-Publication Data

Coordinated portfolio investment survey guide. – [2nd ed.] – [Washington, D.C. : International Monetary Fund, 2002].
p. cm.

Prepared by IMF Task Force on Coordinated Portfolio Investment Survey.
ISBN 1-58906-093-8

1. Securities. 2. Investments. I. IMF Task Force on Coordinated Portfolio Investment Survey. II. International Monetary Fund.
HG4521.C66 2002

Price: $26.00

Please send orders to:
International Monetary Fund, Publication Services
700 19th Street, N.W., Washington, D.C. 20431, U.S.A.
Tel.: (202) 623–7430 Telefax: (202) 623–7201
E-mail: publications@imf.org
Internet: http://www.imf.org

recycled paper

Contents

Tables

Figures

Preface

This second edition of the *Coordinated Portfolio Investment Survey Guide* is provided to assist national compilers in the conduct of the Coordinated Portfolio Investment Survey (CPIS). The CPIS is being conducted under the auspices of the IMF across a wide range of economies. The survey is conducted simultaneously by all participating economies, uses consistent definitions, and encourages best practices in data collection. The CPIS is thus a unique tool in capturing the world totals and the geographical distribution of the holdings of portfolio investment assets, thereby contributing to a better understanding of capital flows.

The CPIS was undertaken in response to concerns about imbalances and gaps in statistics on global capital flows. The idea of conducting the CPIS arose from a recommendation contained in the final *Report on the Measurement of International Capital Flows*, published in 1992, and has been carried forward by the IMF Committee on Balance of Payments Statistics (the IMF Committee). The first CPIS was conducted for year-end 1997 by 29 economies.

Since 1997, the economic importance of securities markets has continued to grow around the world and the need for better statistics has been further highlighted. In the light of the success of the first survey, the IMF Committee recommended that the CPIS be conducted for a second time, with a reference date of year-end 2001. All of the economies that participated in the 1997 CPIS will do so again in the 2001 CPIS and are expected to be joined by about another 35.

This second edition of the *Survey Guide* is the product of a Task Force that was set up by the national compilers of the 1997 CPIS to review the first survey and to prepare for its repetition. I would like to extend my thanks to all the Task Force members for their contributions, and in particular to the Chair, Gunnar Blomberg of the Riksbank, Sweden. An earlier draft was used as a basis for discussion among national compilers at five regional seminars conducted by the IMF's Statistics Department (STA) in early 2001.

The *Survey Guide* was drafted primarily by John Joisce of the Balance of Payments and External Debt Division I of STA, with major contributions from Task Force members, from other national compilers, and from Simon Quin, Robert Heath, Robert Dippelsman, Samuele Rosa, and Alice Lieberman, all of STA. Carmen Diaz-Zelaya and Maria Delia Araneta, also of STA, made valuable contributions to preparing the manuscript, and James McEuen, of the IMF's External Relations Department, edited the manuscript and coordinated publication. The authors drew heavily from the first edition of the *Survey Guide*.

Carol S. Carson
Director
Statistics Department
International Monetary Fund

IMF Task Force on the 2001 Coordinated Portfolio Investment Survey: Terms of Reference and Membership

Terms of Reference

1. To examine the results of the 1997 Coordinated Portfolio Investment Survey
2. To assess the effectiveness of the 1997 Coordinated Portfolio Investment Survey
3. To assess whether a repeat survey should be recommended to the IMF Committee on Balance of Payments Statistics.

Members

Chairman

Sweden	Mr. Gunnar Blomberg Sveriges Riksbank gunnar.blomberg@riksbank.se

Members

Argentina	Mr. Jorge Rodriguez[1] Ministry of Economy and Public Works and Services rodri@mecon.gov.ar
Australia	Mr. Michael Davies Australian Bureau of Statistics michael.davies@abs.gov.au
Austria	Mr. Michael Andreasch Austrian National Bank michael.andreasch@oenb.co.at
Belgium	Mr. Guido Melis National Bank of Belgium guido.melis@nbb.be
Canada	Mr. Eric Boulay Statistics Canada bouleri@statcan.ca
France	Mr. Dominique Rougès Banque de France dominique.rouges@banque-france.fr
Germany	Mrs. Helga Michalik-Ringenaldus Deutsche Bundesbank statistik-s1@bundesbank.de

[1]Mr. Rodriguez replaced Mr. Marcelo G. Dinenzon during the life of the Task Force.

Ireland	Mr. Michael Connolly Central Statistics Office michael.connolly@cso.ie
Israel	Mr. Balfour Ozer Bank of Israel bozer@bankisrael.gov.il
Italy	Mr. Francesco V. Loi Ufficio Italiano dei Cambi loi@uic.it
Japan	Ms. Junko Matsumi Bank of Japan junko.matsumi@boj.or.jp
	Mr. Yoshiaki Ando[2] Ministry of Finance yoshiaki.ando@mof.go.jp
Malaysia	Mrs. Rozainita Shamsudin[3] Bank Negara Malaysia roz@bnm.gov.my
	Mrs. Norhayati Sidi[3] Bank Negara Malaysia yatie@bnm.gov.my
Spain	Mr. Eduardo Rodríguez Tenés Banco de España bal.pagos@bde.es
United Kingdom	Mr. Simon Humphries[4] Office for National Statistics simon.humphries@ons.gov.uk
United States	Mr. William Griever Board of Governors of the Federal Reserve System William.l.griever@frb.gov
BIS	Mr. Denis Petre denis.petre@bis.org
	Ms. Melissa Fiorelli melissa.fiorelli@bis.org
ECB	Mr. Peter Neudorfer peter.neudorfer@ecb.int
OECD	Ms. Ayse Bertrand ayse.bertrand@oecd.org
IMF	Mr. Simon Quin squin@imf.org
	Mr. John Joisce jjoisce@imf.org

[2]Mr. Ando replaced Mr. Koichiro Hayashi during the life of the Task Force.
[3]Mrs. Shamsudin and Mrs. Sidi replaced Mr.Yeo Cheng Yan during the life of the Task Force.
[4]Mr. Humphries replaced Mr. Colin Yeend during the life of the Task Force.

Glossary

ABS	Australian Bureau of Statistics
ADR	American depository receipt
ALPS	Adjustable long-term putable security
ANNA	Association of National Numbering Agencies
B/A	Banker's acceptance
BDR	Bearer depository receipt
BIS	Bank for International Settlements
BPM5	IMF's *Balance of Payments Manual,* fifth edition (Washington: International Monetary Fund, 1993)
CD	Certificate of deposit
CFI	Classification of Financial Instruments
CMO	Collateralized mortgage obligation
CPIS	Coordinated Portfolio Investment Survey
CSO	Central Statistical Office (Ireland)
DL bond	Drop-lock bond
ECB	European Central Bank
ECP	Euro commercial paper
EMI	European Monetary Institute
EMTN	Euro medium-term note
EU	European Union
FECD	Federal Exchange Control Department (Israel)
FHLMC	Federal Home Loan Mortgage Corporation (United States)
FIPS	Foreign interest payment security
FNMA	Federal National Mortgage Association (United States)
FRN	Floating-rate note
FTD	*Financial Terminology Database*
GIAM	Global ISIN Access Mechanism
GNMA	Government National Mortgage Association (United States)
GUN	Grantor underwriting note
IAIM	Irish Association of Investment Managers
IBC	International business company
IFSC	International Financial Services Centre (Ireland)
IIP	International investment position
IMF	International Monetary Fund
IMF Committee	IMF Committee on Balance of Payments Statistics
IO	International organization
ISA	Israeli Securities Authority
ISIN	International Securities Identification Number
ISMA	International Securities Market Association
ISO	International Standards Organization
LEBA	London Eurodollar banker's acceptance
LIBID	London interbank bid rate
LIBOR	London interbank offered rate
LIMEAN	London interbank mean rate
LYON	Liquid yield option note
MBS	Mortgage-backed security

MNC	Multinational corporation
NIF	Note issuance facility
NNA	National numbering agency
NPISH	Nonprofit institution serving households
OECD	Organisation for Economic Co-operation and Development
OEIC	Open-ended investment company
OFC	Offshore financial center
ONB	Oesterreichische Nationalbank (Austria)
ONS	Office for National Statistics (United Kingdom)
PRN	Perpetual-rate note
RCB	Regional central bank
Repo	Repurchase agreement
RUF	Revolving underwriting facility
SEC	Securities and Exchange Commission (United States)
SEDOL	Stock Exchange Daily Official List (United Kingdom)
SEFER	Survey of Geographical Distribution of Securities Held as Foreign Exchange Reserves
SEIFiC	Small economy with an international financial center
SICAF	Société d'investissement à capital fixe
SICAV	Société d'investissement à capital variable
SII	Survey of International Investment (Australia)
SNA	System of National Accounts (EU, IMF, OECD, UN, and World Bank, *System of National Accounts 1993*; Brussels/Luxembourg, New York, Paris, and Washington, 1993)
SPE	Special purpose entity
SSIO	Survey of Geographical Distribution of Securities Held by International Organizations
STA	IMF Statistics Department
T-bill	Treasury bill
TPH	Third-party holdings
TRUF	Transferable revolving underwriting facility
UIC	Ufficio Italiano dei Cambio (Italy)
VRN	Variable-rate note

I. Introduction

This Survey Guide *has been prepared to assist countries to prepare for their participation in the Coordinated Portfolio Investment Survey (CPIS).*

I. Purpose of the CPIS

1.1 The purpose of the CPIS is to improve statistics of holdings of portfolio investment assets in the form of equity, long-term debt, and short-term debt. Specifically, the objectives are:

- to collect comprehensive information, with geographical detail on the country[1] of residence of the issuer, on the stock of cross-border equities, long-term bonds and notes, and short-term debt instruments for use in the compilation or improvement of international investment position (IIP) statistics on portfolio investment capital. The IIP statistics, in turn, can provide information to check the coverage of recorded estimates of portfolio investment financial flows and associated investment income transactions recorded in the balance of payments.
- to exchange the bilateral data. When the results of the CPIS become available, the data may be exchanged among the participating countries as well as with other countries. By exchanging comparable data (subject to confidentiality constraints), participating countries should be able to improve their statistics of nonresident holdings of their portfolio investment liabilities as well as associated financial flows and investment income data. (Information on the geographic distribution of nonresident creditors also becomes known.)

[1]The term "country," as used in this publication, does not in all cases refer to a territorial entity that is a state as understood by international law and practice; the term also covers some nonsovereign territorial entities.

II. Background

1.2 The CPIS is being undertaken in response to the recommendations contained in the *Report on the Measurement of International Capital Flows* (the Godeaux Report), which was published by the IMF in 1992. The report highlighted the increasing importance of portfolio investment across international borders, reflecting the liberalization of financial markets, financial innovation, and the changing behavior of investors. The increased liberalization of international flows, however, has brought measurement difficulties. These difficulties have been reflected in the imbalances at the worldwide level between recorded financial assets and liabilities, with higher flows usually being recorded for liabilities than for assets. Imbalances have generally increased since the publication of the Godeaux Report: between 1990 and 1998, recorded flows in portfolio investment liabilities at the global level exceeded those in portfolio investment assets by an accumulated $950 billion.

1.3 Concerned by these global imbalances and the associated discrepancies in income flows at the global level, the IMF Committee on Balance of Payments Statistics (the IMF Committee) decided in 1993 to promote the idea of an internationally coordinated benchmark survey of long-term portfolio investment holdings to facilitate cross-country comparisons, permit data exchanges, and encourage standardization and best practice. By undertaking a benchmark survey of holdings, it was hoped that many countries, for the first time, would be in a position to obtain a reasonable estimate of the outstanding balances, at market price, of the level of portfolio investment their residents held, rather than merely summing the balance of payments flows. In this manner, a more accurate estimate might be obtained that would reduce to some extent the imbalance at the global level.

1.4 Developing such data was also seen as a basis for future data exchange and possible substitution of asset for liability data, particularly on a bilateral basis.

- One of the problems in recording portfolio investment liabilities on a bilateral basis is that, for reasons of practicality, they are often not allocated to the country of residence of the acquirer of the claim. That is, the country of initial sale is recorded, but subsequent transactions with residents of other countries are frequently not recorded by the compilers in the country of residence of the issuer.
- Moreover, the transaction is frequently recorded with the country of residence of the broker rather than with the country of residence of the beneficial owner, which may be different from that of the broker. Consequently, if a security of country A is sold to a resident of country B, who in turn sells it to a resident of country C, balance of payments compilers in country A may not know that the second transaction has occurred. In addition, if the same security is subsequently sold by the resident in country C to a resident of country A, that, too, may not be recorded, and country A's external liabilities would be overstated.

1.5 As a result of these types of problems, the IMF organized the first internationally coordinated portfolio investment survey, using a common set of definitions and a common reference date. It was conducted as of the end of December 1997 (the 1997 CPIS). All major investing countries had been invited to participate in the 1997 CPIS. In the event, 29 countries[2] took part. The results were published by the IMF in December 1999.[3] The results are summarized in Table 1.1.

1.6 Following the publication of the results of the 1997 CPIS, the IMF published an analysis[4] that explores these results in depth.

III. The 1997 CPIS

1.7 Following the completion of the 1997 CPIS, the national compilers of the participating countries established the Coordinated Portfolio Investment Survey Task Force (the Task Force) to review the results, to examine to what extent the survey had met its goals, and, in the light of that assessment, to determine whether it should be repeated. The composition of the Task Force is shown at the front of this *Survey Guide.* The Task Force was convened in June 1999 and reported to the IMF Committee at its meetings in Santiago, Chile, in October 1999, and in Washington, D.C., in October 2000.

1.8 At the 1999 meeting, the Task Force reported that the 1997 CPIS had produced several benefits, including:

- demonstrating that an organized effort toward standardizing the scope, coverage, timing, definitions, and concepts used in the compilation of data could be successfully coordinated among a large number of countries;
- proving an effective vehicle for establishing and disseminating, on a worldwide basis, appropriately high methodological standards;
- giving higher visibility to the coordinated, cross-country approach and resulting in improved budgetary support for the reporting of data on portfolio investment;
- facilitating a greater understanding of country practices with respect to survey design and alternative approaches to data collection and encouraging exchanges of experience in these matters;
- increasing the confidence of countries in portfolio investment data;
- facilitating data exchange;
- encouraging awareness of the IMF's *Balance of Payments Manual,* fifth edition (Washington, 1993; *BPM5*), and promoting implementation of the methodology and standards presented therein; and
- facilitating the attribution of portfolio investment assets by country, although there were some difficulties relating to issuers resident in small economies with international financial centers.

1.9 The Task Force was of the view that the lessons of international financial crises of 1997 and 1998 reinforced the importance of the 1997 CPIS.

1.10 Notwithstanding the positive aspects of the 1997 CPIS, the size of the resulting global discrepancy (about $1.7 trillion, see Table 1.1) between measured outstanding portfolio investment assets and liabilities indicated that there were significant gaps in coverage, the possibility of overestimation of global portfolio investment liabilities, and other measurement problems. The main gaps in the coverage of the

---

[2]The countries were Argentina, Australia, Austria, Belgium, Bermuda, Canada, Chile, Denmark, Finland, France, Iceland, Indonesia, Ireland, Israel, Italy, Japan, Korea, Malaysia, the Netherlands, New Zealand, Norway, Portugal, Singapore, Spain, Sweden, Thailand, the United Kingdom, the United States, and Venezuela.

[3]See IMF, "Results of the 1997 Coordinated Portfolio Investment Survey," (Washington, 2000).

[4]See IMF, "Analysis of the 1997 CPIS: Results and Plans for the 2001 CPIS," (Washington, 2000).

Table 1.1: Global Portfolio Investment Assets and Liabilities (as of the end of December 1997)
(Trillions of U.S. dollars)

	Assets	Liabilities	Assets less Liabilities
(A)Estimate based on available IIP or cumulated BOP data	6.91	8.90	-1.99
(B)Revisions to basic estimate due to combined CPIS, IMF SEFER, international organizations, and information from the BIS	+0.75	+0.44	+0.31
Final estimate (A) + (B)	7.66	9.34	-1.68

(A) Shows global holdings of portfolio investment assets and liabilities compiled by summing across countries' international investment position (IIP) data and, in the absence of such sources for particular countries, by summing balance of payments flows, or a combination of the most recent IIP data plus accumulated flow data to the end of 1997.

(B) Shows the changes to the data in row A that result from using data from the 1997 CPIS, the international banking statistics system of the Bank for International Settlements (BIS), the results of the IMF Survey of the Geographical Distribution of Securities Held as Foreign Exchange Reserves (SEFER) that was conducted in conjunction with the 1997 CPIS, and data provided by major international organizations on their portfolio investment holdings.

1997 CPIS for portfolio investment assets were believed to comprise:

- the nonparticipation of some important investing countries for which alternative data sources proved inadequate;
- the nonparticipation of a number of countries with offshore financial centers (OFCs; in this *Survey Guide,* the preferred term for these jurisdictions is *small economy with an international financial center,* or SEIFiCs) for which there were no alternative data sources;[5] and
- difficulties faced by many participating countries in capturing cross-border portfolio investment by households (and in some cases, enterprises) that do not use the services of resident custodians.

1.11 Given the underlying reasons for undertaking the CPIS in the first place—global imbalances in financial flows and stocks—the Task Force felt that the results of the 1997 CPIS were an encouraging first step. In light of the positive aspects of the 1997 CPIS and the potential room for improvements, the Task Force recommended to the IMF Committee that the CPIS be repeated, with the reference date of the end of December 2001 (2001 CPIS), and that it be undertaken on a regular basis thereafter. The IMF Committee agreed to the recommendation to conduct the 2001 CPIS and was inclined to support conducting the survey on an annual basis thereafter.

IV. The 2001 CPIS

1.12 It was decided to include cross-border portfolio investment holdings of each of the following items in the 2001 CPIS, on a "mandatory" basis:

- equity securities;
- long-term debt securities; and
- short-term debt securities;
- by country of residence of issuer.[6]

1.13 In addition, it was decided to include the following "encouraged" categories for all countries in a position to provide the data:

- portfolio investment liabilities—equity securities, long-term debt securities, and short-term debt securities (each broken down by country of residence of issuer).[7] The designation of these liabilities as "encouraged" reflected the predominant view that existing collection systems are unlikely to produce a reliable breakdown of portfolio liabilities by country of foreign holder. It was, however, judged useful to compare with partner countries' holdings to determine the size of the discrepancies;
- institutional sector of the holder, as a further disaggregation of the instrument by country of residence of the issuer; and

[5]From a statistical perspective, a SEIFiC may be characterized in terms of the size of its transactions and positions on both sides of the balance sheet with the rest of the world in relation to the size of the domestic economy. From a statistical point of view, SEIFiCs can be characterized as jurisdictions that have financial institutions engaged primarily in business with nonresidents and having financial systems (i) with external assets and liabilities out of proportion to domestic financial intermediation designed to finance domestic economies and (ii) where enterprises owned or controlled by nonresidents play a significant role in providing financial services to nonresidents.

[6]Only equity and long-term debt securities were "mandatory" items in the 1997 CPIS. Short-term debt was a "nonmandatory" item.

[7]These were "nonmandatory" items in the 1997 CPIS.

- currency breakdown of all securities for assets (equities, long-term debt, and short-term debt) in aggregate (i.e., not by counterpart country). Even though it is not directly relevant for the CPIS in constructing a portfolio of assets by counterparty of issuer, the currency breakdown would provide important additional information for the analysis of a country's balance of payments flows and reconciliation with its IIP. The Task Force considered that to include a full currency breakdown within the CPIS framework (i.e., by instrument by country of issuer[8]) would add materially to the collection costs and would make the resulting matrix of data too big to manage or understand.

1.14 To ensure an improved coverage in the 2001 CPIS, the IMF Committee recommended that an effort be made to encourage new participants among major investing countries and SEIFiCs. In addition, a broader participation by countries on a regional basis should be encouraged to ensure a wider application of best practice.

1.15 The IMF Committee recommended that participating countries also supply a geographical breakdown of the value of securities holdings that are included in reserve assets. Accordingly, the Survey of the Geographical Distribution of Securities Held as Foreign Exchange Reserves (SEFER) is being held in parallel with the 2001 CPIS.

[8]And by sector of holder if that encouraged item were also compiled.

1.16 The IMF Committee also recommended that a survey be conducted of large international organizations, the Survey of Geographical Distribution of Securities Held by International Organizations (SSIO), in order to obtain the value of their holdings of securities.

1.17 As with the 1997 SEFER, in order to maintain confidentiality of individual returns, special procedures will be used by the IMF to collect the data from these two surveys. Similarly, data from these two surveys will be published only in aggregated form so that no country's or organization's data will be identifiable. The SEFER and SSIO are discussed further in Chapter 2.

V. Organization of the *Survey Guide*

1.18 The *Survey Guide* is divided as follows. After this introduction, Chapter 2 outlines the scope and modalities of the CPIS; Chapter 3 sets out the concepts and principles; Chapter 4 describes various collection strategies; Chapter 5 describes other practical matters; and Chapter 6 reviews country experiences in conducting the 1997 CPIS. There are several appendices that provide model report forms, definitions and descriptions of instruments, and the International Securities Identification Number (ISIN) code system.

2. Scope and Modalities

This chapter sets out the scope and modalities of the CPIS, SEFER, and SSIO.

I. Scope of the CPIS

A. Participation

2.1 All countries are welcome to participate. The IMF has invited the participants of the 1997 CPIS; 41 other major investing countries that were invited on the basis of the size of reported portfolio investment in their IIPs or balance of payments statistics; and 16 SEIFiCs (in addition to Bermuda, which participated in the 1997 CPIS). Other IMF members have been advised of the 2001 CPIS and are welcome to participate if they wish.

2.2 Each participating country will conduct its own national survey at the **reference date of end-December 2001.**[9] To meet the objectives set by the IMF Committee, each national survey must incorporate certain mandatory features. These mandatory features constitute the framework for the conduct of the CPIS and are incorporated in the model survey forms contained in Appendices I–V. Because the model forms meet the objectives of the CPIS, they may be used to conduct the national survey.[10]

B. Mandatory Items

(i) Date

2.3 The national survey is to be conducted in respect of portfolio investment positions as at close of business, December 31, 2001.

(ii) Assets

2.4 The national survey must cover portfolio investment assets of domestic residents; that is, securities issued by nonresidents and owned by residents[11]—outward investment.

(iii) Type of securities

2.5 The national survey must cover equity securities, debt securities with an original maturity of over one year (long-term), and debt securities with an original maturity of one year or less (short-term) issued by nonresidents and owned by residents of the compiling economy. Equity securities must be reported **separately** from debt securities, and short-term debt instruments should be reported separately from long-term debt instruments. These categories of securities are more fully defined in Chapter XIX of the *BPM5* and in Appendix VI of this *Survey Guide.* Note that the inclusion of short-term debt instruments as a mandatory requirement is a change from the 1997 CPIS, when short-term instruments were not mandatory. Table 3.1 indicates the range of instruments covered by the participants in the 1997 CPIS.

2.6 Unlike the 1997 CPIS, financial derivatives are **not** included in the 2001 CPIS. The three major reasons for this are as follows:

- In the 1997 CPIS, of the 29 countries that participated, only 2 provided any results, and there is the possibility that for the 2001 CPIS, at least, additional information may not be forthcoming.

[9]Where reference is made in this *Survey Guide* to the 2001 CPIS, it should be taken to cover any future CPIS as well, until such time that this *Survey Guide* is superseded.

[10]The forms are not mandatory: they are proposals that countries may use in their entirety, in part or not at all, depending on the situation in each participant's own country. The forms are drawn from the countries with experience in conducting similar surveys.

[11]*Residence* is an important concept in the CPIS and should not be confused with nationality. The economy in which an entity has its center of economic interest is where it resides. Residents need not be nationals of the economy in which they are located. The country of legal incorporation—or in the absence of legal incorporation, legal domicile—is one practical method of determining residence of corporate entities. See Chapter 3, Section III, for further discussion on residence.

- At the time of the 1997 CPIS, financial derivatives were included in *portfolio investment;* since then a new functional category, *financial derivatives,* has been created in *BPM5.*[12] Consequently, as the CPIS is a survey of portfolio investment, financial derivatives do not qualify.
- The IMF Committee felt that it was important to keep the survey to a single, discrete undertaking. For the same reason, direct investment and other investment were excluded.

(iv) Country breakdown

2.7 To enable data exchange, a full geographic attribution of securities issued by nonresidents and owned by residents is a necessary feature of the CPIS. In other words, securities are to be allocated geographically by the country of residence of the issuer, by type of security. In some instances, to reduce respondent burden, a threshold of holdings may be used so that any holdings below that threshold need not be reported separately.

2.8 The country breakdown is to be based on the International Standards Organization (ISO) code 3166. Securities issued by international organizations (IOs) are **not** to be allocated to the country in which the IO is located but rather to a separate IO category. Guidance on geographic attribution is provided in Chapter 3; the model survey forms in Appendices I–V contain the ISO country breakdown.

(v) Methodology

2.9 The concepts and principles underlying the CPIS conform with those contained in *BPM5.* The most important of these, for the conduct of the CPIS, are discussed in Chapter 3 of this *Survey Guide.* When compilers apply the concepts and principles to their surveys, practical reporting issues will arise for which consistent treatment across countries is required. Guidance is provided in Chapter 4. It is important for purposes of data exchange that methodology be applied as consistently as possible across countries.

C. Encouraged Items

2.10 Several elements of the survey are not considered mandatory; countries are encouraged to report these elements if they want to extend the scope of the national survey beyond the mandatory requirements of the CPIS, although, in doing so, the compilers would increase the complexity of the exercise. Hence, it is important that national compilers consider the objectives and scope of their national survey at the outset. Some of these elements are different from encouraged items for the 1997 CPIS.

(i) Liabilities

2.11 Compilers might consider extending the national survey to include securities issued by residents and owned by nonresidents (that is, portfolio investment liabilities of residents—inward investment). The national survey would then cover both outward and inward investment. Compilers could compare the data from the inward survey with that received from the data exchange. However, it is recognized that collecting geographic data on liabilities on the correct basis—the *debtor/creditor* principle—may not be possible. Frequently, countries can only collect information on a *transactor* basis. The *debtor/creditor* principle will attribute the liability to the correct country of holder whereas the data collected on the *transactor* basis are likely to record the country of residence of the first party to acquire the security. Any subsequent trading between nonresidents will not be recorded because the national compiling system may not be capable of obtaining this information. Nonetheless, the comparison may still be useful to indicate the nature and size of discrepancies resulting from the two approaches.

(ii) Currency breakdown

2.12 The national survey could be extended to include a currency breakdown of securities (by type of instrument, not by counterpart country) issued by nonresidents and owned by domestic residents. This provides compilers with more scope to verify income data using position data because the yields calculated will be more accurate if they are computed by currency. However, for countries that do not have or cannot make use of a securities database, or which are collecting data on an aggregate basis (versus a security-by-security approach), it may not be possible to obtain such additional information without substantial additional cost and increased respondent burden.

(iii) Sectoral breakdown

2.13 National compilers may want to identify in their national survey the economic sector of domestic investors: for instance, collective investment schemes

[12] See IMF, *Financial Derivatives: Supplement to the Fifth Edition of the Balance of Payments Manual* (Washington, 2000).

(mutual funds, unit trusts), pension funds, and insurance companies. This would provide analytically useful information. However, the information may be impractical to collect where custodians are the primary source of information. The sectoral breakdown is explored further in Chapter 3.

II. Modalities of the CPIS

2.14 Because a considerable degree of complexity is involved in organizing a portfolio investment survey—no matter which approach is taken—compilers undertaking the survey for the first time are strongly recommended to undertake initial investigations with financial market participants before deciding which approach to take. This issue is discussed in Chapter 4.

2.15 In determining the approach to take, national compilers must focus on two key issues: whom to survey (**coverage**) and the **degree of detail** to request. This will determine the collection methods to use. Guidance on how to make these important decisions is provided in Chapter 4, drawing on practical experiences of countries involved in previous surveys of portfolio investment. Chapter 5 guides compilers on some of the other practical applications and Chapter 6 presents some of the practical experiences countries had compiling the 1997 CPIS. Appendices I–V provide model survey forms.

A. Coverage

2.16 National compilers will have to investigate how to achieve comprehensive coverage of resident investment in securities issued by unrelated nonresidents. They should be mindful that the population of investors is not necessarily the population to be surveyed. Decisions will have to be made on which entities should be surveyed. The possibilities are

- primarily **end-investors** (e.g., banks, security dealers, pension funds, insurance companies, mutual funds, nonfinancial corporations, households);
- primarily **custodians,** who hold or manage securities on behalf of others; and
- a **combination of end-investors** and **custodians.**[13]

2.17 The advantages and disadvantages of each approach are explained in Chapter 4. No matter which approach is taken, it is important that national compilers have a degree of understanding of the relationship between domestic investors and survey respondents, so as to avoid undercounting or double counting.

B. Degree of Detailed Information

2.18 The data required to meet the objectives of the CPIS can be collected through either a **security-by-security approach**—where survey respondents provide information on each holding of securities issued by nonresidents owned by individual instrument held—or an **aggregated approach**—where securities issued by nonresidents owned are reported by survey respondents in aggregate for each counterpart country, in a common (usually domestic) currency.

2.19 The advantages and disadvantages of the two approaches are given in detail in Chapter 4. Whichever approach is taken, it is important that good control checks be established in order to ensure high-quality data (see also Chapters 5 and 6).

C. Other Modalities

2.20 Considerable other preparation is required for a portfolio investment survey: namely, establishing a timetable, taking account of legal and confidentiality considerations, developing a mailing list of survey respondents, choosing and developing computer software to process the data provided, and maintaining quality-control checks. Chapter 5 provides guidance on these modalities.

D. Network of National Compilers

2.21 The Task Force recognized that national compilers, as they prepare for their national survey, might require advice in addition to that provided in this *Survey Guide.* To assist national compilers, a network of contacts has been established, designating compilers with considerable expertise in conducting portfolio investment surveys. This network will be coordinated by the IMF. National compilers who require advice can contact any of the members of the IMF Task Force on the 2001 Coordinated Portfolio Investment Survey, shown at the front of this document, or:

Task Force on the 2001 Coordinated Portfolio Investment Survey
Balance of Payments and External Debt Division I
Statistics Department

[13]An alternative approach is to survey investment managers. Operating within specific contractual guidelines, and in return for the payment of a fee, investment managers buy and sell securities on behalf of their clients to maximize the goals set out under the contract. The investment managers do not take these assets on to their own balance sheets. Surveying investment managers is complex, and this approach is recommended only when compilers have experience in conducting such surveys. For countries interested in exploring this approach further, a discussion of the advantages and disadvantages is presented in Chapter 4, Section II.C.

International Monetary Fund
700 19th Street, N.W.
Washington, D.C. 20431
U.S.A.
Telephone number: (202) 623-7930
Facsimile number: (202) 623-6033
E-mail address: cpis@imf.org

E. Data Exchange

2.22 After the survey data have been collected, validated, compiled, and checked for quality, national compilers will supply them to the IMF, which will facilitate exchange of data among countries. Data can be denominated either in domestic currency or in U.S. dollars (countries will be asked to indicate which has been used). Details regarding data exchange are not included in this *Survey Guide,* but will be finalized before the reference date of end-December 2001. To help ensure international comparability and for future reference, each country will be required to provide documentation—for instance, survey forms or metadata (describing the coverage, approach, collection methods, computer systems, etc.)—to the IMF on how it conducted the survey, in the same fashion as was done with the Country Implementation Reports for the 1997 CPIS.[14] An understanding of the survey procedures and of the overall coverage and reliability is important, not only for users of the data, but also because counterpart countries may wish to use the data in constructing their liability positions. Providing as much detail as possible is essential for that assessment, and countries will be encouraged to be as comprehensive as possible. Moreover, to the extent that there may be data exchange bilaterally, any particular elements of the data that may affect any particular counterpart country should be identified. Data exchange has strong potential benefits between two countries, but each country must be able to provide the other country with additional information—while, at the same time, being able to ensure that any confidentiality concerns are adequately addressed.

F. Timeliness

2.23 It is intended that the results from the 2001 survey be provided to the IMF by the end of September 2002 at the latest. If final data are not available by that date, preliminary estimates will be acceptable. It is expected that the results of the survey, in conjunction with results from SEFER, will be published by the IMF by the end of 2002 or early in 2003. Subsequent surveys will follow the same timeliness.

[14]Country Implementation Reports were prepared by all the participating countries in the 1997 CPIS. These reports provided their metadata, indicating what was covered (the institutional units), the approach(es) taken (aggregate, security-by-security, end-investor, custodian, a combination of these), how nonresponse was addressed, the computer systems used, and similar elements of the survey that are important to understand quality dimensions.

III. Modalities of the SEFER

2.24 SEFER is a survey of the geographical breakdown of holdings of securities held as part of reserve assets. It is related to the CPIS in that it uses the same concepts and definitions and is necessary to give a comprehensive view of securities markets and portfolio investment. However, different collection, processing, and publication procedures are used.

2.25 One of the main objectives of the CPIS is to reconcile portfolio investment asset and liability positions. Although the foreign securities component of reserve assets appear under a separate heading from portfolio investment in *BPM5,* securities held as part of reserve assets are part of the portfolio investment liabilities of the issuers. From the perspective of the issuer, securities that are held as reserve assets are indistinguishable from those held in *portfolio investment.* Moreover, securities held as part of reserve assets make an important contribution to securities markets that should not be ignored. Consequently, for the CPIS project, it is necessary to cover portfolio investment and reserve assets in an integrated way for a comprehensive reconciliation of portfolio investment asset and liability positions.

2.26 One problem in collecting data on the geographical breakdown of securities issued by nonresidents and held as part of a country's reserve assets is that some monetary authorities do not wish to release these data publicly. Since data relating to individual countries' reserve holdings are not required for the CPIS project, reserve assets data can be included in other aggregates. For the 1997 project, two options were used. For some countries, data on holdings of securities held as part of reserve assets were collected by the IMF through SEFER. The data were provided to the IMF on a confidential basis, and were published only in totals together with data on the holdings of portfolio investment of selected large IOs. However, some other countries reported CPIS data total securities holdings that included both portfolio investment and reserve assets, rather than through SEFER. Because of these two treatments used for the 1997 CPIS, it was not possible to make a proper comparison between and among countries with respect to their comparative share of assets held as part of *portfolio investment.* **Accordingly, to avoid this lack of comparability in the 2001 results, all countries will be asked to report CPIS data that exclude reserve asset holdings and to report asset holdings data separately through SEFER.**

2.27 Data reported for the SEFER survey will be treated in a confidential manner. Data reported for SEFER will be handled separately by a small number of IMF staff using secure procedures to ensure confidentiality. Transmission of data will be adequately protected by the confidential classification. The set of guidelines governing the security of information entrusted to the IMF on a confidential basis ensures that necessary and sufficient levels of protection against unauthorized access and disclosure are afforded to all sensitive information. The results of SEFER will be published in aggregate form only. These aggregates will comprise the securities holdings within *reserve assets* of all countries reporting for SEFER, plus the portfolio investment holdings of the international organizations (for which see below, "Modalities of the SSIO"). If any aggregated component is dominated by the holdings of a single or small number of reporters, it will not be published.

2.28 Those countries that wish to publish the geographical breakdown of their securities holdings within *reserve assets* are free to do so. However, to ensure international consistency within the CPIS, they should be prepared to supply to the IMF CPIS data (excluding reserves) and the reserves data separately for inclusion in SEFER results.

2.29 Data reported under SEFER will be aggregated and will be included in the CPIS publication. Therefore, the SEFER data will need to be reported to the IMF in a timely fashion for inclusion with the CPIS published results. It is proposed that all the data from the SEFER will be reported to the IMF by June 28, 2002.

IV. Modalities of the SSIO

2.30 The Survey of Geographical Distribution of Securities Held by International Organizations (SSIO) is a survey of international organizations that are understood to have significant holdings of securities. The survey will be conducted by the IMF on a confidential basis and is designed to obtain the value of these organizations' holdings of securities on a country by country basis. The data will be combined with those from SEFER, and will be published as a single vector, so that no one organization's holdings will be identifiable. It is proposed that all the data from SSIO will be reported to the IMF by June 28, 2002.

2.31 For the purposes of the CPIS, the balance of payments, and the international investment position, pension funds of IOs are treated as residents of the countries in which the international organizations are resident. Consequently, these holdings should be excluded from the SSIO. For further discussion of IOs, see Chapter 3, Section III.C, International organizations and regional central banks, paragraphs 3.28 through 3.32, of this *Survey Guide.*

3. Concepts and Principles

Although the manner in which the national survey is to be conducted is left to the national compiler, the concepts and principles underlying the national survey are to be applied in conformity with BPM5. *To assist compilers in meeting this task, the Task Force identified the following areas where practical guidance is required:*

- *nomenclature,*
- *country attribution/residence,*
- *valuation,*
- *distinction between direct and portfolio investment, and*
- *securities where there is a potential to double-count.*

I. Guidance to Compilers

3.1 The concepts and principles underlying the CPIS are those contained in *BPM5.* As national compilers apply these concepts and principles, some reporting issues may arise: these practical dimensions are addressed in Chapter 4. In addition, to guide compilers, in 1995 the IMF published the *Balance of Payments Compilation Guide,* which describes how the conceptual framework in *BPM5* can be implemented in practice.

II. Nomenclature

3.2 As discussed in Chapter 2, the CPIS is concerned with collecting information on equity securities and on long-term and short-term debt securities issued by nonresidents and owned by residents. *BPM5* defines these securities in Chapter XIX, paragraphs 388 and 390, and discusses the methodological treatment of selected instruments in paragraphs 395 through 408 (see also Appendix VI to this *Survey Guide*).

3.3 Nonetheless, financial markets continually evolve. Consequently, national compilers face changing classification or valuation or other balance of payments accounting problems.

3.4 To provide national compilers in the European Union (EU) with a reference tool and to encourage a consistent approach in classifying financial instruments, the Bank of England, in response to a request from the European Monetary Institute (EMI), the forerunner of the European Central Bank (ECB), created the *Financial Terminology Database*[15] (*FTD*). The database provides the economic rationale and the balance of payments treatment for each financial instrument listed. Where appropriate, the relevant *BPM5* reference is provided; if the instrument is not directly covered in *BPM5,* a treatment in line with the IMF methodology is proposed by the Bank of England.

3.5 For the CPIS, national compilers should endeavor to use the methodology of *BPM5* to classify financial instruments; however, if compilers desire further guidance, they may find the *FTD* a valuable reference. It covers, among other things, various types of equity and long-term and short-term debt instruments.

III. Country Attribution and Residence

3.6 A principal requirement of participation in the CPIS is the provision of a country attribution of residents' investment in securities issued by nonresidents. This requires identification of the residence of the issuer of the security and of the holder of the security so that bilateral information can be exchanged. This section addresses the issues raised by this requirement.

[15] See Bank of England, *Financial Terminology Database* (London, 1997).

3.7 The concept of residence required for the CPIS is in line with that in the *System of National Accounts 1993* (*1993 SNA*)[16] and in *BPM5*. Thus, the economic territory of a country is the basis upon which residence is determined. It includes the geographic territory administered by a government, territorial enclaves, and free zones and bonded warehouses operated by offshore enterprises under customs control. These principles have been applied to SEIFiCs so that they are treated as resident in the economic territory of which they are a part, regardless of their treatment under local exchange control, tax, or employment regulations.[17] Apart from being consistent with the concept of residence recommended in the *1993 SNA* and in *BPM5*, this treatment is critical to ensure consistency in applying a common principle of residence across territories.

3.8 Both the *1993 SNA* and *BPM5* define the residence of units in terms of their center of interest. The application of this concept to individuals and enterprises for the purposes of the CPIS is the same as in the SNA and *BPM5*.[18] Both the *1993 SNA* and *BPM5* recommend that offshore enterprises (which may be engaged in manufacture, trade, and financial services) be treated as resident in the economy in which they are located.[19] *BPM5* gives particular attention to the residence and classification of special purpose entities (SPEs) as direct investment enterprises.[20] SPEs are commonly engaged in providing financial services.

3.9 For the CPIS it is necessary to provide further clarification of the treatment of so-called "brass-plate" companies, "international business companies" (IBCs), "shell companies," and special purpose entities (SPEs) that may have a limited physical presence in the economy in which they are located, may be offshore in the sense just defined, and yet may be significant vehicles for cross-border portfolio investment. To ensure their inclusion in the CPIS, the legal domicile of an enterprise is a preferred indicator of residence. In a typical SEIFiC, the transactors that are likely to meet the test of legal domicile may well include: (i) companies that are incorporated in the jurisdiction (including so-called "international business companies" and "exempt" companies) even though they may be managed or administered in another jurisdiction; (ii) branches of companies incorporated abroad (including financial holding companies); and (iii) unincorporated enterprises that are deemed to be legally domiciled, can produce separate accounts, and are expected to be in business for a period of one year or more. This test of residence is consistent with that followed in the draft interagency *External Debt Statistics: Guide for Compilers and Users* (Washington: IMF, 2002, forthcoming), which treats debt issues on the balance sheet of entities legally incorporated or domiciled in SEIFiCs as external debt of the SEIFiC. However, although international business companies in SEIFiCs are residents of the countries in which they are incorporated, unless they undertake financial intermediation they are not usually regulated and are not usually required to have accounts, so collection of CPIS data on IBCs in SEIFiCs may be very difficult.

3.10 For the CPIS, the residence of individuals that hold securities is established by their center of economic interest, as interpreted by the *1993 SNA* and by *BPM5*. This is determined by the location of their principal residence (as a member of a household) or by their employment status. An individual who is employed for one year or more in a country is deemed to be resident in that country. As explained in *BPM5*, there are specific guidelines for determining the residence of diplomatic staff and technical assistance personnel, but these are unlikely to be critical for the purposes of the CPIS.

A. Country Attribution of the Issuer of a Security

3.11 The issuer of a security is likely to be a government agency, a public or private corporation (including financial institutions), or a branch or subsidiary of a

[16]Commission of the European Communities, International Monetary Fund, Organisation for Economic Co-operation and Development, United Nations, and World Bank, *System of National Accounts 1993* (Brussels/Luxembourg, New York, Paris, Washington, 1993).

[17]Both the *1993 SNA* and *BPM5* say that liability to pay taxes is an **indicator** in helping to determine the residence of an entity. This is so regardless of the rate of tax. The important consideration is whether the entity is subject to the laws and taxes of the jurisdiction in which it is located.

[18]For the purposes of balance of payments statistics, enterprises comprise: "(i) incorporated enterprises (e.g., corporations, joint stock companies, limited liability partnerships, cooperatives, or other business associations recognized as independent legal entities by virtue of registration under company and similar acts, laws, or regulations); (ii) unincorporated enterprises; and (iii) nonprofit institutions" (*BPM5*, paragraph 76).

[19]Although the term "offshore" is used as an adjective in both the *1993 SNA* and in *BPM5*, no definition is given. For the CPIS, an offshore enterprise is one that is wholly or largely owned by nonresidents of the jurisdiction in which it is domiciled and is wholly or largely engaged in providing goods and/or services to nonresidents.

[20]That an SPE may be a direct investment enterprise does not necessarily mean that it is excluded from the CPIS because it is the nature of its assets, not its liabilities, that determines whether or not any holdings of securities are portfolio or direct investment. See Section VI of this chapter for a fuller discussion of the distinction between *portfolio investment* and *direct investment*.

public or private corporation (including a financial institution). Depending on their data sources, CPIS compilers may have difficulty in determining the country of residence of nonresident issuers of securities held by their residents. As noted below, for some multinational companies, there may be difficulty in determining residence, either of the issuer or of the holder.

3.12 Ensuring the correct country attribution of the issuer of a security is a central element of the CPIS. For data to be consistent, each reporter or compiler must attribute the same security issue to the same country, regardless of whether the national survey is being conducted on a security-by-security basis or whether it is on an aggregated basis (see Chapter 4 for the discussion of these approaches).

3.13 The coding systems used by the securities industry to identify securities can help ensure consistency of geographic attribution of securities by compilers across countries. For example, International Securities Identification Number (ISIN) codes are now allocated to many internationally traded long-term securities by national numbering agencies (NNAs), which have the sole right to allocate numbers within their jurisdiction. Each security has its own unique identifier. For equity securities (but not debt securities), the first two digits can be used to identify the country of the issuer. For debt securities, the ISIN code may identify the residence of the lead manager and not the issuer. It is recommended that national compilers, when discussing their national survey with potential survey respondents, evaluate the use of the ISIN code system in their own country and gauge its potential use in classifying securities in their national survey. More information on the coding system and the associated security databases is provided in Chapter 4.

3.14 Large multinational corporations (MNCs) may have more than one center of economic interest; others appear to have more than one head office. However, there are usually either separate corporations that operate within the larger entity or there may be a standard allocation principle among the countries of residence of the different owners, based on their equity shares. Moreover, some companies, listed on major stock exchanges and having all the characteristics of a resident of that economy, may be incorporated in another jurisdiction altogether. In addition, some MNCs may use a "shell company" or an SPE,[21] domiciled and registered in another country or economic territory—typically a SEIFiC—to issue securities, usually debt instruments, even though there is "no physical presence" in the economy or territory. In that instance, the securities should be attributed to the country or territory in which the issuing entity is legally incorporated, as opposed to the country of the parent enterprise, even though the legal entity in the SEIFiC is merely a conduit for raising funds in the parent company.

3.15 Even where the issue is guaranteed by the parent company, either explicitly or implicitly, and the funds are for use by the parent company, the residence of the issuer should be attributed to the place of registration of the special financing vehicle. Even for countries using a security-by-security approach (see Chapter 4), the database should be checked because the country allocation of issuer, especially for such special financing vehicles, is not always attributed correctly.

3.16 Securities issued by international organizations should be recorded as such, and not be attributed to the country in which they are located. Other characteristics of a security, such as the currency of denomination, the market where it is issued, listed, or traded, or the country of the guarantor or underwriter of the issue, should not be used as a substitute for the resident country of the issuer.

B. Country Attribution of the Security Holder

3.17 The holder of a security may be a government entity, a public or private corporation (including a financial institution), a quasi-corporation (including a financial institution), an enterprise as defined in *BPM5*, a nonprofit institution serving households (NPISH), or an individual. For the CPIS, the national compiler needs to be able to identify all resident holders of securities issued by nonresidents. The following addresses problems that may arise when the residence of the holder cannot readily be determined from the available data sources (such as reporting by investment managers, custodians, or settlement agents), problems related to the treatment of nominee accounts, issues concerning the treatment of insurance company technical reserves, pension funds, mutual funds, and trust service providers, and the treatment of defeasance.

3.18 This identification of residence based on beneficial holders is particularly difficult where the information is provided by investment (fund) managers or custodians. They may not be aware that the registered

[21] See paragraph 3.9 for discussion of "shell companies," "brass plate companies," "international business corporations," and SPEs.

owner is not the beneficial owner or, alternatively, they may not know the residence of the beneficial owner if the assets are held by nominee companies or trustees. When investment managers or custodians are asked to report the value of securities they hold on behalf of others, it is important that they be provided with guidelines to determine the basis of residence of the asset holder(s). For the most part, they use postal addresses; however, in some instances, this will be inappropriate for reasons noted above.

3.19 Difficulties also arise in regard to whether custodians can readily identify the residence of the beneficial holder. Custodians will sometimes hold securities on behalf of other custodians. Investors may place their portfolios with "global custodians," which, in turn, use the services of "local" or "sub" custodians. In that case, it is important, where possible, to have the subcustodian ignore its holdings on behalf of the global custodian, which should then be asked to report the information on behalf of the securities' ultimate owners. This is because the global custodian, in this instance, would be aware of that information, whereas the subcustodian would not. However, it is recognized that this exercise may require considerable coordination and involve substantial resources, especially as cross-border dimensions are involved. There is, moreover, considerable risk that double or undercounting may result.[22] Accordingly, it is recommended that this process of "looking through" the subcustodian to the global custodian should be undertaken only where there is a strong likelihood of good interagency coordination and cooperation. If this is not possible, it is probably better not to attempt such an undertaking. Clear instructions to both global and local or subcustodians are necessary to ensure that attribution of country of residence is done consistently between them.

3.20 When using investment brokers or custodians as a data source for the CPIS, problems may arise regarding the treatment of nominee accounts. A nominee account is a device through which an investor acquires ownership of securities without his/her/its name appearing on the security register. Nominee accounts are offered by *nominees*, which are usually nominee companies operated by lawyers, accountants, securities dealers, or financial institutions. In countries that use trusts, the nominee usually holds the assets as a trustee and may have no discretion in the management of the assets. Securities acquired via a nominee are registered in the nominee's name. Nominee accounts are sometimes used to make an initial accumulation of shares, up to the legal limit permitted before disclosure is required, pending a takeover bid. More generally, they are used by investors as a convenient means to buy and sell shares through a securities dealer (which will have its own nominee company). Holdings of securities by a nominee, although registered in the name of the nominee, should be attributed to the country of residence of the beneficial owner. The nominee should always know this information. If the beneficial owner of the securities is a nonresident of the compiling economy, the holdings of the portfolio investment assets should not be included in the portfolio investment assets of that economy. However, if the data are collected from custodians[23] rather than directly from the nominee, it may be very difficult for the custodian to determine who the beneficial owner is because the custodian's records may only record the legal owner (i.e., the nominee). Where the nominee is a resident of the compiling economy and the beneficial owner is a nonresident, ownership of portfolio investment assets may be incorrectly attributed to the resident economy. On the other hand, where the nominee is a nonresident and the beneficiary is a resident, unless the custodian is aware of that situation, the portfolio investment asset holdings will be excluded from the CPIS—thereby understating the compiling economy's assets because the respondent will be instructed to include holdings of residents only.

3.21 The treatment of pension funds in the CPIS is fully consistent with the *1993 SNA* and *BPM5*. Pension funds to be included as respondents comprise those that are constituted as separate institutional units from the units that created them. Sometimes, the management of pension funds takes place in another jurisdiction from that in which the pension fund itself is resident. For the CPIS, in all such instances the ownership of the pension funds should be attributed to the country in which the pension fund is resident.

3.22 The treatment of collective investment schemes (such as mutual funds) in the CPIS is fully consistent

[22] For example, if the subcustodian does not remove its holdings on behalf of the global custodian and the latter reports the holdings as well, overcounting will result, while undercounting will result if both the subcustodian and the global custodian make the adjustment.

[23] Custodians hold securities on behalf of investors. These securities may be held in physical form, although nowadays they are overwhelmingly "dematerialized"—that is, in electronic form. Custodians qua custodians do not actively trade securities, though they may perform that function separately as investment managers or brokers.

with the *1993 SNA* and *BPM5*. For mutual funds, it is not uncommon, especially in SEIFiCs, for them to be registered in one jurisdiction, managed in another, and administered in a third. "Managing" means the buying and selling of the assets and other front office activity, such as market research and economic analysis. "Administering" in this context means the bookkeeping, legal, and other "back room" activities. Collective investment schemes that are legally incorporated or registered in an economy are deemed to be residents of that economy, even if the managing or administration is undertaken in another economy. It is important that respondents to the survey understand that, for the CPIS, it is the economy of registration of a collective investment scheme that is its domicile.

3.23 Trusts are arrangements where one party (the *trustee/s*) has the legal title to, and often control of, a portfolio of assets while others (the *beneficiary/ies*) have the right to benefits of the portfolio or income generated by it. Trusts in this use of the term are usually found only in Anglo-American legal systems. The trustee is subject to fiduciary obligations to protect the beneficiaries' interests (e.g., the trust property is kept separately from the personal property of the trustee). The assets are held off the trustee's balance sheet. Because their essential aspect is the separation of different aspects of ownership, trusts give rise to questions on the attribution of their ownership and residence.

3.24 A general treatment of trusts as units is not given by the *1993 SNA* and *BPM5* (which refers to investment trusts along with mutual funds as collective investment schemes). This is because they are not a separate group of units in themselves but, rather, trusts are treated in the same way as entities that undertake equivalent economic functions with different legal structures. This is based on the principle that economic function of the entity is relevant in economic analysis, rather than the particular legal structure that is used. The relevant aspects for identification of the economic function for statistical units are, first, the degree of separation of the unit from others that established and own it, as evidenced by its decision making and whether it has its own accounts and, second, the nature of the activities it undertakes (viz., financial intermediation, market production of goods and services, general government operations, nonprofit production, or simply holding assets).

3.25 Trusts that are used to undertake production of goods and services resemble businesses that use a corporate structure and will usually be treated as nonfinancial corporations. By reasons of the fiduciary duties of the trustee, the trust will have its own accounts and maintain a separate identity from both the trustee and the beneficiaries. Similarly, trusts that undertake financial intermediation (securitization, collateralized securities, and investment pools, such as collective investment schemes) are often found to be separate units and resemble their corporate equivalents undertaking the same activities. For example, unit trusts (which are unincorporated) and mutual funds (which are incorporated) have different legal forms, but both are collective investment vehicles that perform the same economic function. Similarly, pension funds that use corporate structures should be treated the same way in economic statistics as those that use trusts.

3.26 Trusts are also sometimes used solely to hold assets for a small group of people and, in this case, may not be open to the public or be large enough to qualify as a collective investment vehicle.[24] Such trusts are often set up by one or more family members for their relatives (and possibly themselves). However, they can also be used as vehicles for small groups of unrelated investors. Trustees may be relatives of the beneficiaries or professional trustees, such as lawyers or licensed trustee companies established for the purpose. In some cases, the trustee has legal title without decision-making power, as the trust deed requires that the trustee follow the instructions of the beneficiary/ies. In these cases, which include nominee companies, the trust is not the effective decision-making unit. However, in other cases, the trustee has independent control of the assets.[25] Trusts are often managed by professional trust service providers, who may be potential data sources. Such a collection approach is analogous to custodians, which are used as a convenient data collection point in many countries. The treatment for these trusts is not clearly stated in international standards, but would appear to point to treating the assets as if they were held directly by the beneficiaries. When the trust and beneficiaries are in the same country, this does not present practical problems. However, in practice, beneficiaries and the trust are often located in different countries, particularly for the many trusts operating in SEIFiCs. In these cases, it is unlikely that any data can be collected by the country of the beneficiaries. Nor is it proposed for the 2001 CPIS to collect data in the country of the trust, whether a SEIFiC or not.

[24] Similarly, shelf companies are often used only to hold financial assets.

[25] Indeed, the objective of many trusts is to take advantage of the trustee's asset management skills or to protect the beneficiaries from their lack of management skills (for example, infants or the not yet born).

3.27 Defeasance requires a particular mention. Defeasance is an arrangement whereby a debtor sets up a device ("defeasance") into which it places assets of equal value and income stream to match an outstanding liability. Certain countries have practices that permit "defeased" assets and liabilities to be taken off the balance sheet. However, under national accounting, balance of payments, and the CPIS concepts, both the assets and liabilities should be regarded as being on-balance sheet of the defeasing party.

C. International Organizations and Regional Central Banks

3.28 In balance of payments statistics and the CPIS, international organizations (IOs) are not treated as being residents of any country. Although physically located in a given country, they are always treated as nonresident for statistical purposes because they are created by agreements between governments and are outside the authority of an individual government. Any assets or liabilities they may hold are **not** the assets or liabilities of the countries in which they are physically located. However, it should be emphasized that any **pension funds** operated by IOs are considered to be residents of the country in which the pension funds are located.

3.29 The IMF will conduct a survey of the portfolio investment assets **held by** international organizations to complement the results of the CPIS. They will be included in the global CPIS results, as was done in the 1997 CPIS publication.[26] Portfolio investment assets of IOs should **not** be included in national CPIS data because their inclusion would result in double counting. For countries that are hosts to IOs, the IOs' portfolio investment assets should not be included in their national data. Similarly, any securities issued by residents that are held by an IO are liabilities of the issuing country to a nonresident. Correct classification may be an issue if data are obtained through custodians, and IOs may be incorrectly identified as residents if the classification is based on their physical location.

3.30 Similarly, for the CPIS, holdings of securities **issued by** international organizations should be reported as a separate category under a specific code for international organizations (code "XX," the last code in the list of countries in the model forms), rather than under the host country of the international organization.

[26]The data will be reported on a confidential basis to the IMF and will be included in the published results in a single separate vector, so that confidentiality is maintained.

3.31 Securities held by **regional central banks** (RCBs) may be included in both foreign exchange reserves and portfolio investment **asset** holdings. For example, pension fund portfolio investment assets holdings (if not held in a separate institutional unit) or securities held for monetary policy purposes may be recorded as *portfolio investment* rather than as *reserve assets.* In some cases, RCBs may hold securities issued by member countries of the RCB. These latter securities are usually not included in the RCB's reserve assets. In that case, these securities should be reported by the RCB as securities claims on the member countries of the RCB as part of their portfolio investment asset holdings.

3.32 Securities issued by RCBs do not appear to be significant at present, but the holder of any such securities should report them in its portfolio holdings in the "international organizations" line in the country allocation. RCB securities should not be allocated to the member countries of the bank and they should always be treated as having been issued by a nonresident. If securities issued by RCBs become significant in the future, it would be desirable to add a specific line or lines for them in CPIS codes and report forms.

IV. Valuation

3.33 In paragraph 468, *BPM5* recommends that stocks of assets (and liabilities) be valued at current market prices[27] at the appropriate reference date; it also provides advice on how to value securities:

> *For equities that are listed on organized markets or are readily tradable, the value of outstanding stocks should be based on actual* [market] *prices. The value of equities that are not quoted on stock exchanges or otherwise traded regularly should be estimated by using the prices of quoted shares that are comparable as to past, current, and prospective earnings and dividends. Alternatively, the net asset values of enterprises to which the equities relate could be used to estimate market values if the balance sheets of enterprises are available on a current value basis. For debt securities that are listed in organized markets or are readily tradable, the outstanding value of stocks also*

[27]Defined in *BPM5* as prices that willing buyers pay to acquire something from willing sellers.

should be determined on the basis of current market prices. For debt securities that are not readily tradable, the net present value of the expected stream of future payments or receipts associated with the securities could be used to estimate market value. (The net present value of any future receipt is equal to the value of that receipt when discounted at an appropriate interest rate.)

3.34 It is essential that, as far as possible, there be consistency of reporting across countries. For those securities that are traded, which should be the majority by far, prices should be commonly available from bond and stock exchanges, commercial vendors (for instance, Reuters and Bloomberg), or organizations that maintain security databases (for instance, the International Securities Market Association [ISMA] and Telekurs) (see Box 4.1). Where the bid and asking prices are both quoted, the midpoint should be used. The market value should be that as at the close of business on December 31, 2001[28] (or any subsequent year if the decision is made to conduct the survey on an ongoing basis) in each compiling country. What this means is that there may be price differences across countries in different time zones for the same securities quoted in different markets. However, for the time being, given that the survey is to be used as input to a country's international investment position (IIP), the relevant price for that economy is the market price at close of business in that economy. Accordingly, this timing difference is a valuation inconsistency that should be recognized, but at present, it is one that cannot be addressed.

3.35 *BPM5* recommends that interest accrued, but not yet payable, be included in the price of the debt security (see *BPM5*, paragraphs 121 and 396): the so-called "dirty" price. In line with that recommendation, this survey should be conducted on the basis that debt securities are to be reported on a dirty price basis. This is particularly important for zero coupon or deep discount instruments with terms to maturity of greater than one year, where the accrual of interest can be large in relation to the initial funds advanced. However, in many countries, the market price of debt securities excludes interest accrued but not yet due: the so-called "clean" price. Wherever possible, data on debt securities, reported on a clean price basis, should be converted to a dirty price basis, but it is recognized that this may not always be possible, especially for countries that use an aggregate approach. Compilers are asked to provide methodological notes setting out the basis of reporting, together with the methods used, if any, to adjust the data to a dirty price basis.

3.36 Respondents may record their security holdings, especially debt instruments on a variety of different valuation principles, notably par value, acquisition cost, amortized value, or market price, depending on the purpose of the investment and the accounting practices of the institution or economy. Compilers should make every effort to endeavor to have securities holdings reported at market prices.

3.37 Market price valuation is recommended because it is

- the recommended basis in *BPM5*;
- the only manner in which assets and liabilities can be valued on the same basis;
- the basis for economic and portfolio investment theory: for the creditor, it reflects the command it has over resources, while for the debtor, it is the measure of the amount of funds required to eliminate the liability under current market conditions. This is increasingly important in an era where debtors are becoming active liability managers.

3.38 Accordingly, wherever possible, respondents should be asked to report their holdings at market price.

3.39 In some cases, securities have been issued at a substantial premium, as the coupon is much higher than the market rate of interest at the time of issue. The security should be reported at market price, which should approximate the present value of the future stream of payments, discounted by an appropriate current rate of interest.

3.40 Survey respondents may face the same problems that compilers face in obtaining good information on market valuation (Box 3.1). Therefore, when compilers rely on respondents to provide information on the market value of securities, it is important that some method of quality control be introduced. When survey respondents report on a security-by-security basis, compilers are advised to request additional information: for example, the number of equities held, by issuer; or the face value of the debt instru-

[28] In some markets, December 31 is a very light day of trading, or no trading is undertaken at all. In cases where there is very light volume on December 31 for any given security, it may be preferable to use an average (perhaps weighted by volume) of the three days up to the end of the year or the last two trading days in 2001 and the first two trading days in 2002 (and similarly in following years, should the CPIS become an annual survey).

Box 3.1: Approaches to Approximating Market Prices

Where market prices are not available for securities (e.g., in private placements and in organized exchanges where they are not actively traded), valuing securities may create difficulties for national compilers.

In France, which has a security-by-security approach, in the absence of a readily observable price, custodians reporting security holdings of clients are instructed to value listed securities at the price chosen for the annual valuation of the respondent's portfolio for unlisted securities. In Australia—which has an aggregated approach—respondents are given a range of possibilities with which to value both equities and debt; the order of preference is based on the recommendations of *BPM5* (including the method of valuing securities issued at a discount, which is outlined in paragraph 396), viz., in descending order of preference: a recent transaction price, directors' valuation, or net asset value.

Choosing the market price of a comparable company (in the same industry, of similar size, with a comparable number of shares on issue) is not a recommended option since there are too many other factors (not least, the management) that are imponderables and that could produce a considerable distortion in the valuation. At the same time, illiquidity itself tends to depress the price of a security.

ment and the price used to value it. With this information, compilers could confirm that the price looks appropriate, either by using their own knowledge or by comparing prices quoted for comparable or the same securities by other respondents. For infrequently traded securities, the problems are more severe.[29] The compiler could use a price index to provide a means for revaluation to market prices if nominal values are provided by the respondent. The index could vary in complexity between that based on similar maturities in the same currency and that which identifies individual issues that mirror the characteristics of the unpriced security. If national compilers intend to create their own price index from information already available, they need to carefully consider technical complexities. See Box 3.2 for some of the problems associated with valuation of a particular type of instrument: asset-backed securities.

3.41 Regarding those respondents who report on an aggregate basis, the compilers' scope for independently verifying that securities have been correctly valued is more restricted. If the data are being collected within an integrated system, the compiler could, as in Australia, request that the reporters reconcile transactions and position data on the same survey form; alternatively, the compilers themselves could, as in the United Kingdom, reconcile transactions and position data (see Chapters 5 and 6 for more information on quality control). Independent information, such as an entity's published balance sheet or statement of assets under management or under custody, could also be used. However, it is important to bear in mind when making these comparisons that like be compared with like: accordingly, if the published balance sheet is for the consolidated group's global activities, it is unlikely to be appropriate for the purpose of this survey (or for balance of payments or the IIP) if there have been issues by nonresident subsidiaries that will be included in that consolidated balance sheet. In addition, for assets under management (or held in custody), it is important that the data adequately reflect what is managed on behalf of residents and what is managed on behalf of nonresidents. If this distinction cannot be made, the comparison for verification purposes is limited. In all cases, where comparison is made, it is necessary that the alternative source of data provide the basis for valuation in notes to the balance sheet or statement of assets under management to ensure that the comparisons with the CPIS are on the same valuation basis.

3.42 Countries that intend to conduct an aggregate survey, particularly a first-time survey targeted at custodians, are advised to gain some idea of the reported value of securities not revalued to end-period market prices. One approach is to ask respondents to report this information (such as holdings at acquisition price) on the survey form. This information could be requested as supplementary to the main data for the CPIS: for example, in the model survey forms in Appendices I and V, this information could be collected at the end of the forms on equities, long-term debt securities, and short-term debt securities as items "of which value of total securities issued by nonresidents held on respondent's books or on behalf of residents that is not recorded at market price." Alternatively, the total value of all equity and long- and short-term debt securities could be recorded separately from the information for individual countries' issues. These figures might provide only a rather rough indication of the size of the problem in value terms, but they may serve as a useful basis for the CPIS because they would help compilers identify, contact, and, perhaps, directly assist those survey respondents who have the most difficulty revaluing securities.

[29]The boundary between securities and loans, may, in certain circumstances, be difficult to draw. In principle, one of the defining features of securities is that they are tradable, whereas other instruments are not. However, recently there have been instances where loans have been sold to third parties, usually at a discount to their nominal value. Unless there is evidence that these transactions are likely to prompt similar types of sales, the loans should not be reclassified to securities.

Box 3.2: Valuation of Asset-Backed Securities

The vast majority of asset-backed securities are U.S. securities backed by pools of residential mortgages. As of March 2000, there were approximately 900,000 such securities outstanding, with nonresident ownership estimated at approximately $360 billion.

These securities present a special problem, given that there can be partial repayments of principal at any time. Because the market price is a function of market interest rates and perceived creditworthiness, not just the amount of principal outstanding, simply revaluing the original face value to end-period market prices will cause an overvaluation of position data if there has been a partial repayment. The compiler need only revalue the face value of the remaining amount outstanding—the so-called "factor value." For example, if the original face value of a security is $1,000,000, and $700,000 of the principal has been repaid, the "factor value" is 0.300.

Problems have arisen—at least when collecting data from U.S. custodians—because some custodians keep track of only the original face value amount of principal outstanding on the security, whereas other custodians keep track of only the remaining principal outstanding. Thus, when collecting data on a security-by-security basis from custodians, compilers are advised to ask for both the original and the remaining principal outstanding; if only one is available, the compiler should at least be clear as to which has been reported so that the appropriate adjustments can be made. If data are collected on an aggregate basis, prior consultation with major respondents is recommended to decide upon the appropriate course of action.

V. Sectors

3.43 For some purposes, knowing the sector of the holder is useful for analysis. For custodian or asset manager surveys, providing definitions by sector may help if the compiler is contemplating asking the custodian/asset manager for sectoral information. Because there are a variety of different types of institutions, especially financial, the more detailed sectors set out in the *1993 SNA* may be more appropriate than the more limited version in *BPM5*. Should compilers feel that the more detailed breakdown of the *1993 SNA* is too complicated to collect or process yet still seek some sectoral split, the *BPM5* sectors (or a still smaller sectoral split) may still provide useful additional information. Alternatively, as the "other sector" of *BPM5* covers many different sectors and subsectors in the *1993 SNA*, compilers may wish to provide some limited breakdown (of the financial sectors, for example) without adopting the full *1993 SNA* sectoral detail.

A. Monetary Authorities

3.44 *BPM5*, paragraph 514, describes monetary authorities as follows:

The monetary authorities sector, which is based on a functional concept, includes the central bank (or currency board, monetary agency, etc.) and certain operations that are usually attributed to the central bank but are sometimes carried out by other government institutions or commercial banks. Such operations include the issuance of currency; maintenance and management of international reserves, including those resulting from transactions with the IMF; and operation of exchange stabilization funds. Such transactions are, in effect, rerouted through the central bank.... In the SNA, the central bank is a subsector of the financial corporate sector.

As discussed in Chapter 2, it is recommended that securities held as part of reserve assets be reported to the IMF under the confidential survey, SEFER.

B. General Government

3.45 *BPM5*, paragraph 515, gives the following description of the general government sector:

The general government sector, with the exception noted in the previous paragraph, is consistent with that sector in the SNA. General government consists of (i) government units that exist at each level—central, state, or local—of government within the national economy; (ii) social security funds operated at each level of government; (iii) nonprofit institutions that are majority financed and controlled by government units; and (iv) unincorporated enterprises that are owned and operated by government units and that produce goods and services, including collective services or public goods. (However, if it is appropriate under SNA guidelines to treat unincorporated enterprises as quasi-corporations, such enterprises are allocated to the financial or nonfinancial corporate sectors.)

3.46 The *1993 SNA* (paragraphs 4.104 and 4.105) describes general government as follows:

Government units may be described as unique kinds of legal entities established by political processes which have legislative, judicial or executive authority over other institutional units within a given area. Viewed as institutional units, the principal functions of govern-

ment are to assume responsibility for the provision of goods and services to the community or to individual households and to finance their provision out of taxation or other incomes; to redistribute income and wealth by means of transfers; and to engage in non-market production. In general terms:

(a) A government unit usually has the authority to raise funds by collecting taxes or compulsory transfers from other institutional units...a government unit...must also be able to borrow funds on its own account;

(b) Government units typically make three different kinds of final outlays:

(i) The first group consists of actual or imputed expenditures on the free provision to the community of collective services such as public administration, defense, law enforcement, public health, etc. which, as a result of market failure, have to be organized collectively by government and financed out of general taxation or other income;

(ii) The second group consists of expenditures on the provision of goods or services free, or at prices that are not economically significant, to individual households. These expenditures are deliberately incurred...by government in the pursuit of its social or political objectives, even though individuals could be charged according to their usage;

(iii) The third group consists of transfers paid to other institutional units, mostly households, in order to redistribute income or wealth.

Within a single country, there may be many separate government units when there are different levels of government—central, state, or local government. In addition, social security funds also constitute government units.

Excluded from government are government-owned (more than 50 percent of voting shares[30]) entities that charge economically significant prices for their output. These units are to be included in either financial or nonfinancial corporations, depending on the nature of the unit's activities. For example, government owned entities that provide export insurance, housing programs, housing finance, are excluded from general government and included in financial corporations if the programs' costs are priced in such a fashion as to influence the extent of demand. Similarly, government owned transportation systems, or utilities (such as electricity supply or telephone companies) should be included in nonfinancial corporations if the output is priced so as to recover at least 50 percent of operating costs.

[30]If general government has a holding in another institutional unit of less than 50 percent, that unit is not considered to be a government owned enterprise.

C. Banks

3.47 *BPM5*, paragraph 516, describes the banking sector as follows:

The banking sector is identical with the "other (than the central bank) depository corporations" subsector of the financial corporate sector in the SNA.... Included are all resident units engaging in financial intermediation as a principal activity and having liabilities in the form of deposits or financial instruments (such as short-term certificates of deposit) that are close substitutes for deposits. Deposits include those payable on demand and transferable by check or otherwise usable for making payments and those that, while not readily transferable, may be viewed as substitutes for transferable deposits. Thus, in addition to commercial banks, the banking sector encompasses institutions such as savings banks, savings and loan associations, credit unions or cooperatives, building societies, and post office savings banks or other government-controlled savings banks (if such banks are institutional units separate from government).

3.48 The *1993 SNA* (paragraphs 4.93 and 4.94) goes on to describe these institutions as follows:

Deposit money corporations...consist of resident depository corporations and quasi-corporations which have liabilities in the form of deposit payable on demand, transferable by check or otherwise usable for making payments. Such deposits are included in the concept of money in the narrow sense. These corporations include so-called "clearing banks" which participate in a common clearing system organized to facilitate the transfer of deposits between them by checks or other means.

[Other depository corporations]...consist of all...resident depository corporations and quasi-corporations which have liabilities in the form of deposits that may not be readily transferable or in the form of financial instruments such as short-term certificates of deposit which are close substitutes for deposits and included in measures of money broadly defined. These corporations compete for funds with deposit money corporations in financial markets even if they are unable, or unwilling, to incur liabilities in the form of transferable deposits. They may include corporations described as savings banks (including trustee savings banks and savings banks and loan associations), credit cooperatives and mortgage banks or building societies. It must be emphasized that such corporations are described in different ways in different countries and they can only be identified by examining their functions rather than their names. They may also include post office savings banks or other savings banks controlled by the government, provided these are separate institutional units from government. As a result of financial innovation, improved technology in the field of computers and communications, and also financial deregulation in many countries,...drawing a clear distinction between "deposit money corporations" and "other" depository corporations may be too blurred to be operational in some countries.

D. Other Sectors in *BPM5*

3.49 *BPM5* (paragraph 517) describes "other sectors" and their components as follows:

The other sectors category is comprised of nonfinancial corporations (private, public, and quasi-corporations), insurance companies, pension funds, other nondepository financial intermediaries, private nonprofit institutions, and households.

(i) Other financial intermediaries, except insurance corporations and pension funds (1993 SNA, *paragraph 4.95)*

This subsector consists of all resident corporations and quasi-corporations primarily engaged in financial intermediation except depository corporations, insurance corporations and pension funds. Financial corporations included under [this] heading are those which raise funds on financial markets, but not in the form of deposits, and use them to acquire other kinds of financial assets. The types of corporations which may be included under this heading are those engaged in financing investment or capital formation; for example, investment corporations, corporations engaged in financial leasing, hire purchase corporations and other corporations engaged in the provision of personal finance or consumer credit.

Most mutual funds (unit trusts) are also included.

(ii) Insurance corporations and pension funds (1993 SNA, *paragraphs 4.97 and 4.98)*

This subsector consists of insurance corporations and quasi-corporations and autonomous pension funds. Insurance corporations consist of incorporated, mutual and other entities whose principal function is to provide life, accident, sickness, fire or other forms of insurance to individual institutional units or groups of units. Pension funds included...are those which are constituted in such a way that they are separate institutional units from the units which create them. They are established for purposes of providing benefits on retirement for specific groups of employees. They have their own assets and liabilities and they engage in financial transactions in the market on their own account. These funds are organized, and directed, by individual private or government employers, or jointly by individual employers and their employees; and the employees and/or employers make regular contributions. They do not cover pension arrangements for the employees of private or government entities which do not include a separately organized fund nor an arrangement organized by a nongovernment employer in which the reserves of the fund are simply added to that employer's own reserves or invested in securities issued by that employer.

(iii) Financial auxiliaries (1993 SNA, *paragraph 4.96)*

This subsector consists of all resident corporations and quasi-corporations engaged primarily in activities closely related to financial intermediation but which do not themselves perform an intermediation role. They consist of corporations such as securities brokers, loan brokers, flotation corporations, insurance brokers, etc. They also include corporations whose principal function is to guarantee, by endorsement, bills or similar instruments intended for discounting or refinancing by financial corporations, and also corporations which arrange hedging instruments such as swaps, options, and futures or other instruments which are continually being developed as a result of wide-ranging financial innovation.

(iv) Nonfinancial corporations (1993 SNA, paragraphs 4.68 and 4.69)

Nonfinancial corporations or quasi-corporations are corporations or quasi-corporations whose principal activity is the production of market goods or nonfinancial services. The nonfinancial corporations sector is composed of the following set of resident institutional units:

(a) All resident nonfinancial corporations, irrespective of the residence of the shareholders;

(b) All resident nonfinancial quasi-corporations including the branches or agencies of foreign-owned nonfinancial enterprises that are engaged in significant amounts of production on the economic territory on a long-term basis [i.e., more than one year];

(c) All resident nonprofit institutions [NPIs] that are market producers of goods or nonfinancial services.

Some nonfinancial corporations or quasi-corporations may have secondary financial services: for example, producers or retailers of goods and services may provide consumer credit directly to their own customers...Such corporations or quasi-corporations are nevertheless classified as belonging in their entirety to the nonfinancial corporate sector provided their principal activity is nonfinancial. Sectors are groups of institutional units, and the whole of each institutional unit must be classified to one or another sector...even though that unit may be engaged in more than one type of economic activity.

That having been said, however, if a financing arm of a nonfinancial corporation or quasi-corporation maintains a separate set of books from its parent, and can acquire financial and nonfinancial assets and liabilities in its own name then it should be treated as a separate institutional unit and be classified to financial corporations.

(v) Nonprofit institutions serving households (NPISHs) (1993 SNA, paragraphs 4.161 and 4.162)

The NPISH sector comprises legal or social entities that are nonmarket producers of goods and services (i.e., which provide their output free of charge or at prices that are not economically significant) and which are not financed or controlled by government. Their status does not permit them to be a source of profit. The NPISH sector includes two main kinds of NPISH:

(a) Trade unions, professional or learned societies, consumers' associations, political parties (except in single-party states), churches or religious societies (including those financed by governments), and social, cultural, recreational and sports clubs;

(b) Charities, relief and aid organizations financed by voluntary transfers in cash or in kind from other institutional units.

While NPISHs are separate institutional units, for most statistical systems it is very difficult to separate them, so they are usually included with households as a result.

(vi) Households (1993 SNA paragraph 4.132)

A household may be defined as a small group of persons who share the same living accommodation, who pool some, or all, of their income and wealth and who consume certain types of goods and services collectively, mainly housing and food. In general, each member of a household should have some claim upon the collective resources of the household. At least some decisions affecting consumption or other economic activities must be taken for the household as a whole. Households often coincide with families, but members of the same household do not necessarily have to belong to the same family so long as there is some sharing of resources and consumption.

Members of the household who have resided abroad for more than one year are considered to be nonresidents and do not form part of the resident household, unless the member of the household is studying abroad or is a medical patient abroad. In these cases, students and patients remain residents as long as their center of economic interest remains with the resident households.

Households sometimes establish trusts. See the discussion on trusts, paragraphs 3.23 through 3.26.

E. Offshore Financial "Sector"

3.50 There is no offshore financial sector, in either the *1993 SNA* or *BPM5*. However, in economies that have

(a) a financial services industry that is primarily engaged in business with nonresidents,

(b) where the institutional units in this industry have assets and liabilities out of proportion to the domestic financial intermediation designed to finance domestic economies, and

(c) where many or most of these institutional units are direct investment enterprises,

the authorities may wish to distinguish between an "onshore" and an "offshore" financial sector, even though all the institutional units are considered residents. Users can then choose to ignore or include this "sector," as they prefer, in their analysis of the national accounts, the balance of payments, the IIP, and the CPIS.

VI. Distinguishing Between Direct and Portfolio Investment in Securities

3.51 The objective of the CPIS is to collect data on residents' investment in securities issued by nonresidents for use in the compilation of portfolio investment data. If the securities held are considered to be issued by an enterprise that is in a direct investment relationship with the holder, they should be excluded. Hence, not all holdings of securities issued by a nonresident come under the auspices of the CPIS.

3.52 The definition of direct investment is in Chapter XVIII of *BPM5* and in the *OECD Benchmark Definition of Foreign Direct Investment* (third edition; Paris: OECD, 1996).

3.53 Paragraph 359 of *BPM5* describes direct investment as follows:

> Direct investment *is the category of international investment that reflects the objective of a resident entity in one economy obtaining a lasting interest in an enterprise resident in another economy. (The resident entity is the direct investor and the enterprise is the direct investment enterprise.) The lasting interest implies the existence of a long-term relationship between the direct investor and the enterprise and a significant degree of influence by the investor on the management of the enterprise.* Direct investment *comprises not only the initial transaction establishing the relationship between the investor and the enterprise but also all subsequent transactions between them and among affiliated enterprises, both incorporated and unincorporated.*

3.54 This description is elaborated further in paragraph 362 of *BPM5*:

> *...[A] direct investment enterprise is defined in this* Manual *as an incorporated or unincorporated enterprise in which a direct investor, who is resident in another economy, owns 10 percent or more of the ordinary shares or voting power (for an unincorporated enterprise). Direct investment enterprises comprise those entities that are subsidiaries (a nonresident investor owns more than 50 percent), associates (an investor owns 50 percent or less* [but usually more than 20 percent]*) and branches (wholly or jointly owned unincorporated enterprises) either directly or indirectly owned by the direct investor....Subsidiaries in this connotation also may be identified as majority owned affiliates.*

3.55 Therefore, **both** the **equity** held that establishes the direct investment relationship and any other holdings of equity or **debt**[31] that are issued by the direct investment enterprise or the direct investor or its affiliates and owned by them should be excluded from the CPIS. The one exception is transactions between affiliated financial intermediaries. Only those securities that can be regarded as permanent debt (loan capital reflecting a permanent interest) and equity (share capital) are to be classified as direct investments. Other securities transactions of related financial intermediaries are classified as portfolio investment (see *BPM5*, paragraphs 365 and 372). In practice, the method by which they are excluded may well depend on the general collection method adopted.

[31]Already held when the threshold of 10 percent is reached or other securities acquired subsequent to the reaching of that threshold.

3.56 In an end-investor survey, the reporting instructions should be clear as to what should be included and what should be excluded. Because end-investors are best informed about the composition of their investments, they should be able to distinguish portfolio from direct investment assets. Indeed, as direct investment statistics themselves are commonly collected through a survey of investors, the reporting instructions can make clear to respondents that securities reported as direct investment should not be reported as portfolio investments. Countries usually require separate reporting of direct and portfolio investment data. The compiler can also compare the direct and portfolio investment returns for each respondent as an additional check.

3.57 In a custodial survey, the instructions should also clearly state that securities that have been issued by an enterprise that is considered to be in a direct investment relationship with the holder should be excluded; however, the applicability of these instructions might well vary among countries. The experience among Task Force members is that, in some markets, investors tend to hold all portfolio investment securities with custodians, whereas securities issued by an enterprise in a direct investment relationship are frequently held separately from their portfolio investments and away from custodians. It is recommended that national compilers conducting a custodian survey evaluate market practice in their own country and ensure that custodians understand the direct investment relationship and that any holdings of securities between direct investment enterprise and the direct investor are to be excluded from the survey. In markets where investors tend to hold all securities with custodians, compilers collecting data for the CPIS from custodians will need to be particularly vigilant in ensuring that securities that should be classified as direct investments are excluded.[32] (Alternatively, as a quality check, such securities could be identified separately as a memorandum item.) This could take the form of monitoring particularly large holdings of securities and comparing data from direct investment survey returns with those from the CPIS. Box 3.3 illustrates how Austria ensures that direct equity investment securities are excluded from its survey of portfolio investment.

[32]Surveys that give the number of securities held can provide a useful check against the total number of shares on issue to determine whether any one investor holds more than 10 percent.

Box 3.3: Austria's Experience in Excluding Direct Investment from the National Survey Results

In Austria, custodians provide the Oesterreichische Nationalbank (ONB) with information on individual securities at par value. The custodians are not able to distinguish between portfolio investment securities and securities held for direct investment purposes. Hence, all securities are included in the report by custodians, and the data are adjusted by the ONB using an estimate of direct investment securities held with domestic custodians.

As in many countries, the data on outward direct investment in Austria are based on reports by the domestic direct investors. The ONB, using these reports, chooses a sample of domestic companies—based on their size, the type of industry, the geographical breakdown of their investment abroad, and so on—and requests that they provide information on the custody of their direct investment equity securities. The approximate breakdown was as follows:

	Percent
No equities issued	11
Equities held in safekeeping abroad	12
Equities held in custody with nonresident banks	29
Equities held in domestic safekeeping	20
Equities held in custody with domestic banks	28

It is assumed that the sample is representative of all domestic companies that held direct investment securities. Consequently, 28 percent of the total amount of the nominal capital of outward direct investment—the amount of equities held in custody with domestic banks—is deducted from the custodians reports on residents' holdings of nonresident-issued equities.

3.58 Finally, national compilers—whether they approach end-investors or custodians—need to be careful when classifying securities issued by entities based in offshore centers. If held by the parent enterprise or associated affiliate, these securities should be classified under direct investment. As noted in paragraph 3.55, an exception is made for some holdings by financial intermediaries when the nonresident entity that issued the security and the resident owner of the security are affiliated financial intermediaries.

VII. Treatment of Securities Where There Is Potential for Double Counting

3.59 In this section, four types of transactions of growing importance, which could lead to potentially significant under- or double counting of securities holdings between countries, are identified. These types of transactions are (i) repurchase agreements, (ii) securities lending agreements, (iii) depository receipts, and (iv) stripped securities.

A. Repurchase Agreements

(i) Definition

3.60 A *repurchase agreement*[33] (repo) is an arrangement involving the sale of securities at a specified price with a commitment to repurchase the same or similar securities at a fixed price on a specified future date or on demand. A reverse repo is the same transaction seen from the other side; that is, an agreement whereby a security is purchased at a specified price with a commitment to resell the same or similar securities at a fixed price on a specified future date or on demand. Repos sometimes require that the value of the security be greater than the cash provided, to provide (initial) margin against the possible default on the part of the repo party. If the value of the security falls, additional securities (variation margin) may be required; on the other hand, if the value of the security rises, part of the original margin may be returned to the repo party (depending on country practice). In other cases, substitution of the security provided is permitted (which may arise if the security goes "special" or if the repo party needs the security to make delivery on another contract).

3.61 There is more than one type of repo. In some repo transactions, ownership of the underlying security remains with the seller; in others, the underlying security is, in essence, held by a third party for safekeeping (so-called tri-party repos); and in others, the ownership of the underlying security changes hands. Some repos are "cash driven"; that is, the primary purpose of the transaction is for the repo party to acquire cash. In other instances, the transaction may be "security driven"—that is, where the reverse-repo party has need for a particular security, if the security has gone "special" or the reverse-repo party needs to make delivery on a contract. Provided that cash is exchanged, regardless of whether the transaction is "cash driven" or "security driven," the economic nature is the same, and both types of transaction are treated in the same manner as collateralized loans (see ahead). Regardless of the type of repo transaction, the market risks of owning the security and all significant benefits remain with the "seller."

[33]Also included are sale/buy backs, carries, and bond/stock lending against cash, which, while having some minor technical differences, are essentially the same transaction as a repo.

(ii) Potential for double counting

3.62 Repurchase agreements were developed primarily as a method of financing security positions. Hence, they have been used as a means of leverage,[34] but they also have become a method by which investors can borrow securities to cover "short positions." Accounting practice in many countries is to regard the securities involved in repo transactions as remaining on the books of the seller and to record the cash received as a collateralized loan. On the other hand, some countries—for institutional, legal, or other reasons—treat repos, where ownership changes hands, as transactions in the underlying security; that is, as an outright sale of the security for cash. The subsequent repurchase is regarded as a separate and independent security transaction. The IMF Committee, at its 2000 meeting, endorsed an IMF recommendation that a repo be treated as a collateralized loan, reflecting the economic nature of the transaction.

3.63 In practice, national compilers in some countries find that they have no realistic choice other than to require data on security holdings (and transactions) to be reported in line with the accounting or regulatory conventions prevailing in their countries. It appears that the vast majority of countries prefer that repos be treated as collateralized loans (so that the "seller," not the "buyer," reports the holding).[35] Only a few countries record repos as a transaction in securities; however, it is also probable that in many countries, the recording practices are not universally applied, so compilers should be very careful in their preparation for the survey to be sure that the respondents know what is required and can comply. This concern applies particularly to countries that obtain the data for the CPIS from custodians (see the next section, "Treatment of repos in the CPIS"). Compilers are encouraged to discuss the nature of recording of these transactions with custodians and to see to what extent they can be identified and reported on the basis required for the CPIS. In particular, it is important that reporting of repos (and securities lending) is consistent within an economy.

[34]Repo is a common means whereby a mutual fund may leverage investors' funds. As a consequence, an investment of $100 million in securities may be used, via repo, to increase the value of the fund several times over the initial investment. In these instances (sometimes known as "hedge funds"), the survey should collect data on the fund's total portfolio investments, including those on repo.

[35]If the "buyer" on-sells the security acquired under a repo to a third party, then a negative or "short position" in the security should be reported; otherwise, the holding of the security will be double counted (see Box 3.6).

(iii) Treatment of repos in the CPIS

3.64 Because of the ambiguity of the nature of the transaction—they are, in part, transactions in securities, where there has been a legal change in ownership; equally, by their nature, they are more akin to a financing activity and should therefore be classified as collateralized loans—differences in the statistical recording of repos can lead to miscounting of cross-border holdings of the securities involved. Accordingly, the Task Force recognized that a practical and consistent approach should be adopted regarding the reporting of securities holdings underlying repos. It is recommended, at least for the purposes of this survey, and in line with the endorsement of this approach by the IMF Committee at its 2000 meeting, that repo transactions be recorded as collateralized loans. However, implementing this proposal is not always straightforward, particularly in countries where accounting and statistical practices are not in line with this proposal, or where there is asymmetry in the recording of repos versus the recording of reverse repos. There is an added problem in countries where custodians are a primary source of information as securities on repo are not necessarily identified or identifiable by the custodian (for either the repo party or the reverse-repo party). In that case, the custodian may only be able to report what is held in custody at any one time—therefore, a security on repo may not be identifiable and will be excluded from the custodian's (and, consequently, the repo party's) holdings. Similarly, a security acquired under reverse repo may not be identifiable as such on the books of the custodian and may, therefore, be recorded inappropriately as part of the custodian's holdings on behalf of clients (and hence the reverse-repo party's holdings).

3.65 There are several elements to this exercise. As a first step, national compilers are encouraged to obtain some idea of the importance of the securities repurchase market in their own economy. If it is significant, then national compilers should gain an understanding of the market.

3.66 Second, compilers should ascertain the recording practices of respondents and attempt to ensure internal consistency within the economy. If the treatment of repo holdings is not consistently applied among all respondents within a creditor country, claims on the debtor country will be inaccurately measured. Box 3.4 explains the reasoning behind these conclusions. However, ensuring internally consistent instructions is not necessarily straightforward, particularly for those countries that conduct a custodian survey. They will, for instance, need to capture "short positions"; otherwise, the security holdings could be double-counted (see Box 3.4). Boxes 3.5 and 3.6 provide examples of some of the problems that can result from the measurement of repos (and securities lending).

3.67 For those countries that collect data through an end-investor survey, the respondents should be asked to report repos and reverse repos as collateralized loans, in other words, as if the security has not changed hands. If the reverse-repo party then repos the security, the transaction should be treated in the same manner—as a collateralized loan. However, if a security acquired under reverse repo is sold outright, the reverse-repo party should record a short position (as described in Box 3.4). Where, due to accounting and legal requirements, the practice in the country is to record repos as transactions in securities, end-investor respondents should be asked to make every effort to report them as collateralized loans. It is especially important that there be consistency within an economy on the treatment of repos of nonresident-issued securities to ensure that the overall position of that economy vis-à-vis the issuing economy is correctly stated. If some respondents report on one basis (as collateralized loans) and others on another basis (as transactions in securities), the result could be a substantial over- or underestimate of the claims on the issuing economy.

3.68 Countries that collect data from custodians will need to discover whether their custodians are able to separately identify securities held under repo agreements when reporting clients' holdings. (This should not be an issue with regard to their own account holdings, where securities on repo or acquired under reverse repo should be clearly identifiable.) In some countries, the custodian of the repo party will know that the security is on repo because the records are set up to identify securities on repo to ensure that they are not sold twice. However, in these countries, even the custodian for the reverse-repo party frequently will not be aware that the security has been acquired under reverse repo. There is no need for the custodian to know this information in many instances: if the security can be on-sold, to all intents and purposes as far as the custodian is concerned, the security acquired is no different from any other transaction in a security and can be sold in the same way. Moreover, in many countries, the custodian will not know whether a security is on repo. Accordingly, in all

Box 3.4: Statistical Treatment of Repurchase Agreements

Explaining the possible statistical entries arising from repurchase agreements (repos) can soon become immensely complicated, not least because there are frequently three variables to consider: the two counterparties to the repo transaction and the issuer of the underlying security (and, in a tri-party repo, the custodian holding the security).

Provided that both the counterparties are domestic residents and provided that their statistical treatment of repos is identical (that is, national compilers ensure that all respondents have the same instructions), then claims vis-à-vis the country of issuance of the underlying security remain unchanged. For example, in the example in Box 3.5, if resident X of country A repos 100 security liabilities of country B to resident Y of country A, then regardless of whether X maintains this holding on its books and Y does not, or vice versa, country A has a claim of 100 on country B; that is, only one entity in country A has a reported claim on country B.

If, however, resident X treats repos as a collateralized loan, and resident Y treats repos as a purchase of securities, then country A's claim on B will be incorrectly measured at 200; that is, both X and Y report a claim on country B. Similarly, if resident X treats repos as a sale of securities and resident Y treats repos as a collateralized loan, then country A's claim on B will be incorrectly measured at zero, since neither X nor Y reports a claim on country B.

However, holdings data may not necessarily be "correct" even if both X and Y treat repo transactions in a consistent manner. Assume that X and Y both treat repos as collateralized loans, but Y on-sells the securities outright, not as a repo, to fellow resident Z. Y's sale of the security may be accurately reported in the transactions data, but given that Y has sold a security that was not on its balance sheet, then Y has a "short" or negative position. If country A's collection system cannot record negative positions, then country A's claim on country B will again be incorrectly measured at 200, because both X and Z will report claims on country B, even though only one claim exists.

The potential reporting possibilities become more complex if one of the counterparties is a nonresident (see Box 3.5). From the viewpoint of the CPIS, the residence of the counterparty to the repo transaction is not directly relevant. It is rather the residence of the issuer of the security used for the repo that is relevant, because the CPIS is measuring security claims on nonresidents. However, the residence of the counterparty is of relevance to the extent that the treatment of the securities underlying repos differs between countries. To the extent that national compilers adopt different treatments, there is potential for under- and overrecording at the global level for the same reasons as explained above in the domestic context.

The same considerations that apply to repos also apply to securities lending.

instances where custodians are principal sources of information, compilers should explain to custodians the importance of being able to identify securities on repo or reverse repo, and ways should be sought to ensure that they can meet the survey's needs.

3.69 An additional avenue to ensure consistency across borders in the recording of repos is for national compilers to consult their counterparts in the appropriate foreign country(s)—where the issuer(s) of the securities is (are) resident—to discover whether both countries are treating repos in a consistent manner. Different approaches can lead to asymmetric reporting of securities holdings; given the size and growth of the repo market in the 1990s, this could cause problems when the results are aggregated and when data are exchanged. Bilateral exchanges of additional information might be required to meet both countries' needs.

3.70 Because of the overwhelmingly common practice of treating repos (and reverse repos) as collateralized loans, and because of the IMF Committee's endorsement of this approach, that is the recommended approach for the CPIS and is used in the model survey forms (Appendices I to V).

3.71 Finally, information on how countries are intending to treat repo holdings should be supplied to the IMF (along with other documentation regarding the conduct of the survey at the national level) so that inconsistencies in approach between countries can be monitored and, if need be, brought to the attention of the relevant national compilers.[36]

3.72 A further complication may be the manner in which repo data are collected for balance of payments purposes, which may influence the way the data are collected for the IIP and for the survey. For example, repos with nonresidents may be reported by securities dealers and banks as transactions in securities but then reclassified as collateralized loans by a compiler who uses a program that identifies all trades and treats all matches of similar characteristics and counterparty; this can only be done ex post facto. Therefore, if any repo agreement is still extant at the reference date, it will not be known that it is to be reversed until the next reporting period. If that

[36]Cross-border transactions in repos have been growing so rapidly in recent years that it may be valuable for countries to collect this information for balance of payments purposes in its own right, given the importance of repos as a financing and leveraging tool.

Box 3.5: Repurchase Agreements: Examples of International Position Data-Reporting Possibilities of Portfolio Investment

A. Resident of A repos securities worth 100 issued by a resident of country C with a resident of B

Method of treatment	Country A claims on C	Country B claims on C	Reported nonresident claims on C
1. Both countries treat repos as collateralized loans	100	0	100
2. Both countries treat repos as sales and purchases of securities	0	100	100
3. Country A treats repos as collateralized loans, B as sales and purchases of securities	100	100	200
4. Country A treats repos as sales and purchases of securities, B as collateralized loans	0	0	0

B. Resident of A repos securities worth 100 issued by a resident of country B with a resident of B

Method of treatment	Country A claims on B	Reported nonresident claims on B
1. Both countries treat repos as collateralized loans	100	100
2. Both countries treat repos as sales and purchases of securities	0	0
3. Country A treats repos as collateralized loans, B as sales and purchases of securities	100	0
4. Country A treats repos as sales and purchases of securities, B as collateralized loans	0	100

C. Resident of A repos securities worth 100 issued by a resident of country A with a resident of B

Method of treatment	Country B claims on A	Reported nonresident claims on A
1. Both countries treat repos as collateralized loans	0	0
2. Both countries treat repos as sales and purchases of securities	100	100
3. Country A treats repos as collateralized loans, B as sales and purchases of securities	0	100
4. Country A treats repos as sales and purchases of securities, B as collateralized loans	100	0

occurs, and if the repo transactions that have not had their reverse leg completed are large, the compiler is asked to provide revisions to the IMF as soon as they become available.

3.73 From the foregoing, the importance of recording repos on a consistent basis, and preferably as collateralized loans, can be appreciated.

3.74 However, as noted in Box 3.6, a country's debt security liabilities may be overstated when a reverse repo is followed by an outright sale. If both the original holder and the final purchaser are nonresidents and the security has been issued by a resident, the security holders will both record ownership. This issue is one that requires continuing work to resolve. A Technical Group set up by the IMF Committee is exploring means to overcome the potential double counting.

B. Securities Lending

(i) Definition

3.75 Securities lending is an arrangement whereby the ownership of a security is transferred usually in return for collateral,[37] typically another security, under the condition that similar securities are returned to the original owner on a specified future date or on demand.[38] If cash exchanges hands, the transaction has the same economic nature as a repo and should be treated as a repo. A fee is paid by the "borrower" to the "lender."

(ii) Potential for double counting

3.76 Securities lending is an activity usually associated with securities dealers needing to meet commitments to deliver securities that they have sold but do not own—that is, covering a "short" position. Basically, a securities loan, in the absence of cash collateral,[39] involves swapping the borrowed securities for other acceptable securities (or other acceptable collateral). Depending on the nature of the transaction and the relative credit risks of the parties involved, the value of securities received as collateral may be the same or greater than the value of the securities "lent." As with repos, the market risks of owning the securities involved in a

[37]In some instances, no collateral is provided.

[38]Often, the collateral provided to the securities "lender" cannot be on-sold except on default by the "borrower."

[39]If cash is given as collateral, the transaction should be treated as a repo.

Box 3.6: Example of a Reverse Repo Followed by Outright Sale

Treating a repo as a collateralized loan may result in an incorrect statement of a country's external securities liability.

Where a nonresident repos a security issued by a resident to another resident, who in turn sells outright the security so acquired to another nonresident, an overstatement of the country's securities liabilities will result.

A resident in country A repos a security worth 100 issued by the government of country B to a resident of country B. In turn, the security acquired under this reverse repo is sold outright to a resident of country C. Country B's external securities liabilities would be recorded as follows under a collateralized loan approach, while, at the same time, recording a "short" position:

Securities liability to country A (under the collateralized loan approach)	100
Securities liability to country C (as recorded through the outright sale)	100
Total securities claims by nonresidents on country B	200

Even though the resident of country B who on-sells the security acquired under the reverse repo with the resident of country A will record his or her claim on the issuer of the security (a resident of country B) as a short position, the nonresidents' claims in the form of securities will be overstated by 100.

Country B's IIP will not be overstated, however, because the resident of country B (the reverse-repo party) will record a loan asset receivable under the reverse repo with the resident of country A that offsets the overstatement of the securities liability.

The same situation applies with a securities loan of a resident-issued security by a nonresident "lender" to a resident "borrower," who followed the loan with an outright sale to another nonresident.

Other circumstances may produce a similar overstatement of a country's debt securities liabilities.

securities loan (and all significant benefits) remain with the original owners. In all cases, the ownership of the securities "lent" changes hands. Unlike repos, the methodological treatment of securities lending is not covered in either *BPM5* or the *1993 SNA*.

3.77 In most countries, the statistical practice is to regard the securities (both those lent and those provided in return as collateral) as remaining on the books of the original owner. If a borrowed security is on-sold (which is usually the case), then both the original owner and the third party will each regard itself as owning the security, while the "borrower" will regard itself as having a negative holding (a "short" position). In essence, what this means as far as the initial "borrowing" is concerned is that no transaction is recorded—the nature of the initial "borrowing" is similar to that of a repo, without cash being exchanged. Because it is only the cash portion of a repo that is recorded—the exchange of ownership of the securities is ignored—for securities lending, the same applies. Therefore, since no cash is involved in securities lending, to be consistent with the treatment of repos, no transaction is recorded for the exchange of securities under securities lending. This treatment was endorsed by the IMF Committee at its 2000 meeting. However, in some countries, the practice is to regard securities lending as a transaction in its own right: the lent security becomes owned by the "borrower," and the collateral becomes owned by the "lender," even where there is an imbalance between the value of the security provided and the value of the security received. If a "borrowed" security is on-sold outright, then the "borrower" (the reverse repoing party) should record a "short" position. From the above, it can be readily seen that, as with repos, there is the possibility of asymmetric reporting within and among countries.

(iii) Treatment of securities lending in the CPIS

3.78 The preferred treatment for the purposes of the survey is for securities lending/borrowing to be regarded as an off-balance-sheet transaction—that is, that it not be recorded as a transaction so that the original owners continue to report that they still hold the security. If (when) the security is on-sold, the "borrower" of the security should record a "short" position.

3.79 As can be seen, the issues for securities lending are similar to those for repos, and the importance of both internal and external consistency of approach is equally valid. Therefore, the recommendations with regard to repos apply equally to securities lending: the importance that the market be assessed; internally consistent reporting instructions, developed after consultation with potential survey respondents; investigation of the scope for the lending to nonresidents of securities issued by nonresidents; bilateral contacts established with national compilers in the appropriate countries; and information on the intended treatment sent to the IMF. The problems of collecting information from custodians are similar for both repos and security lending: custodians, especially for the "borrower," may be unaware that a security has only been "lent/borrowed" and may have no means of identifying that the security is to be returned, or that a "short" position should be recorded, in the event of an on-sale. It is strongly recommended that compilers make every effort to ensure that the custodian understands the requirements and can provide the information on the bases recommended. It is suggested that contacts with all respondents regarding securities lending and repos, but especially for custodians, be undertaken simultaneously.

C. Depository Receipts

(i) Definition

3.80 *Depository receipts* are securities that represent ownership of securities held by a depository.[40] The country of residence of the issuer of the underlying securities is different from the country in which the receipts are issued.

(ii) Potential for double counting

3.81 The issuance of depository receipts is becoming increasingly prevalent: issuers and intermediaries are finding that investors frequently prefer to acquire securities in the financial markets where payment and settlement systems, registration procedures, and so on are familiar, rather than in the home market of the issuer, where systems and procedures may not be as familiar or as efficient. The potential for double counting lies in the existence of both the underlying security, held by the depository, and the depository receipts. That is, two securities could be reported as held, but only one liability exists. Clear guidance to survey respondents is required in order to avoid double counting.

(iii) Treatment of depository receipts in the CPIS

3.82 The way in which depository receipts should be recorded is that the financial institution "issuing" the receipts should be "looked through"; that is, the holder of the receipts should be taken to have a claim on the unit that underlies the receipts.

3.83 The reporting should follow the guidelines below.

3.84 Depository receipts are certificates that represent ownership of securities held by a depository. These receipts should be allocated to the country of residence of the issuer of the original (or underlying) security and not to the residence of the financial intermediary that issues the receipts. In other words, American depository receipts (ADRs) are liabilities of the non-U.S. enterprise whose securities underlie the ADR issue and not of the U.S. financial institution that issued the ADRs.

3.85 Financial intermediaries should not report holdings of any securities issued by nonresidents against which depository receipts have been issued and sold. If a depository receipt has been issued before the financial institution arranging the issue has acquired the original (or underlying) securities, then that financial institution should report a negative holding in the original (or underlying) securities.

D. Stripped Securities

(i) Definition

3.86 *Stripped securities* (strips) are securities that have been transformed from a principal amount with periodic coupons into a series of zero-coupon bonds, with the range of maturities matching the coupon payment dates and the redemption date of the principal amount. Strips can be created in two ways. Either the owner of the original security can ask the settlement or clearinghouse in which the security is registered to create strips from the original security, in which case the strips replace the original security and remain the direct obligation of the issuer of the original security; or the owner of the original security can issue strips in its own name, backed by the original security, in which case the strips represent new liabilities of the owner of the original securities and are not the direct obligation of the issuer of the original security.

(ii) Potential for double counting

3.87 The issuance of stripped securities is becoming more prevalent. The creation through strips of zero-coupon bonds eliminates the reinvestment risk inherent in a bond with a coupon and allows investors greater leverage; that is, less money needs to be invested to gain the same market exposure as with an equivalent bond with a coupon. When the entity issuing the strips is creating new liabilities, double counting does not arise. The potential for double counting arises when the strips have replaced the

[40]A depository is an entity to whom securities are entrusted for safe-keeping.

Box 3.7: Treatment in 1997 CPIS of Financial Transactions That May Lead to Under- or Double Counting

Portugal—Reporting instructions on these issues were drawn up according to the *Survey Guide* (note, however, that stripped securities were not covered in the Portuguese Survey). Any question could be clarified with the Banco de Portugal and contacts with major reporters were made, so the reported data provided guarantees that double counting was excluded. Double counting is also avoided because the resident custodians report to the Banco de Portugal the number of the opened dossiers of foreign securities (this is attributed by the Banco according to its technical instructions); that number is also used in the direct report by final investors. Each dossier number of the foreign securities is given an enterprise register number that allows the Banco to identify the underlying client. This feature allows the implementation of a quality control and data capture system. Furthermore, these aspects are in accordance with the collection and statistical production of the balance of payments system, which assures better reconciliation of flows and stocks.

United States—Respondents were instructed to report as if repo and securities lending activities do not exist. That is, if a custodian has securities that are temporarily involved in a repo agreement, they are to report these securities as if they are continuously held. Further, the counterparty is instructed not to report these securities that they have temporarily acquired. Collateral received as part of the repo agreement is not to be reported, and collateral given is to be reported as continuously held. Likewise, securities lent are to be reported as continuously held, securities borrowed are not to be reported, and any collateral involved is to be reported as if held by the original owner (in the same manner as for repos).

original security even though the latter has not been redeemed. In essence, the original security is "dormant" in the settlement or clearinghouse, until such time as it is reconstituted or redeemed.

(iii) Treatment of stripped securities in the CPIS

3.88 The reporting instructions should follow the guidelines below.

3.89 If strips have been issued by an entity in its own name, then the residence of the issuer is that of the entity that issued the strips, and the issuing entity should report its holdings of the existing securities issued by nonresidents.

3.90 If strips have been created from a nonresident security and remain the direct obligation of the original issuer, then the residence of the issuer remains the same as for the original security.

3.91 Dealers who request that a settlement or clearing house create strips from an existing nonresident security should not report their holdings of the underlying nonresident security after the strips have been created.

3.92 Strips with an original maturity of less than one year are money market instruments. If identifiable, they should be reported as such.

3.93 Box 3.7 indicates the experience in two countries in the 1997 CPIS in attempting to avoid double or undercounting of holdings that may result from repo, securities lending, depository receipts, and stripped securities.

VIII. Instruments

3.94 Appendix VI to this *Survey Guide* describes in detail many of the instruments that are available to investors. The information may assist both compilers and respondents to classify these instruments as equity or long-term or short-term debt. Table 3.1 sets out the instruments covered by all of the participants in the 1997 CPIS.

Table 3.1: Instruments Covered by Participants in the 1997 CPIS

Instruments	Argentina	Australia	Austria	Belgium	Bermuda	Canada	Chile
Equity securities	[1]						
Shares and stocks (excluding nonparticipating preferred shares)		X	X	X	X	X	X
Participation documents		X	X	[2]	X	X	X
Depository receipts		X	X	X	X	X	X
Shares in mutual funds and investment trusts		X	X	X	X	X	X
Other		[3]	—	[4]	—	[5]	—
Long-term debt securities	[1]						
Nonparticipating preferred stocks or shares		X	—	X	X		X
"Straight" (coupon) bonds		X	X	X	X	X	X
Convertible bonds and bonds with optional maturity dates, the latest of which is more than one year after issue		X	X	X	X	X	X
Negotiable certificates of deposit with maturities of more than one year		X	X	X	X		X
Dual currency bonds		X	X	X	X	X	X
Zero coupon bonds and other deep discount bonds		X	X	X	X	X	X
Floating rate bonds		X	X	X	X	X	X
Indexed bonds		X	X	X	X	X	X
Asset-backed securities, such as collateralized mortgage obligations (CMOs) and participation certificates		X	X	X	X	X	—
Other		[3]	—	[4]	—	[6]	—
Money market instruments	[1]						
Treasury bills		X	X	X	—	X	—
Commercial and finance paper		X	X	X	—	X	—
Bankers' acceptances		X	X	X	—	X	—
Negotiable certificates of deposit with original maturity of one year or less		X	X	X	—	X	—
Short-term notes issued under note issuance facilities (NIFs)		X	X	X	—	X	—
Other		[3]	—	[4]	—	—	—

Instruments	Denmark	Finland	France	Iceland	Indonesia	Ireland	Israel
Equity securities							
Shares and stocks (excluding nonparticipating preferred shares)	X	X	X	X	X	X	X
Participation documents	X	X	X	X	—	X	X
Depository receipts	X	X	X	X	—	X	X
Shares in mutual funds and investment trusts	X	X	X	X	—	X	X
Other	—	—	—	—	—	—	—
Long-term debt securities							
"Straight" (coupon) bonds	X	X	X	X	X	X	X
Nonparticipating preferred stocks or shares	X	X	—	X	—	X	X
Convertible bonds and bonds with optional maturity dates, the latest of which is more than one year after issue	X	X	X	X	X	X	X
Negotiable certificates of deposit with maturities of more than one year	X	X	X	X	—	X	X
Dual currency bonds	X	X	X	X	—	X	X
Zero coupon bonds and other deep discount bonds	X	X	X	X	X	X	X
Floating rate bonds	X	X	X	X	—	X	X
Indexed bonds	X	X	X	X	—	X	X
Asset-backed securities, such as collateralized mortgage obligations (CMOs) and participation certificates	X	X	X	X	—	X	X
Other	—	—	[7]	—	—	—	—
Money market instruments							
Treasury bills	—	X	—	—	—	—	X
Commercial and finance paper	—	X	—	—	X	—	X
Bankers' acceptances	—	X	—	—	—	—	X
Negotiable certificates of deposit with original maturity of one year or less	—	X	—	—	X	—	X
Short-term notes issued under note issuance facilities (NIFs)	—	X	—	—	—	—	X
Other	—	—	—	—	—	—	—

(Table continues on following page)

Table 3.1 *(continued)*

Instruments	Italy	Japan	Korea	Malaysia	Netherlands	New Zealand	Norway	Portugal
Equity securities								
Shares and stocks (excluding nonparticipating preferred shares)	X	X	X	X	X	X	X	X
Participation documents	X	X	X	X	X	X	X	X
Depository receipts	X	X	X	X	X	X	X	X
Shares in mutual funds and investment trusts	X	8	X	X	X	X	X	X
Other	—	9	10	—	—	—	X	11
Long-term debt securities								
"Straight" (coupon) bonds	X	X	X	X	X	X	X	X
Nonparticipating preferred stocks or shares	X	—	X	X	X	X	X	12
Convertible bonds and bonds with optional maturity dates, the latest of which is more than one year after issue	X	X	X	X	X	X	X	12
Negotiable certificates of deposit with maturities of more than one year	X	13	X	X	X	X	X	X
Dual currency bonds	X	X	X	X	X	X	X	12
Zero coupon bonds and other deep discount bonds	X	X	X	X	X	X	X	12
Floating rate bonds	X	X	X	X	X	X	X	12
Indexed bonds	X	X	X	X	X	X	X	12
Asset-backed securities, such as collateralized mortgage obligations (CMOs) and participation certificates	X	X	X	X	X	X	X	X
Other	—	14	15	—	—	—	—	12
Money market instruments								
Treasury bills	X	X	X	X	—	—	—	X
Commercial and finance paper	X	X	X	X	—	—	—	X
Bankers' acceptances	X	X	X	X	—	—	—	—
Negotiable certificates of deposit with original maturity of one year or less	X	10	X	X	—	—	—	X
Short-term notes issued under note issuance facilities (NIFs)	X	X	X	X	—	—	—	—
Other	—	—	—	—	—	—	—	16

Instruments	Singapore	Spain	Sweden	Thailand	United Kingdom	United States	Venezuela
Equity securities					17		
Shares and stocks (excluding nonparticipating preferred shares)	X	X	X	X	X	X	X
Participation documents	X	X	18	X	X	X	X
Depository receipts	X	X	X	X	X	X	X
Shares in mutual funds and investment trusts	X	X	X	X	X	X	X
Other	—	19	—	—	—	—	—
Long-term debt securities					20		
"Straight" (coupon) bonds	X	X	X	X	X	X	X
Nonparticipating preferred stocks or shares	X	X	X	X	X	X	X
Convertible bonds and bonds with optional maturity dates, the latest of which is more than one year after issue	X	X	X	X	X	X	X
Negotiable certificates of deposit with maturities of more than one year	X	X	—	X	—	X	X
Dual currency bonds	X	X	X	X	X	X	X
Zero coupon bonds and other deep discount bonds	X	X	X	X	X	X	X
Floating rate bonds	X	X	X	X	X	X	X
Indexed bonds	X	X	X	X	X	X	X
Asset-backed securities, such as collateralized mortgage obligations (CMOs) and participation certificates	X	X	X	X	X	X	X
Other	—	21	—	—	—	—	—
Money market instruments					22		
Treasury bills	X	X	X	—	X	—	X
Commercial and finance paper	X	X	X	—	X	—	X
Bankers' acceptances	X	X	—	—	—	—	X
Negotiable certificates of deposit with original maturity of one year or less	X	X	—	—	X	—	X
Short-term notes issued under note issuance facilities (NIFs)	X	X	X	—	X	—	X
Other	—	23	—	—	—	—	—

Note: X = country did cover instrument in 1997; — = country did not cover instrument.

[1] No "CPIS forms" were used; portfolio investment data that had already been collected pointed mainly to shares, depository rights, treasury bonds, treasury bills, and negotiable certificates of deposit (CDs).

Table 3.1 *(concluded)*

[2]None (treated as direct investment).
[3]The Survey of International Investment is specifically designed to collect data necessary to support *BPM5* requirements. The format and wording used in the collection forms, together with the wording in the detailed Explanatory Notes that are supplied to all respondents, are closely aligned to the wording in the *BPM5*. The Explanatory Notes provide numerous examples of what should be included (and excluded) under each type of instrument. Copies of the survey forms and the Explanatory Notes were used during the December quarter 1997.
[4]As far as they meet the *BPM5*'s definition.
[5]Installment receipts and preferred stocks or shares (participating and nonparticipating distinction rarely available).
[6]Negotiable CDs with maturity of more than one year (information on maturity often missing).
[7]Fixed-rate bonds and any bond not described above; medium-term notes.
[8]Excluding open-end unincorporated investment trusts.
[9]Preference shares.
[10]Equity securities that were sold under repos and equity securities that have been lent under securities lending arrangements.
[11]Subscription rights.
[12]A general category of "bonds" was reported, which might include other types of long-term debt securities. Additional detail is also available for public and guaranteed bonds.
[13]Only assets.
[14]Open-end unincorporated investment trusts.
[15]Debt securities that have been sold under repos and debt securities that have been lent under securities lending arrangements.
[16]A residual category "other" has been reported, which might include other types of short-term debt securities.
[17]U.K. data include all categories listed.
[18]Not implicitly mentioned in the CPIS form.
[19]All quoted equity securities were included.
[20]U.K. data included all categories. Bonds with less than one year's maturity were also included (on existing survey forms institutions are asked to report all bonds as debt securities regardless of maturity as result of implementing *European System of Accounts 1995*).
[21]All quoted long-term debt securities were included.
[22]Collected for banks only. Banks were requested to classify all CDs, regardless of original maturity, as money market instruments.
[23]All quoted short-term debt securities were included.

4. Collection Methods

A considerable degree of complexity is involved in organizing a portfolio investment survey to ensure good-quality data. Therefore, compilers should carefully consider all possibilities before deciding on the collection system. To ensure both consistency and quality of reporting across the participating countries in the CPIS, this chapter covers certain practical issues that go beyond those covered in the IMF's Balance of Payments Compilation Guide *(Washington, 1995).*

This chapter provides guidance for compilers on the following issues: choosing a collection system (preliminary investigations, coverage, and degree of detail required), security databases, thresholds, and third-party holdings.

I. Data Considerations

4.1 Although it is essential that CPIS data are comparable across countries—for the data exchange as much as for international comparability—it is **not** necessary that all countries use the same data collection systems. Instead, national compilers should tailor their collection systems to meet their own circumstances.

4.2 Experience in conducting the 1997 CPIS indicated that the national survey can target primarily any of a number of groups: (i) end-investors; (ii) custodians (financial institutions that administer or manage securities issued by nonresidents on behalf of domestic residents); (iii) a combination of both end-investors and custodians; and (iv) investment managers in combination with either custodians or both end-investors and custodians. However, because of the special and complicated nature of surveying investment managers, targeting this group is not recommended for countries that have not conducted a portfolio investment survey before. A discussion of the advantages and disadvantages in conducting a survey using investment managers is included later in this chapter.

4.3 Data can be collected either on a **security-by-security** or on an **aggregated** basis. So, to guide national compilers, this chapter specifies considerations to take into account when deciding which type of collection system to use for the CPIS. It also discusses the difficulties inherent in covering investment by the household sector.

II. Choosing a Collection System

4.4 Choosing the appropriate collection system is central to the success of the CPIS. It is probably the single most important decision that national compilers will need to make. Difficult technical issues, such as the possibility of under- or double counting, have to be resolved regardless of which system is chosen. Consequently, before deciding on the type of collection system to use, national compilers should undertake some preliminary investigations, particularly among financial institutions, taking into account both the objectives for the CPIS and their own information requirements.

A. Preliminary Investigations

(i) General issues

4.5 As a starting point, issues that need to be explored both within the compiling agency and with market participants are as follows:

- What objectives are being established for the survey at the national level? For instance, what type of information is being sought? How important are timeliness of results and frequency of the survey?[41]

[41]The CPIS is likely to be repeated on a regular basis; therefore, it is important to advise respondents of this so they can set up their information systems to report regularly. If respondents are under the impression that the survey is to be conducted on one occasion only, they may not set in place systems that can be used in subsequent surveys, which may cause them additional expenses were the survey to be repeated.

- What, if any, is the legal authority that governs the collection of the information?
- Which residents invest in and/or own securities issued by nonresidents? In a broad sense, which are the largest investors?
- How do residents arrange for the custody of their holdings of securities issued by nonresidents: with domestic custodians, directly with nonresidents, in their own custody, or some combination of these?
- How are data currently collected on securities issued by nonresidents, for both transactions and position? Is it possible to adapt an existing survey, or is there a need to develop a new approach?
- What are the record-keeping and internal arrangements of potential survey respondents? What type of survey would most easily and efficiently fit these arrangements?
- Should the data be collected security-by-security or in aggregate? Would one type of collection system be more efficient in terms of producing good-quality data at lower cost than the other? What is the view of market participants? What budget and resource constraints does the compiler face?

4.6 The answers to the above questions will assist compilers in making an informed decision about the type of collection system to adopt.

What objectives are being established for the survey at the national level? For instance, what type of information is being sought? How important are timeliness of results and frequency of the survey?

4.7 The objectives of the survey may be circumscribed by the resources available to the compiler. In principle, the survey is aimed at collecting data on all resident holdings of securities issued by unrelated nonresidents (equities and long- and short-term debt), by country of issuer. However, it is not always practical to attempt to cover all holdings of all sectors, especially if the survey is being conducted for the first time. The decision of what to cover may well be based on two critical criteria: the budget available to the compiler and materiality. That is, what can realistically be surveyed with the resources available and which are the most important sectors/respondents to cover with those resources to maximize the benefit of the expense, while minimizing the costs to the respondents? At the same time, the issue of timeliness and frequency of data collection must be addressed as part of this process. Data not available for more than a year after the reference date may be too late for CPIS purposes, while the frequency of providing and processing the data needs to be considered if the survey is to be conducted on an ongoing basis (i.e., can the respondents and the compiling agency afford to collect the data regularly?).

What, if any, is the legal authority that governs the collection of the information?

4.8 In many countries, a statistics act or the legislation under which the central bank or national statistical office operates will provide the legal authority for the collection of the information. The legal authority should require that reporting of statistical information is mandatory, that it should be provided accurately and within a reasonable time of the request, and that there can be sanctions for failure to comply. The legislation should also indicate that the individual data are confidential to the compiling agency and that there should be no means through which any individual respondent's data can be identified (without the express approval of that respondent).

4.9 In countries where the legislation is insufficiently clear or where sanctions are missing, the authorities may wish to seek improvements to the law. Other countries may lack legal authority; in these cases the survey has to be conducted on a voluntary basis, and a good working relationship between the compiling agency and the potential respondents is essential for the success of the exercise. To that end, it is valuable to employ the good offices of industry associations to facilitate the implementation of the survey and, possibly, act as a go-between for collection of the information from individual respondents or to process the returns. The association(s) could then forward the aggregated data to the compiling agency. This approach may result in lower-quality data (there is no means of adequately verifying the data), but it may provide information that might otherwise not be available. In any event, even when there is adequate legal authority to collect the data on a mandatory basis, involving industry associations is often a useful tactic and a valuable public relations exercise—it may help relations with individual respondents if the association is seen to be actively involved and can see the benefits of the undertaking.

Which residents invest in and/or own securities issued by nonresidents? In a broad sense, which are the largest investors?

4.10 A useful starting point may be to review the data sources for portfolio investment that are provided for the balance of payments or the international investment position (IIP) to find out which investors are the most important and what existing data can be built on for the CPIS. In addition, discussions with market participants provides a useful additional source of information—since the compiler may not be aware of some avenues of investment or some players in international investment activity.

How do residents arrange for the custody of their holdings of securities issued by nonresidents: with domestic custodians, directly with nonresidents, in their own custody, or some combination of these?

4.11 This issue should also be explored with institutional investors and others with a knowledge of local market conditions and investment conduits. See the discussion later in this chapter on the pros and cons of using an end-investor survey, a survey of custodians, or a combination.

How are data currently collected on securities issued by a nonresident, for both transactions and positions? Is it possible to adapt an existing survey, or is there a need to develop a new approach?

4.12 If data for either portfolio investment in the financial account of the balance of payments or in the IIP are presently collected from resident sources, a review of what information is available, how it is collected, and the bases of valuation will give an indication of the types of institutions that could be approached (the periodicity with which revaluation of the portfolio is undertaken is very important).

4.13 However, these sources of data are usually insufficient without additional information being collected. Given that one of the objectives of the CPIS is to gain information on a geographic basis, if information for an IIP is presently collected, obtaining the geographical breakdown for the CPIS may not involve much additional burden on respondents, depending on how the respondents maintain their records. This should be undertaken with a recognition of the materiality of the data. If holdings are small in some countries, an appropriate threshold may be established if by so doing a significant reduction in respondent burden results. Determining a threshold (if any) should be done following discussions with investors to identify what might represent a reasonable cut-off point while still maintaining substantial coverage and geographical detail (see below).

What are the record-keeping and internal arrangements of potential survey respondents? What type of survey would most naturally fit these arrangements?

4.14 Discussions with respondents about their internal record keeping is important in order to determine the best and easiest way to obtain the information on the bases required. In some countries, information that is central for the CPIS may be available, in one form or another, in many large financial institutions. Other investors in securities issued by unrelated nonresidents may need more assistance. Some investors classify their exposure to various investment markets on the basis of a number of variables, such as country of parent, currency, region, industry, credit rating, and country of issue (which may not necessarily be the country of residence of the **issuer**). The concept of residence that is central to the balance of payments, the IIP, and the CPIS is not necessarily always used. This concept should be clarified (see the discussion on residence in Chapter 2), and its importance reinforced. In some cases, if the respondents prefer, it may be easier for them to provide the complete file of their holdings to the compiler, if adequate safeguards can be provided. (See the discussion on the security-by-security approach later in the chapter.)

Should the data be collected security-by-security or in aggregate? Would one type of collection system be more efficient in terms of producing good-quality data at lower cost than the other? What is the view of market participants? What budget and resource constraints does the compiler face?

4.15 The best way to obtain the data is not something that can be decided in advance. Factors that should be taken into account include what resources are available to the compiler and what is the easiest and cheapest way for the respondents to provide the data. If the compiler's resources are limited, using the aggregate approach may be the better choice, but the drawback is that the respondents may be required to do a considerable amount of reordering and reaggregating of their data that they might not otherwise have to do (depending on their internal management and accounting information systems). In addition, the data cannot usually be checked readily by the compiler. On the other hand, providing data on a security-by-security basis may reduce respondent workload (depending on the existing means through which data are collected) but increase the workload of the compiler. The ultimate choice will depend on an assessment of the costs and benefits of the alternative approaches for both the compiler and the respondents.

4.16 In addition, choosing an end-investor approach, a custodian approach, or a combination of the two will depend on the extent to which the compiler is able to determine the best coverage while minimizing overlap. Clear instructions and discussions with respondents will result in better data. See the discussion later in this chapter on the merits and disadvantages of an aggregate versus a security-by-security approach.

(ii) Sectors to consider in the survey

4.17 In undertaking the above process, compilers may wish to bear in mind the sectoral dimension, not only for analytical purposes but also to ensure maximum coverage without double counting. A description of the sectors is given in Chapter 3, Section V.

4.18 National compilers are advised to examine domestic sources of information to establish, in a broad sense, the saving pattern of the four major sectors of their respective economy: **households, financial institutions, nonfinancial corporations**, and **general government**. This examination might provide some indication of which sectors are likely to be the largest owners of securities issued by nonresidents. In this regard, it is particularly important to gauge the extent to which the household sector acquires securities issued by nonresidents, and where these securities are held.

4.19 Financial institutions are usually major investors either on their own account or as agents on behalf of others (usually the household sector) through collective investment schemes, life insurance companies, or pension funds. Monetary authorities hold international reserve assets that should be kept separate from portfolio investment but reported through a separate collection vehicle, SEFER. See the discussion on SEFER in Chapters 1 and 2.

4.20 The **general government** sector is not usually a major investor in international portfolio markets, although governments are frequently major issuers of debt instruments acquired by international investors. (Holdings of international reserves are not recorded as being the holdings of the general government sector. These holdings are included with monetary authorities—see *Financial institutions,* above.)

4.21 It is uncommon for **nonfinancial corporations** to have large holdings of portfolio investment assets (although, like governments, they may well have substantial portfolio liabilities). International investment by nonfinancial corporations is more likely to take the form of direct investment (see the discussion on separating direct investment from portfolio investment, in Chapter 3, and on experiences of various countries, in Chapter 6).

4.22 The **household** sector is generally a major source of saving in most economies, but it is difficult to survey directly, given the size of the potential reporting population and the inherent problems in building a representative sample. Thus, national compilers are encouraged to investigate the channels through which this sector invests in and holds securities issued by nonresidents. *Does the household sector own securities issued by nonresidents through domestic pension funds and mutual trusts? Do custodians and fund managers manage securities issued by nonresidents directly for the household sector? Does the household sector transact and hold securities directly with nonresident financial entities, not least for tax minimization reasons?*

4.23 In the experience of the Task Force, national compilers may take various approaches to covering private household sector holdings of securities issued by nonresidents. One approach is to survey collective investment funds—for instance, mutual funds and investment trusts—used by households to invest in securities issued by nonresidents. In these cases, the households' interests are indirect—that is, claims on the resident funds that hold nonresident security assets. A second approach is to survey financial entities, such as custodians who hold securities issued by nonresidents for households or fund managers who manage holdings on behalf of households. The next section places these various options in context.

4.24 The problem remains, however, of covering household holdings in securities issued by a nonresident held directly with nonresident financial entities. In some countries, this is an insignificant issue; in others, it is very significant. For the latter group of countries, there is no simple solution.

4.25 One approach would be to try to estimate the extent of investment made by domestic households that is held directly abroad on the basis of domestically available statistical information. To this end, comparisons could be made between (i) the net savings of households measured by the production, income, and use of income accounts as the difference between income and spending and (ii) household saving as measured by financial accounts. Such comparisons could, together with an analysis of net errors and omissions of the balance of payments, indicate whether household saving held directly abroad is a significant problem. At best, it could give some indication of the amount of this kind of saving. It is unlikely, however, that comparisons of this kind could contribute to the CPIS, which requires details regarding country breakdown of portfolio assets.

4.26 Another approach would be to rely upon international cooperation and the exchange of information between countries. Through this approach, countries to which nonresident households directly entrust their portfolio savings would collect information on these so-called third-party holding and share that information with partner countries. The partner country would, in turn, be able to add this information to its portfolio assets. Given the lack of experience in collecting third-party holding data for this purpose, the complexity and potential for double counting,[42] and the possible lack of legal authority to collect information that is unrelated directly to domestic policy needs, countries considering this approach are advised to make careful investigations and preparations. Some of the practical and methodological problems connected with undertaking a third-party holdings (TPH) survey are described in Section V of this chapter.[43]

B. Coverage (End-Investors, Custodians, or Both)

4.27 The most suitable approach to ensuring comprehensive coverage of securities issued by nonresidents that are owned by residents varies according to a given country's circumstances. Countries differ in their financial structure for legal, institutional, and historical reasons. The types of residents that invest in securities issued by nonresidents and how they arrange for the custody of their securities vary from country to country. Nonetheless, experience suggests that most countries will rely primarily on either (i) end-investors to report their own account holdings, (ii) custodians to report their own account and client holdings, or (iii) a combination of the two.[44] Set out below are the advantages and disadvantages of these three approaches.

[42]For example, both a local and a global custodian could report the same holdings when the latter has placed securities in the custody of the former; or an end-investor could report the same holdings as a custodian in a third country.

[43]The IMF has set up a Technical Group to explore the possibilities of collecting data from third-party holdings, but it will not be able to provide assistance in time for the 2001 CPIS.

[44]Investment (or fund) managers may also sometimes be approached.

(i) An end-investor survey

4.28 An end-investor survey approaches directly the owner of securities issued by nonresidents. This approach should provide good coverage when investment in securities issued by nonresidents is concentrated in institutional investors, such as banks, security dealers, mutual funds, and pension and insurance funds. The quality of the data provided should also be good because end-investors are probably best informed about the size, composition, and value of their own portfolio. They should also be the best source on repos, which would help ensure that repos are reported as collateralized loans.

4.29 In addition, if the current method of collecting portfolio investment data is through an end-investor survey, and if it is considered that coverage is comprehensive, and it is possible to amend or supplement existing statistical collections, then continuing to use this approach should be the most cost-effective method. Data from the survey could be cross-checked against existing returns as a method of quality control (see Chapter 5).

4.30 If, however, collecting portfolio investment data through an end-investor survey is a new approach for the national compiler, additional preparation will be required. Most important, the compiler will need to prepare a comprehensive register of potential survey respondents and engage in extensive discussions with the institutions most likely to hold securities issued by nonresidents. Otherwise, there is the possibility of undercoverage (see Chapter 5 on the issues related to establishing and maintaining a register). Creating and maintaining the register will require resources. National compilers must also avoid either double counting or overrecording of securities holdings. For instance, in their reports, entities might consolidate holdings of resident subsidiaries that report separately to the national compiler (double counting) or holdings of subsidiaries located outside the resident economy (overrecording). Essentially, compilers should know whose holdings are covered by the survey respondent. Moreover, compilers should be alert to the possibility that entities not familiar with completing portfolio investment survey forms may have difficulty in reporting the required information and may require advice. Indeed, regular contact and follow-up visits to potential respondents is a very worthwhile exercise that is often indispensable for a first, or even second or third, survey until respondents are comfortable with the survey's requirements. An end-investor approach also gives a better means of determining the holdings by sector. Although an end-investor approach is likely to provide good coverage of large institutional investors, however, securities owned by households are not captured because it is usually too difficult and expensive to conduct a survey of households.

4.31 Valuation by end-investors may also vary among holders and even within a respondent's own accounts. Some end-investors mark their holdings to market daily; others do it weekly, monthly, quarterly, or annually. Others may not do it on any regular basis, depending on what their needs are. Some investors may hold both a trading account and an investment account. In these cases, investment accounts are sometimes not marked to market because they are to be held to maturity or are held for other purposes (such as reserve or capital requirements). Respondents should be asked to specify where they maintain valuation on a different basis from that required for the survey (i.e., market price on the reference date). Where valuation is provided on a different basis from market price, efforts should be made whenever possible to revalue the securities to market price.

(ii) A custodian survey

4.32 A custodian survey focuses primarily on those financial institutions that hold securities issued by nonresidents on behalf of end-investors. In other words, the survey population is not the same as the population of domestic investors. This type of collection system should provide good coverage when residents mainly hold their securities issued by nonresidents with domestic custodians. Because the number of survey respondents will be fewer than the number of end-investors, the difficulties inherent in identifying and maintaining the appropriate reporting population are much reduced compared with such difficulties for an end-investor survey.

4.33 However, to compile good-quality data from a survey of custodians, the national compiler must be aware of the potentially complex relationships between end-investors and custodians and among custodians. Because of the hierarchy of custodians (the investor may deal with a primary custodian who in turn deals with a global custodian, or vice-versa[45]), the possibility that a security holding may be double counted is ever present and should not be underestimated. Essentially, national compilers should understand the structure of the custodian business, know who should report, and write very clear instructions on the survey form. National compilers may find flow charts useful.

4.34 Custodians may encounter difficulties in (i) distinguishing between holdings of residents and nonresidents (unless they have a reason, such as for tax purposes, to make such a distinction), (ii) providing details of the geographic breakdown of resident holdings of securities issued by nonresidents, and (iii) valuing some securities at market value. In other words, they may store information in a format that makes it difficult for them to extract the data required by the national compiler. **Hence, it is essential that those countries undertaking a custodian survey conduct presurvey consultations with domestic custodians.** As with a survey of end-investors, ongoing contact and follow-up visits are an important mechanism to ensure that data are reported as required. Such quality-control checks are essential (see Chapter 5).

(iii) Combined custodian/end-investor survey

4.35 Surveys that included domestic custodians only would miss any securities owned by domestic residents that are held directly with nonresident custodians or in own custody. More complete coverage would be obtained by a survey that included domestic custodians who hold securities issued by nonresidents owned by residents as well as end-investors who hold securities issued by nonresidents. Countries that use combined custodian/end-investor surveys have adopted the approach of collecting data primarily from custodians (and from end-investors only when the end-investors do not use domestic custodians or have own custody). These countries have found that the vast majority of securities issued by nonresidents owned by residents are entrusted to domestic custodians.

4.36 With this approach, there is a clear danger of double counting; domestic investors might erroneously report securities deposited with domestic as well as with nonresident custodians. Hence, compilers will need to take particular care in defining the respondent population[46] and in writing very clear

[45]A global custodian manages the custody of end-investors' securities via a global subcustodian network of subsidiaries and correspondent agent banks. A primary or local custodian may not have a global subcustodian network and, therefore, may subcontract the safekeeping of the client's securities to a domestic global custodian.

[46]Chapter 6 provides guidance on compiling a register of potential survey respondents.

reporting instructions. In some countries, national compilers require the custodian to indicate the name of the end-investor on the behalf of which the securities issued by nonresidents have been entrusted. In addition, the end-investor could be asked to report a breakdown of holdings of securities issued by nonresidents that are (i) held with domestic custodians, (ii) held with nonresident custodians, and (iii) held in own custody. This helps reduce under- or double counting. However, it should be recognized that custodians, in particular, may be very reluctant to provide such information, and quality-control checks are essential (see Chapters 5 and 6).

C. Advantages and Disadvantages of Surveying Investment (Fund) Managers

4.37 This chapter has explored various types of surveys: end-investor surveys, custodian surveys, and combined custodian/end-investor surveys. One can, however, collect data from still another source: investment managers.

4.38 Investment managers are individuals or groups providing investment advice and management for a fee. The funds that investment managers invest remain the assets of their clients and are not brought on to the balance sheet of the investment manager. The ultimate responsibility for the investment remains with the client. For example, when a pension fund has all or part of its assets invested through investment managers, the trustees of the pension fund remain responsible for the investments, not the investment manager.

4.39 The advantage of including investment managers is that more complete coverage might thereby be obtained. The disadvantage is that both the complexity of the survey and the possibility of double counting or undercounting are increased.

4.40 A typical coverage gap—even in the case of combined custodian/end-investor surveys—is small business enterprises and individuals with high net worth who own securities issued by unrelated nonresidents, particularly if they entrust these securities directly to foreign-based custodians. Although it is not usually practical to include such investors directly in asset surveys, these investors sometimes employ the services of domestic investment managers to manage their portfolios. The leading investment managers can often be identified and included in the survey because in many countries investment managers must register with a government agency and disclose the amount of funds under their control.

4.41 Yet investment managers are not employed only by individuals and small companies; they are also used by large institutions whose assets are already being measured by the survey, so care must be taken to carefully delineate and explain reporting responsibilities.

4.42 The following sections discuss the advantages and disadvantages of various approaches.

D. Advantages and Disadvantages of Surveying End-Investors Only

4.43 This type of survey typically collects data from the largest domestic sources of foreign portfolio investment, such as mutual funds, insurance companies, pension funds, government institutions, banks, and other large corporations. Survey respondents report their holdings regardless of whether their assets are held by domestic or foreign custodians. The assets of smaller institutional and corporate investors, as well as those of the household sector, are typically not measured by this type of survey if they invest directly in securities issued by unrelated nonresidents.

4.44 If investment managers are included in the survey, the coverage gap can be decreased. End-investors might be instructed to report their foreign holdings regardless of whether they employ domestic investment managers. Domestic investment managers might then also be instructed to report on all securities issued by nonresidents that they hold on behalf of domestic clients. They might also be instructed to provide the name(s) of the institution(s) on whose behalf they are acting and the amount(s) held for each client. They may be required to indicate whether they are acting on behalf of private individuals and to disclose the amount invested for all private individuals combined without disclosing individual identities. In this way double counting can be avoided.

4.45 A complicating factor is that sometimes custodians pass on all or part of the assets under their management to other domestic custodians. In such cases, instructions must be given to specify which custodian is to report these foreign holdings to avoid either gaps or double counting. It might be preferable to have the custodian in direct contact with the investor report, because otherwise the second custodian may be unaware whether the investor is a resident of the economy (or be unable to allocate to the appropriate institutional sector, if reporting encouraged items). In such cases, custodians should be instructed not to include those holdings that they receive from other custodians. On the other hand, it might be better to have the custodian that is providing the safekeeping services provide the information on holdings of securities issued by nonresidents, while advising the first custodian to report the name of the custodian to whom it has entrusted the securities. Whichever approach is chosen, it is important that the compiler discuss the reporting arrangements with the respondents and that the instructions be clear to avoid any misreporting.

E. Advantages and Disadvantages of Surveying Custodians Only

4.46 This type of survey collects data from major domestically based custodians. Holdings of all sectors of the economy—large and small institutions and corporations, government organizations, and the household sector—are captured to the extent that they entrust their securities issued by nonresidents to domestically based custodians. All securities entrusted directly to foreign-based custodians by any sector of the economy are missed. However, if investment managers are added to this type of survey, then that portion of foreign holdings entrusted directly abroad that is managed by domestic investment managers would be captured.

4.47 As with an end-investor-only survey, care would need to be taken to avoid double counting or undercounting. Only securities issued by unrelated nonresidents managed by a domestic investment manager and not entrusted to a domestic custodian should be reported by the investment manager. Instances of multiple domestic investment managers would need to be accounted for, as discussed in the section on end-investor surveys.

4.48 In addition, at times multiple domestic custodians are involved in the safekeeping of the same securities issued by nonresidents. This occurs when a domestic custodian (Custodian 1) that is not in the foreign custody business nonetheless accepts the custody of securities issued by a nonresident. In such cases, the securities might in turn be entrusted to another domestic custodian (Custodian 2) that provides international custody services. This creates a situation where two domestic custodians have records pertaining to the same securities issued by nonresidents. Reporting instructions must specify how each custodian is to report in such cases. This might be handled by instructing the custodian who provides the safekeeping of the securities issued by nonresidents (Custodian 2) to report these holdings on the survey, and to instruct the custodian who passed on safekeeping responsibilities (Custodian 1) not to report such holdings, while instructing Custodian 1 to report the name of Custodian 2 and the amount entrusted for cross-checking purposes. Alternatively, it might be preferable to have the custodian that is in direct contact with the investor to report, so that there is no possible misallocation of residence. Whichever approach is chosen, the instructions should be clear to avoid misreporting.

F. Advantages and Disadvantages of Surveying Both Custodians and End-Investors

4.49 This type of survey has the most comprehensive coverage because it collects data from both custodians and end-investors. However, because it already collects data from two different data sources—which requires coordination to avoid double or undercounting—adding investment managers into the mix further complicates the situation.

4.50 Let us assume that primary reporting responsibility is placed with custodians. In this case reporting instructions might be as follows:

(a) Domestic custodians that provide international custody services are instructed to report all holdings of securities issued by nonresidents on behalf of residents.

(b) Domestic custodians that accept securities issued by nonresidents for safekeeping but in turn pass them on to another domestic custodian are instructed not to report these holdings or are instructed to report only the name of the custodian they passed the securities on to and the amount passed on. Alternatively, the custodian that is in direct contact with the investor might be asked to report because he or she would be in a better position to determine whether the investor is a resident of the economy (or to allocate to the appropriate institutional sector, if encouraged items are being reported). Custodians who receive securities from other custodians should be advised not to include those holdings in their own reports.

(c) Investment managers are instructed to report holdings of securities under their management that were issued by nonresidents and not entrusted to other domestic investment managers or to domestic custodians.

(d) Investment managers that pass on assets under their control to other domestic investment managers are instructed not to report these securities.

(e) End-investors are instructed to report only their holdings of securities issued by nonresidents that are not under the control of a domestic investment manager and also not entrusted to a domestic custodian.

4.51 Extensive coverage is achieved with this approach, but the possibility of errors arising from misunderstood reporting requirements is increased. The situation could arise in which a domestic end-investor employs a domestic investment manager who employs another domestic investment manager who employs a domestic custodian who in turn employs another domestic custodian. Five different domestic entities that are potential reporters thus have information pertaining to the same securities issued by unrelated nonresidents, but only one must report in the survey.

G. Degree of Detail Required (Security-by-Security or Aggregate)

4.52 The degree of detail required for the CPIS can be met by collecting data either on a **security-by-security** basis or on an **aggregate** basis. Deciding which approach to take depends on the degree of detail required by the national compiler for domestic statistical purposes, on the costs involved, and perhaps on the type of respondent being approached.

(i) Security-by-security basis

4.53 Collecting data on a security-by-security, rather than on an aggregate, basis provides more information and allows greater possibility for data verification.[47] This approach not only provides the building blocks required to construct the geographically allocated position data and allows for verification of certain variables, such as price and country of issuer, but it can also provide additional information—for instance, on currency attribution, industry/sector of the issuer, yields on securities, and so on. It could also help identify direct investment securities.[48] An additional side benefit of a security-by-security approach, in conjunction with a securities database, is that other data series may be constructed from it or be used to supplement information required for other statistics, such as external debt data or the data template of reserve assets and foreign currency liquidity. But the national compiler will probably need to acquire a database that provides information on individual securities so that securities can be correctly allocated and valued.[49] Before making a decision, the compiler needs to decide whether the extra information is required.

4.54 The decision whether to collect data security-by-security will also depend on the costs involved and whether respondents are prepared to provide the information on that basis. Such a survey is, however, usually cheaper and easier for respondents: the additional costs fall on the compiling agency. This, in turn, relates to how frequently the national survey will be repeated—if the survey is likely to be a continuing exercise,[50] the initial investment in setting up a securities database to be used in conjunction with the security-by-security approach may be amortized over several years, whereas a one-time security-by-security survey is almost certain to be more expensive and take longer to conduct. Given the considerable amount of information to be collected, this type of survey probably needs to be conducted by electronic means, which involves developing compatible software to receive and process the information from survey respondents and to provide a link between the reported data and the securities database.

(ii) Aggregate basis

4.55 In contrast, an aggregated survey relies on the survey respondent to perform the aggregation, allocation, and valuation of securities, thus entailing relatively less involvement from national compilers. (However, if the security-by-security survey is repeated on a periodic basis—for instance, once a year—experience suggests that the marginal costs fall while the benefits of extra detail are maintained.)

4.56 There is also the issue of data quality. An end-investor survey should produce good-quality data reported on an aggregate security basis, provided that

[47] In an integrated end-investor survey system that collects aggregate data, some of the additional detail may be collected on other survey forms.

[48] See Chapter 5.

[49] See next section for more detail on securities databases.

[50] It is probable that the CPIS will become a regular undertaking.

the national compiler ensures that survey respondents are fully aware of the survey requirements; for instance, regarding market valuation and country attribution of issuer. This is because end-investors are the best informed about the size, composition, and value of their portfolios, and there is a direct link with their balance sheet data. Hence, end-investor surveys tend to be associated with an aggregated approach.

4.57 In contrast, to ensure that (i) double counting is kept to a minimum, (ii) securities are correctly valued, and (iii) quality is maintained, the evidence from those countries collecting data from custodians is that it is advisable to collect data at the individual security level. The U.S. experience is that initial reports from custodians contain frequent, serious inaccuracies. In the 1997 CPIS, the U.S. compilers estimated that relying on these initial data would have led to an overestimation of U.S. holdings of securities issued by nonresidents by a factor of two. Detailed security information helped the U.S. compilers identify possible sources of error and thus was necessary to ensure good-quality data.

4.58 Nonetheless, aggregate custodian surveys are conducted. A key factor in ensuring success appears to be the experience of the national statistical agency in organizing custodian surveys. The greater the experience, the deeper the knowledge. The more frequent the survey, the more reliable the data from an aggregate security survey of custodians.

III. Securities Databases

4.59 The Association of National Numbering Agencies (ANNA) has a database covering equities and debt securities for those of its 60 members that accept International Securities Identification Number (ISIN) codes. This database is available to central banks, though at a cost. (See Appendix VII for more details.) It contains information on securities provided on a voluntary basis by some of the country institutions that assign security identification codes. Coverage and completeness vary by country. Securities are identified by ISIN codes. Key information on each security is generally available, but there is no information on prices or on holders. At present, the database can only be accessed online one security at a time, but it may become possible in the future to obtain complete copies of the database.

4.60 Before acquiring a database, national compilers should be aware of one potential difficulty: different respondents could submit different security identifiers for the same security because any widely traded security could be allocated identifiers by more than one coding system. Indeed, in the model survey form in Appendix I, survey respondents are given the option of reporting either an ISIN code or a code allocated by another of a number of coding systems. National compilers should discuss this issue with potential survey respondents; the allocation exercise becomes more straightforward and efficient if national compilers can rely on survey respondents to use primarily one coding system—ISIN, for instance. If not, then the agency is advised to acquire a database that contains all the various identifier codes that a given security has been assigned by the different coding systems, and then build links between all these data and the reported information.

4.61 Some countries use ISIN codes as their only securities identification system. However, many countries—especially the industrial countries—developed their own national numbering systems prior to the introduction of ISIN codes, and these have remained in widespread use in many cases. As a result, private firms have adopted a variety of different securities identification systems as their primary identifier. Thus, some national compilers have respondents that report securities identified by several different security identification systems, such as SEDOL (United Kingdom), CUSIP (United States), or VALOR (Switzerland), as well as ISIN. This can result in identical securities being reported by different respondents with different security identification codes, since the same security might trade in different countries using different codes.

4.62 Having a database that contains all of the various worldwide identification codes that each security is identified by can be very useful. This makes it possible to know when the same security is being reported regardless of whether it is identified by an ISIN code or a SEDOL code or yet another code. Without such a cross-reference database, the value of having a securities database (as discussed earlier) is significantly reduced. Cross-reference databases are generally available from the same commercial firms that provide international securities databases. (See Box 4.1.)

4.63 Some national numbering agencies issue ISIN codes to neighboring or related jurisdictions that do not have a national numbering agency of their own. For example, securities issued by crown

Box 4.1: Commercial Databases

Numerous commercial databases exist. Below is an alphabetical list of those commercial databases containing international securities that have been or are being used by at least one organization represented on the Task Force. However, the Task Force makes no recommendations, and the list is provided for information only. Compilers who approach a commercial database vendor will need to make their own judgments about whether the product being offered meets their needs.

- Bloomberg, 499 Park Avenue, New York, New York 10022, USA
- Euromoney Bondware, Nestor Avenue, Playhouse Yard, London EC4V 5EX, England
- Interactive Data, 96 Hayden Avenue, Lexington, Massachusetts 02173-9144, USA
- International Financing Review, 33 Aldate High Street, London EC3N 1DL, England
- International Securities Market Association, Seven Limeharbour, London E14 9NQ, England
- Muller Data, 90 Fifth Avenue, New York, New York 10011, USA
- Reuters, 85 Fleet Street, London EC4P 4AJ, England
- Icovam, 5 Rue du Centre, Noisy le Grand, 93167, France
- Telekurs, Postfach 8021, Zurich 8005, Switzerland
- Wertpapiersammelstelle Frankfurt, Dusseldorfer Strasse 167, Frankfurt am Main D-60329, Germany

dependencies and territories of the United Kingdom are likely to be assigned a United Kingdom ISIN code.

4.64 Table 4.1 provides an indication of the 10 countries in the 1997 CPIS that used a securities database (whether it was a commercial database or an in-house system), the use made of the Ufficio Italiano dei Cambi (UIC) database, and the extent of coverage it provided.

4.65 Box 4.2 provides information on the BIS securities database that is available to central banks on request and, depending on circumstances, to statistical agencies.

IV. Reporting Thresholds

4.66 To limit the amount of respondent burden, it may be appropriate to establish reporting thresholds. A reporting threshold is a value that, if exceeded, indicates whether a respondent will be required to report its holdings of portfolio investment. The threshold can be for a minimum of total holdings of nonresident-issued securities or for the level of holdings by country. The manner in which a threshold is established and the way it may be used depend to a certain extent on the way in which the survey is conducted.

4.67 The survey may be conducted first by mailing all on the register of potential investors (or their agents) in securities issued by nonresidents (see Figure 5.1, Chapter 5) to ascertain the level of holdings, without any detail being sought. The mailing may be structured to "cast the net as widely as possible"—that is, to include all possible investors, without any knowledge of the holdings of many on the register. In this way, maximum coverage may be established, but there will also probably be many institutional units that will report zero, or a very low level of, holdings of securities issued by nonresidents.

4.68 To avoid collecting information from a great many units with very small holdings (which, therefore, add very little to the result), some countries may decide that a threshold of total holdings should be established. This could be set at a certain percentage of total value reported from the survey (e.g., 95 percent), and then a grossing up done for the balance. Alternatively, it could be set at the largest units (e.g., the top 100 or 500) as the maximum that the compiler is able to process. (See Chapter 6 on experiences that three countries had in grossing up results in the 1997 CPIS.)

4.69 Another threshold is for geographical detail. This is especially important in small jurisdictions with limited statistical office capacity or where respondent burden is a major consideration. In such situations, it may be appropriate to determine, in conjunction with respondents, a certain limited geographical detail covering the countries where a high percentage of investments are made (e.g., 90 percent plus) and to have the balance be reported as a residual. For respondents who may require considerable manual input to extract the geographical detail, such a threshold could prove a very valuable means of reducing respondent burden and, coincidentally, possibly increasing data quality for the countries for which the detail is provided.

4.70 One of the drawbacks of using thresholds is that it limits the usefulness of the data for counterparties. Country A may have established a threshold that is appropriate for its own purposes (to limit respondent burden or the burden on the compiler's own resources) but excludes information for country B. In view of the cooperative nature of the CPIS, it may be useful for discussions to be held between and among countries in order to set thresholds that maximize the benefits to the countries setting thresholds while minimizing the disadvantages for countries using the results (as their counterpart liabilities).

Table 4.1: Countries in the 1997 CPIS Using a Securities Database, by Type of Database and Extent of Coverage

	Type of Database				Percentage Coverage of Such Database, by Type of Securities			
Countries	(I)	(II)	(III)	(IV)	Equity securities	Long-term debt securities	Short-term debt securities	Total
Austria	—	X	—	—	90	99	95	95
Canada	—	(1)	X	(2)	26	5	3	N/A
France	X	X	—	—	100	100	—	N/A
Israel	(Partial)	(Planned)	—	—	(Mostly)	—	—	N/A
Italy	—	X	X	—	N/A	N/A	—	99
Malaysia	—	—	X	—	N/A	N/A	N/A	N/A
Portugal (3,4)	—	—	X	—	82	58	—	70
Spain	—	—	X	—	N/A	N/A	N/A	N/A
United States	X	—	—	—	69	52	—	66
Venezuela	X	—	X	—	10	60	10	30

Type of database:
(I) A commercial financial instrument database
(II) An in-house financial instrument database
(III) The Ufficio Italiano dei Cambi (UIC) database
(IV) Other (please specify)
N/A: Not available.
Notes:
(1) The in-house database acts as a "dictionary" in which more than 90 percent of the issuer information is stored. Because ISINs were not always available, names are used to identify issuers. The database focuses on the different ways to identify an issuer name more than on listing the different issues. Attached to the issuer information are the country and standard industrial classification of the issuer. The UIC database was used extensively to identify the issuer. Therefore, although more than 90 percent of the issuers end up in the database, it is not possible yet to precisely quantify the percentage of issues covered. Statistics Canada estimates that the database covers between approximately 30 percent and 40 percent of the issues.
(2) Monthly security trading from a balance of payments survey.
(3) Coverage is expressed in number (not in value) of securities.
(4) The UIC database was updated with information available to Banco de Portugal.

V. Third-Party Holdings Survey

A. Background

4.71 Experience from the 1997 CPIS shows that nearly all countries are unable to survey directly domestic households regarding holdings of securities issued by unrelated nonresident entities. Practical difficulties in targeting and surveying a relevant sample of households, the sensitivity of the information hampering the response rate, and the quality of the responses received are the main reasons for this inability. Insofar as domestic households hold their portfolio investment directly with nonresident financial entities, there will be gaps in the coverage in the CPIS. Coverage of other investors (such as small companies and nonprofit organizations) may also be incomplete. These shortages in the coverage of assets in the CPIS often reflect deficiencies in other national statistics like balance of payments and national accounts. For such countries this would hamper the analysis of the level and composition of savings. It furthermore causes errors and omissions in the balance of payments and in the national accounts. The country's IIP would be understated as well.

4.72 A TPH (third-party holdings) survey is a way of obtaining information on holdings in securities issued by nonresident entities and held directly with nonresident financial entities in the countries where these investments are held or entrusted.[51] This requires international collaboration and exchange of information in which the countries where these investments are held or entrusted conduct TPH surveys and share the results on a bilateral basis with the asset holding countries.

4.73 Below, some issues are described that need consideration before embarking on the task of conducting a TPH survey.

B. Preparatory Investigations

4.74 Because of the lack of experience with TPH surveys, thorough preparatory investigations are necessary. The following describes the preparations that should be undertaken by a compiler conducting a

[51] For a TPH survey to provide as much information to the third party as possible, securities issued by entities resident in the same jurisdictions as the custodian and held on behalf of nonresident investors should also be included.

Box 4.2: The BIS Securities Database

The Bank for International Settlements (BIS) maintains a security-by-security database covering international debt securities. Under the contractual terms negotiated with the BIS data providers, this database can be shared with the central bank community.

The BIS bases its security classification as international (as opposed to domestic) on three characteristics: the location of the transaction, the currency of issuance, and the residence status of the issuer. International issues comprise all foreign-currency issues by residents and nonresidents of a given country and all domestic-currency issues launched by nonresidents. Additionally, domestic securities specifically targeted at international investors are also considered to be international issues in the BIS database.

International securities comprise international bonds, notes, and money market instruments. New issues of international bonds are derived from market sources such as Dealogic Capital DATA (Bondware) and Thomson Financial Securities Data (Platinum). The Bank of England provided the bulk of the historical data before 1996. The OECD provided data on some issues for the 1970s. The information on the events occurring in the lifetime of international bonds (e.g., exercised call and put options, sinking funds, early redemption) is reported by the International Securities Market Association (ISMA). The data on international notes and money market instruments are derived from data files made available by Euroclear, which provides the BIS with new issues as well as with information regarding events that occur over the lifetime of the securities.

At the end of September 2001, the BIS international securities database covered 72,887 international bond issues (of which 32,553 were outstanding) and 339,227 international notes and money market instrument drawings (of which 45,113 were outstanding).

The following details are available for the securities stored in the BIS database: the International Securities Identification Number (ISIN) key; the name of the borrower; its country of residence; its country of nationality; the business sector of the immediate borrower (issuer), the business sector of the ultimate borrower (parent company of the borrower or guarantor); the issued amount expressed both in local currency and in U.S. dollars; the currency of issue; the announcement, completion, and maturity dates; the type of security; and the type of interest rate. In addition, the following information is available for international bonds only: rating and rating source; all features and options attached to the bond; call, put, and early repayment dates; and issue price and coupon.

The main activity of the BIS in the field of international debt securities consists of merging the information received from the different data sources, identifying and removing duplicates, correcting mistakes, ensuring a consistent classification of issuers across the different sources, and performing general quality control. The content of the BIS international debt securities database is aggregated as time series across eight dimensions and is published in various BIS reports, mainly in the *Quarterly Review: International Banking and Financial Market Developments*. The following dimensions are available: the measure (announced, completed and net issues, early and scheduled repayments, and amounts outstanding), the type of security, the business sector of the immediate borrower; the country of nationality, the country of residence, the market of issue, the rate of structure, and the currency of issue. These series are also disseminated to the member central banks via the BIS Data Bank.

TPH survey in which nonresident investors' holdings of securities entrusted directly with local custodians are to be covered.

4.75 A TPH survey has to be adapted to the institutional arrangements through which nonresident investors hold or entrust their securities to domestic financial entities. Nonresident investors can arrange for their securities investments directly with local custodians in different ways. The following are two examples:

- Possibly the most widely used approach is the one in which a nonresident investor entrusts securities issued by a nonresident directly to a resident custodian for safekeeping. Nonresident investors in this case act as customers vis-à-vis the custodian and do not make use of intermediaries in their own country. To cover these positions, the compiler conducting the TPH survey has to approach the local custodians.
- Alternatively, a nonresident investor could directly entrust asset management to an investment manager abroad. These assets are not on the balance sheet of the investment manager that administers the assets by investing the funds and entrusting securities to a local (to the investment manager) custodian for safekeeping on behalf of the customer. Investment management services are commonly provided by banks, but some investment managers operate independently from banks.

4.76 By investigating how market players use these kinds of financial services vis-à-vis nonresident customers, the compiler will be able to design and target the TPH survey to obtain maximum useful output.

4.77 If both custodians and investment managers are approached in a TPH survey, there is a distinct possibility of double counting. If the investment manager, acting on behalf of nonresidents, has entrusted securities to local custodians, instructions should be clear as to who is to report the information to the compiler.

4.78 A TPH survey also has to be designed within the legal provisions of the country. Many countries have no legal provisions authorizing the collection of information on holdings by nonresidents. In these countries, the TPH survey will have to be conducted on a voluntary basis.

4.79 It is also necessary to initiate contacts with players in the market. In the first place, compilers need to gauge the availability of information regarding residence of nonresident customers and residence of the issuer of the securities owned by them. Another issue is whether the respondents are able to distinguish private persons among their nonresident customers, and whether they are able to distinguish in more detail different kinds of nonresident customers, such as institutional investors and nonfinancial companies. The quality of the data is also affected by whether this information is readily available in the records of the respondents or if it is necessary for them to make additional calculations or estimations.

C. Scope

4.80 A TPH survey could also be designed to take into account the needs of the partner countries with whom the information from the survey is to be shared. In many of the countries that participated in the 1997 CPIS, one of the major problems encountered was the coverage of the household sector because many households had entrusted their holdings directly with nonresident custodians. To maximize the benefits of a TPH survey requires targeting the holdings of nonresident households—the *household approach.*

4.81 However, depending on the survey system in place in partner countries (end-investor survey, custodian survey, or a combination of the two), the extent of the lack of coverage can differ and may not be confined merely to the household sector. Gaps in coverage of portfolio assets can also be related to other noninstitutional investors, such as securities issued by trade unions, religious societies, and nonfinancial companies that are held abroad by nonresidents. This would imply the need, from the partner country's view, to have the coverage of the TPH survey extended to include nonresident investors other than those in the household sector—the *extended approach.*

4.82 One issue connected with the scope of the TPH survey is how to define which sectors are to be covered. Another issue is how households should be defined. The most reliable way for respondents to distinguish households from other entities would be to define them in terms of private persons. This would also be fully in line with the *1993 SNA*, where the household sector is defined as all resident households consisting of private persons and any unincorporated business owned by them that does not maintain a separate set of accounts, including a balance sheet.[52] This is distinct from the sector of nonprofit institutions serving households (NPISHs). The NPISH sector includes such potentially important investors as trade unions, churches, and religious societies.

4.83 If the extended approach is chosen, it is not possible to give advice on the coverage and breakdown of categories of nonresident investors. These issues have to be decided after consultations with partner countries. It is in any case very important to have a consistent treatment in the TPH survey and in the partner country to avoid double counting.

4.84 In considering whether to conduct a TPH survey, the national compiler has to take into account the complexity of the extended approach. First of all, the extended approach is very demanding for the respondent, requiring a breakdown of its nonresident customers into different subcategories.

4.85 The extended approach is also associated with an increased risk of double counting by the partner country. The risk that the information shared with the partner country is to some extent already covered in the partner country's own compilation, leading to double counting, must always be carefully watched. Extending the survey beyond the household sector would increase this potential for double counting.

4.86 The household approach is less demanding for the respondents that merely have to focus on nonresident private persons, and it would in general be easier to control the risk of double counting. On the other hand, the information from the household approach would not satisfy the information needs of the partner countries in all cases.

D. How to Avoid Double Counting

4.87 Another issue is how to make sure that the risk of double counting is minimized.

[52]In other words, those unincorporated businesses that are not quasi-corporations.

4.88 In the example presented in Figure 4.1, the compiler of economy A is undertaking a TPH survey (the **household approach**), approaching local custodians, and asking them about securities entrusted to them by nonresident private persons. The issue is which of the compilers in the different economies is to collect the information on the holdings of Mr. Peterson and which is to collect those of Mr. Andersson. Mr. Andersson and Mr. Peterson have entrusted their securities in different ways.

4.89 Mr. Peterson, a resident of economy B, has entrusted his securities to a subcustodian within his own economy (Custodian W), who in turn entrusts them to Global Custodian X, who is a resident of economy A. In this case the compiler in economy B will cover the assets of Mr. Peterson in the standard CPIS, provided that domestic custodians are covered. The information on Mr. Peterson's holdings, even though held with Custodian X in economy A, should still be available to Custodian W in economy B.

4.90 Mr. Andersson, on the other hand, has entrusted his securities directly to Custodian X, who, in turn, placed them with Custodian Y, another resident of economy A. However, Custodian Y then placed them with Custodian Z, a resident of economy B. In this case, the compiler of economy B will not be able to trace these holdings (since there is no direct survey of households) and so is dependent on the information from the third-party holdings survey, if any, conducted by the compiler in economy A.

Figure 4.1: Potential Double Counting in Compiling Third-Party Holdings Surveys

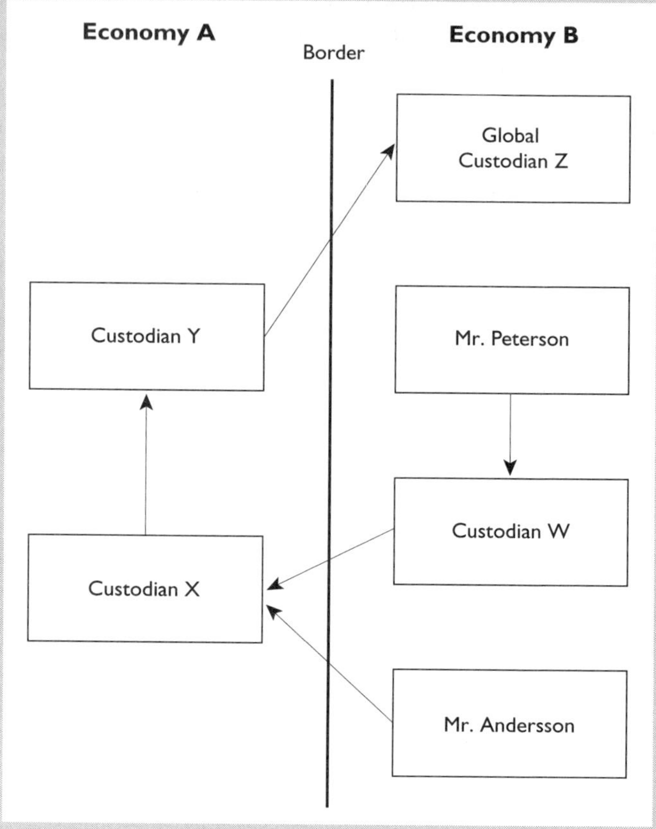

Note: For explanation, see paragraphs 4.88 through 4.94.

4.91 Thus, if compilers in economy A were to undertake a TPH survey, it should cover only those securities that have been entrusted directly by nonresident households. If securities indirectly entrusted (through an intermediary, Custodian W) by a nonresident household (that of Mr. Peterson) are also covered in the third-party holdings report by Custodian X to the compiler in economy A, double counting of third-party holdings in economy A will occur because Mr. Peterson's holdings will also be reported by Custodian W to the compiler in economy B. Accordingly, the instructions for the custodian survey in economy A should make clear that any securities that have been entrusted to them by another custodian, whether resident or nonresident, should be excluded.

4.92 The clarity of instructions is particularly important in this example because of the sequence of on-entrustment. If Custodian Y reports (to the compiler in economy A) its holdings of nonresident-issued securities on behalf of residents of economy A and also reports the holdings entrusted to it by Custodian X, and if Custodian X were to include in its report to the compiler in economy A these same securities, the holdings of residents of economy A of securities issued by nonresidents of economy A would be overcounted. At the same time, if Custodian Y were unaware that some of these securities were owned by a nonresident (Mr. Andersson), there would be an additional overstatement of economy A's securities holdings.

4.93 The situation is further compounded in this example because Mr. Andersson's securities were placed with Custodian Z, a resident of economy B. In this instance, if Custodian Z were to report nonresident ownership of those shares placed by Custodian Y (a resident of economy A), the effect would be to overstate economy A's holdings of nonresident-issued securities because the report would include the holdings of a nonresident of economy A (Mr.

Andersson) to the extent that Mr. Andersson's shares were not issued by residents of economy A.

4.94 To make sure that only directly entrusted securities are covered in a TPH survey, it is crucial for the compiler to keep track of the custodian chain within the compiler's own economy. Custodian X is acting as first custodian vis-à-vis Mr. Andersson and is in the best position to supply the compiler with correct detailed information. Therefore, in a TPH survey, custodians in the retail business acting directly for nonresident customers have to be approached.

E. What Information to Collect

4.95 After the compiler has targeted the population of custodians and the respondent has identified the nonresident households among its counterparts, then the issue arises of what is to be reported.

4.96 The reporting should contain, for nonresident households in each country, a breakdown of types of securities (equity, long-term debt, and short-term debt securities) and for each of these categories a breakdown of country of issuer. An important difference, compared with the standard CPIS, is that the TPH survey should also cover domestic securities—that is, securities issued by residents of the same economy as the compiler. On the other hand, holdings by nonresident households of securities issued by residents of their own economy do not have to be reported. In the example above, Custodian X would not report any holdings of residents of economy B of securities issued by other residents of economy B. Such holdings do not represent any claim on nonresidents from the partner country's perspective and are not relevant for CPIS or IIP purposes. However, for simplicity, it may be easier for the custodian to report all holdings of securities owned by nonresidents, including securities issued by residents. As geographical detail of all holdings, by residence of issuer, and by residence of holder,[53] would thus be provided, any resident-to-resident claims would be identified and could be eliminated for the purposes of the CPIS (but that information may be valuable for other statistical purposes).

VI. Conclusions

4.97 National compilers are advised to choose the method of collection that best suits their domestic circumstances, ensures good-quality data, and meets the objectives of their national survey. As mentioned in Chapter 1, the IMF has established a network wherein compilers with considerable expertise in conducting portfolio investment surveys can provide advice, especially on the choice of collection system (the contact address can be found in Chapter 2).

4.98 In Appendices I through V of this *Survey Guide,* model survey forms cover (i) mixed custodian/end-investor surveys on a security-by-security and on an aggregate basis and (ii) an end-investor survey on an aggregate security basis (as well as specifically designed forms for small economies, such as SEIFiCs).

[53] While observing confidentiality.

5. Other Practical Issues

Considerable logistics are required before a national survey can be conducted. This chapter provides some practical advice based on the experience of Task Force members. The chapter covers:

- *a timetable;*
- *legal and confidentiality considerations;*
- *compiling, maintaining, and using a register of respondents;*
- *choosing and developing a computer package to process the survey results; and*
- *quality control.*

I. Logistical Issues

5.1 The CPIS requires considerable preparation by individual national compilers if it is to be a success: from preparing a timetable, to consulting potential survey respondents, to deciding on the software packages that can be used to process the survey returns. This chapter discusses some of the preparatory steps and provides practical advice based on the experience of the experts on the Task Force. In the event that national compilers might also require additional advice, a network has been established to link compilers with considerable expertise in conducting portfolio investment surveys with those who need guidance in conducting such surveys. Compilers may contact any of the members of the IMF Task Force on the 2001 CPIS (shown at the front of the document) or the project manager at the IMF (the address is provided in Chapter 2, Section II.D).

II. Timetable

5.2 In preparing for the CPIS, one of the national compiler's first steps is to produce a timetable. It serves two main purposes: tasks are identified, and their sequencing is established. A timetable will help ensure the success of a national survey.

5.3 Each country's own timetable will depend on its circumstances. For example, those countries that have never organized a portfolio investment position survey will have a different timetable from those countries that conduct them regularly. Nonetheless, based on collective experience of the countries represented on the Task Force, a broad framework is set out below (and given visually in Figure 5.1), which can be adapted and, if necessary, expanded to meet local circumstances. The timetable uses the survey's reference date as a guide for surveys beyond the 2001 CPIS.

About 12 months before the reference date of the survey:

- Begin preliminary discussions with potential respondents to provide a broad overview of what is to occur by the survey date and to help determine the type of survey to be undertaken; that is, (i) end-investor; custodian, investment (fund) manager, or a combination of these; and (ii) aggregate or security-by-security.
- Determine under whose authority the survey will be conducted; if needed, seek agreement from the appropriate regulatory bodies.
- Prepare draft survey forms and discuss them with a sample of potential respondents.
- Determine approximate quantity and type of data to be collected and undertake initial investigations on how the data should be reported and processed. In this regard, consult with a sample of potential respondents.
- Begin development of a detailed register of potential respondents.
- Inform all potential respondents of the survey.

About nine months before the reference date of the survey:

- Begin seminars and other programs to educate respondents about the survey.
- Finalize survey forms and send them to all respondents so that they can set up the computer systems and other tools they will need to complete the survey.

Figure 5.1: Indicative Time Line for Conducting the CPIS

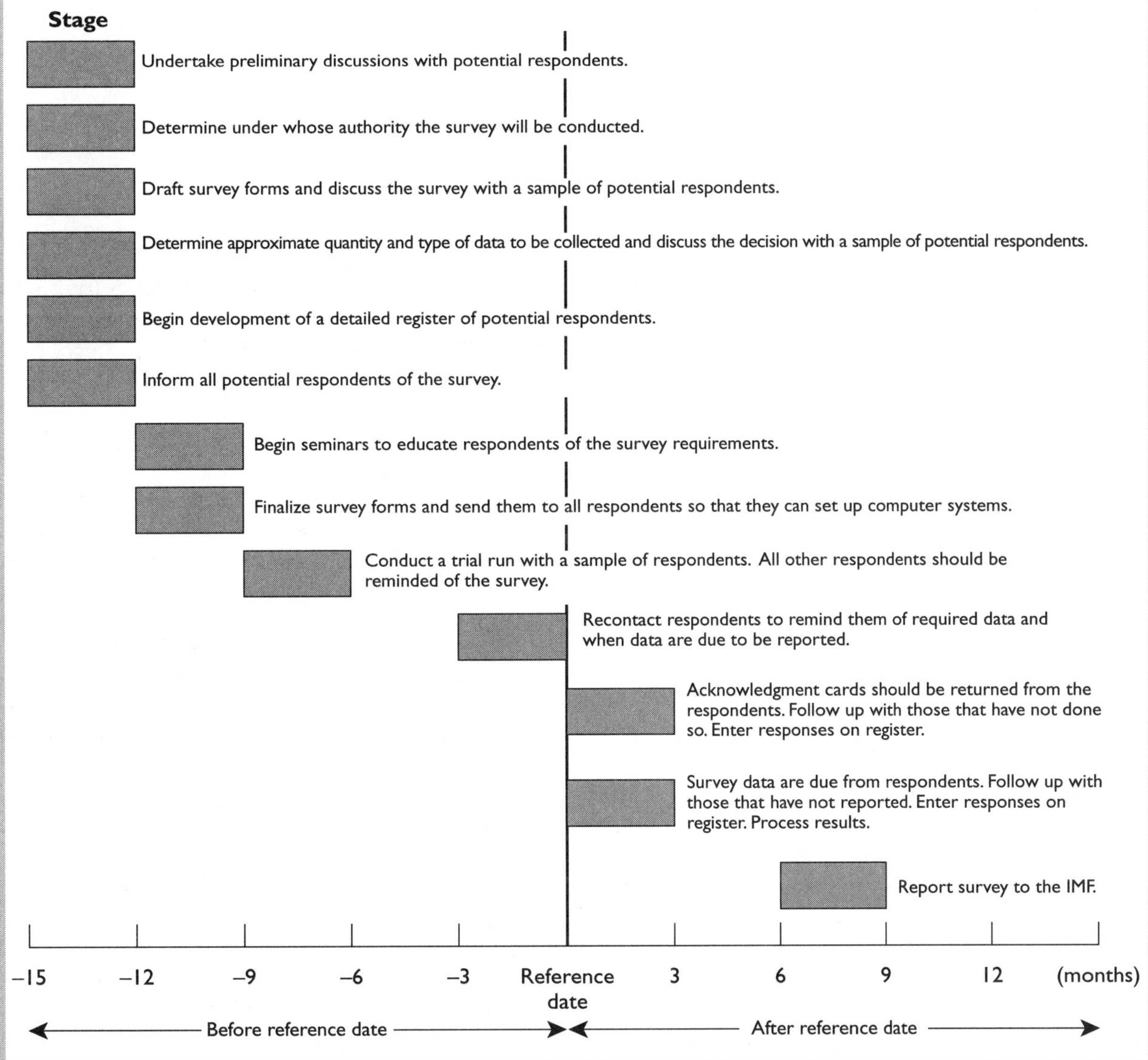

About six months before the reference date of the survey:

- Conduct a trial run with a sample of respondents. All other respondents should be reminded of the survey.

About one month before the reference date of the survey:

- Recontact (by mail) respondents to remind them of the survey's reference date and when data are due to be reported.

About one month after the reference date of the survey:

- Acknowledgment cards should be returned from the respondents. Follow up with those that have not done so. Enter responses on register. See Appendix I, Model Form 1a.[54]

About three months after the reference date of the survey:

- Survey data are due from respondents. Follow up those that have not reported. Enter responses on register. Process results.

[54]Use of an acknowledgment form, such as that shown in Appendix 1, Model Form 1a, is a valuable survey control technique because it ensures that all respondents, whether they are required to provide the

Nine months after the reference date of the survey:
- Report survey data to the IMF.

III. Legal and Confidentiality Considerations

5.4 Wherever possible, it is very important for countries to have the appropriate legislation in place so that the CPIS can be conducted on a mandatory basis and to cover concerns survey respondents may have about the confidentiality of data supplied. See the discussion on the appropriate legislative authority in Chapter 4, Section II.A.

5.5 Each country is unique in regard to these considerations. Italy's position is presented as an example.

5.6 In Italy, the regulations for the collection of data on cross-border and foreign-currency activity are contained in Article 21 of Law No. 148/1988:

> Article 21: Information on currency movements for statistical purposes
>
> (1) For the purposes of statistical information, the Italian Foreign Exchange Office may require authorized banks, other authorized institutions, and operators,[55] and other concerned parties to send data and information (periodically or in samples) on foreign exchange and cross-border transactions in which they have, in whatever capacity, been involved.
>
> (2) Information and data collected shall be processed for each bank, class of transaction, and operator without naming the operators themselves and then stored in archives to which the Bank of Italy may have access insofar as the execution of its duties requires.
>
> (3) Information and data shall be treated as Official Secrets until they are published; they shall be made available, upon request, to the Minister of Foreign Trade and to the Treasury Minister, who may use them in the preparation of the Treasury's biannual report to Parliament on currency movements.
>
> (4) Statistics produced by aggregating data from at least three subjects and excluding references to a single operator may also be made available by the Italian Foreign Exchange Office to the Central Statistics Institute, to national and international public institutions, to authorized banks, and, upon payment, to research organizations and other private sectors.

5.7 The regulations were extended in May 1990 when a Ministerial Decree, put forward by the Interministerial Committee for Credit and Savings, enabled the Italian authorities to collect transaction data from nonbank operators. In October 1995, another directive from the same Committee enabled the Italian Foreign Exchange Office to collect position data from nonbanks.

5.8 In preparing for their national survey, the Italian authorities needed to address the issue of confidentiality. Article 21 guarantees the anonymity of the data supplied by operators. Confidentiality is not simply entrusted to a generic "official secrecy" rule or even to a more specific rule of "statistical secrecy" (i.e., the prohibition of disclosure of data referring to a single person) but, rather, is embodied in the very rules of collecting, processing, and storing the data. The second paragraph of Article 21 states, "the information and data collected shall be processed for each bank, class of transaction and operator without naming the operators themselves...." Furthermore, to meet the legal requirements, the Italian Foreign Exchange Office cancels respondents' names immediately after the data reported have been validated.

IV. Compiling, Maintaining, and Using a Register of Respondents

5.9 Producing a register of survey respondents (register) is an important function for the conduct of any national survey; however, countries participating in the CPIS will need to ensure that any register complies with the relevant data protection legislation. In some countries, if a register is maintained on a computer system and includes information about any identifiable individual, that information may be used only for an authorized purpose.

5.10 This section, based on the practical experience of Task Force members, presents some background on compiling and maintaining a register, ideas about what can be stored on the register (and on a computerized

value of the portfolio investment holdings or not, have received the form and are aware of their responsibilities regarding the survey. Failure to receive the form back from the respondent within a limited and specified time requires follow-up to make certain that the respondent has received the form and is aware of the survey's requirements.

[55] According to directives from the Interministerial Committee for Credit and Savings.

register), and finally an explanation of how the register can be used during the national survey. No register can be developed until national compilers decide how they intend to achieve comprehensive coverage of domestic residents' holdings of securities issued by nonresidents, whether primarily through an end-investor survey, custodian survey, investment (fund) manager survey, or a combination of these options.

A. Compiling a Register

5.11 The sources of information on potential survey respondents are varied, and the work required to compile a register will depend on the extent to which a register already exists in the statistical agency. Box 5.1 provides guidance on how to compile a register, including the possible sources of information, based on the experience of the Australian Bureau of Statistics. In addition, national compilers should read Chapter XVIII of the IMF's *Balance of Payments Compilation Guide* (Washington, 1995) and particularly paragraphs 853 through 862. Table 5.1 sets out the sources of information used to maintain registers in countries that participated in the 1997 CPIS.

5.12 The next step, after the initial examination of the sources of information, is to produce a detailed list of potential survey respondents. The national compiler must be careful to select the "correct" population. To do so, the compiler should engage in some preliminary discussions with the largest institutional investors, such as pension funds, mutual funds, banks, insurance companies, and so on, as well as the appropriate trade associations. The discussions should make these institutions aware of the national survey and help the national compiler to decide upon the design of the survey.

5.13 If national compilers decide to conduct an aggregate survey primarily targeted at end-investors, they must decide whether to set a minimum threshold that excludes units with low-value investments in securities issued by nonresidents. For instance, the number of potential survey respondents identified in the review of sources may be very high, but in practice a significant proportion of investment in securities issued by nonresidents may be undertaken by, or channeled through, a relatively small number of large investors or financial institutions. A minimum threshold may reduce the respondent burden without adversely affecting quality; if necessary, the compiler might consider requiring reports from a sample of these "smaller investors." However, if there is to be a minimum threshold, the national compiler must be careful not to exclude potentially important respondents. See also the discussion on reporting thresholds in Chapter 4, Section IV.

5.14 If the national compiler decides to conduct a survey targeted primarily at custodians but one that also covers end-investors, it is important to understand the relationship between major investors in securities issued by nonresidents and custodians to avoid omission or duplication of data. This point is emphasized in Chapter 4, Section II.B and II.C. One approach to this issue is to require all large investors to identify their domestic custodians, as well as to indicate any holdings of securities issued by nonresidents that they maintain with nonresident custodians. The relationship between end-investors and custodians could also be kept on file, but updating this could prove time-intensive.

5.15 Care is also needed in choosing which respondents to approach; an awareness of the operations, record keeping, and accounting practices of the target businesses is required. The unit from which data are to be collected—that is, the statistical unit—should reflect the level within the business structures at which portfolio investment position data are available and are appropriate, given the consolidated reporting obligations of business. Similar businesses will often have different internal arrangements, which necessitates special reporting arrangements (based perhaps on the degree of centralization or autonomy of related businesses). It may be necessary, therefore, to recognize reporting units inside the standard statistical unit. When approaching an end-investor that is also a custodian, it is of particular importance to ensure that it reports its own account holdings as well as those held on behalf of other residents. Again, it is recommended that national compilers consult the IMF's *Balance of Payments Compilation Guide* (Washington, 1995), paragraph 849.

5.16 The treatment and capture of data from unincorporated entities needs particular care. Because these entities may not prepare full sets of accounts, their investment in securities issued by nonresidents on their own account or as an intermediary may be missed or duplicated in the survey.

5.17 The register will need to be maintained given the likelihood that the survey will be performed on a continuing basis; otherwise, information regarding the entities to be surveyed and the statistical unit to be approached can quickly become out of date. Media reports are a good and timely source of updates for significant businesses, but a review of the sources

Box 5.1: Australia's Experience in Compiling a Register: Practical Advice

Australia has no central repository or transaction system for identifying or reporting international investment position (IIP) statistics. Australia has had an open economy with a freely floating exchange rate for nearly two decades, and no controls or approvals are required for investment flows (although some investment targets in Australia require approval of foreign ownership). To run surveys to measure international investment, it has therefore been necessary to compile a register of organizations from which the data can best be obtained. Some organizations are targeted for their role as end-investors/investees, whereas others are targeted as intermediaries (fund managers or custodians) to report on behalf of their clients.

The Australian Bureau of Statistics (ABS) has long experience in compiling and maintaining registers for statistical surveys. The main ABS business register is used for surveys of the economy and is generally sourced from business taxation reports. But this register is more focused on operating businesses with employees, rather than enterprise groups, and is deficient for those financing company parts of businesses that may have no employees but channel all the international finance accessed by the group. Even if this register were to be augmented with financing units, any survey drawn randomly from such a large register would be inefficient in terms of reporting load and public resources because of the large numbers of nil responses from organizations that have no international investment. Quality assurance is also difficult for international investment measures drawn from such surveys.

The ABS has therefore built a separate register of enterprise groups with international involvement. The enterprise groups that report are the Australian head offices on behalf of all branches, subsidiaries, and consolidated associates, rather than each legal entity that might have an element of overseas investment or debt. This group approach limits the number of organizations that need to be contacted to those that can best report the information.

Sources of information for enterprises for this specialized international investment register are as follows:

- Existing registers of businesses maintained by the statistical agency or other government agencies, which can be approached with brief debt coverage surveys;
- Existing business data collections already run by the statistical agency or other government data collection agencies. Information necessary for an international investment register may be elicited from another survey, either by direct inspection of the other survey's register or by adding one or two exploratory questions to that survey. A range of ABS surveys include questions that can identify potential respondents to debt surveys and vice versa.
- Government administrative sources. Depending on legislation and administrative arrangements or the authority of the collection agency, these sources might include:
  (a) taxation records, files, or lists;
  (b) information held by foreign investment approval or monitoring boards;
  (c) information held by other regulatory authorities, such as lists of entities coming under their supervision and data monitored through supervision requirements (e.g., registered banks, other deposit-accepting institutions, securities brokers, investment managers, investment advisers, and authorized pension or mutual funds);
  (d) listings of registered custodial businesses that can hold debt securities and other assets on behalf of nonresidents, and lists of registered fund managers that can act on behalf of nonresidents;
  (e) statutory company reports and company registration details; and
  (f) records held in foreign exchange control or international transaction reporting systems (e.g., records identifying the originators or recipients of large portfolio investment flows [not available in Australia]).

Other official and regulatory sources, many publicly available, include annual statutory accounts for public companies held by the Australian Securities and Investment Commission, submissions made to the Foreign Investment Review Board, various material held by the Reserve Bank of Australia, and annual reports of other government bodies.

Media reports. Newspapers and periodicals are particularly useful sources of information on potential reporting entities. A high proportion of significant transactions are reported in the media, and these reports are used not only to update the register, but also to confirm data reported in the Survey of International Investment (SII). Apart from significant transactions, the media cover many smaller transactions as well as a high proportion of unusual transactions. The use of traditional print media is being supplemented with information obtained electronically from commercial business news services and via the Internet.

Publicly available databases. A wide variety of information is available from public databases. The information differs in completeness, accuracy, and the extent to which it is of use for a survey of international investment. These sources include the stock exchange register, possibly packaged by the stock exchange with additional information; commercial equity registries' information services; international credit rating agencies' publications (e.g., Moody's, Standard and Poor's); and market research reports or services, such as reviews by accounting or brokerage firms. The ABS uses several Australian Stock Exchange products, such as monthly updates of share issues listed on the exchange and their prices and indices.

Industry associations. These associations and their reports and releases can be a useful source. Apart from the public relations and liaison aspects of a close relationship between the statistical agency and industry associations, many either list members publicly or can make available lists of members, often with indications of their importance or the range of services provided. Particularly in the financial sector, their members are also likely to be significant users of official statistics and thus have a vested interest in accurate data and in assisting statistical or data collection agencies.

referred to in Box 5.1 might be appropriate at discrete intervals, especially close to the time of dispatch of the survey forms.

B. Details Stored on a Register

5.18 The register should contain more than a simple list of names and addresses; it should also (i) include relevant information on each reporting entity, (ii) control the mail-out and receipt of survey forms, and (iii) provide information on the status of the response. A possible list of items that can be stored is indicated in Box 5.2, and Box 5.3 indicates the kind of information that is stored by Statistics Canada and Singapore's Department of Statistics.

5.19 Computerizing the register should save compilers time and effort and reduce the scope for error in dealing with survey respondents when the survey is in operation. (See Box 5.2 for information that can be stored on computerized registers.) However, if a computerized register is to operate efficiently, careful planning and careful maintenance are required; the importance of this cannot be overestimated. The type of issues and tasks that national compilers need to consider include the following:

- taking account of the information flows to and from the database (the use of charts and diagrams is highly recommended in the planning phase);
- taking account of the specifications for interrogations and reports to be generated;
- devising a coding structure that embodies the defining characteristics of each respondent in its unique identification number (this is important because it allows the sorting and analysis of respondents and the tracking of nonresponse);
- ensuring that supporting hardware and software are sufficient for the task—for instance, that the memory and processing capabilities are such that response and retrieval times are acceptable;
- allowing time for a thorough tryout of the system before "live" use;
- backing up copies of data and software on a regular basis and storing them both on-site and at a remote location so that the files can be restored in the event of a system breakdown;
- ensuring appropriate systems security and access authorization;
- producing thorough documentation on the system; and
- providing for a suitable filing system for associated papers, not least the completed survey forms.

C. Use of the Register

5.20 Once the national survey is under way, the benefits of an efficient computerized register become apparent. The benefits accrue both at the initial stage of sending out survey forms and at the follow-up stage and beyond.

5.21 At the initial stage, compilers need to print and dispatch the survey forms and letters. To do so, they can generate the mailing labels from the computerized register. At the same time, a record can be written noting which survey respondents will be sent a questionnaire (e.g., set mail status to "yes"). Compilers can also perform a quality check to ensure that the right respondent is receiving the right survey form(s). This is particularly important if the mailing includes more than one type of survey form. It is very useful to include a postcard with the survey form (or use some similar technique) that respondents use to acknowledge receipt of the questionnaire and identify the person to contact. In this way, compilers can quickly identify problems and initiate follow-up action.[56] The national compiler should note in the response log those entities that have returned the postcard. National compilers should record the return of the completed survey form in the response log, along with the date of receipt. Any changes required to the register (for instance, name and address) could then be made. Compilers could run a report to verify that the correct entries have been made. Thereafter, they could distribute survey forms to the appropriate person for data capture and editing.

5.22 Respondents may need to contact the compiler for a number of reasons. The compiler should keep a record of each telephone call or correspondence, either in a manual file or as a note against the appropriate record in the response log file. If a survey respondent requires more time to complete the survey form, the compiler should note this information so that reminders are not sent. In such a case, the response log status is changed to indicate "in contact," and follow-up procedures are suspended for a specified period. When new copies of the survey forms are requested, a re-mail is initiated, and additional forms are sent to the respondent with the follow-up procedures kept in place. The compiler must update the register if updated information is provided and run a check to confirm that correct details have been stored.

5.23 When the closing date for the return of completed survey forms has passed, the national compiler can select the overdue survey respondents from the response log, on the basis of the response status of "outstanding" and the mailing date, and prepare labels for envelopes and follow-up documents.

5.24 A number of reports can be produced on a regular basis to assess the status of the survey, including the following:

- *transaction reports:* lists of changes sorted by name, ID code, date, and so on.

[56]The U.S. authorities have found it useful to publish a legally binding notice about the survey, which announces it and states that any institution meeting the reporting guidelines is legally required to report, whether or not the institution is sent a survey questionnaire. This approach might bring in some firms that are not on the register. Whether this approach can be undertaken in other jurisdictions depends on local institutional and legal arrangements.

Table 5.1: Sources Used to Build a Register or to Maintain It over Time

(M = main; S = secondary; O = occasional)

	Government Administrative Sources								Publicly Available Databases						
Countries	(a)	(b)	(c)	(d)	(e)	(f)	(g)	(h)	(i)	(j)	(k)	(l)	(m)	(n)	(o)
Argentina				M	M										
Australia	M	O	O	M		M			M	M	S	S	M	O	
Austria	M														
Belgium				M	M	M									
Bermuda				M					O					M	
Canada	M	O			M			S(1)					S	S	
Chile															
Denmark	M			M			M								
Finland					M		M		S				S		
France				M	M										
Iceland				M		O									
Indonesia	S			M	S										
Ireland	M		M	M	M	O			O	O	O	S	O	O	
Israel		S	S	S	S	M			S	S			S		
Italy	S			M	M	M	S		M						
Japan				S			M								
Korea							M								
Malaysia				M	M	O	M		S						
Netherlands				M		O									
New Zealand	M	O	O	O	S	S			S	O	O	O	S		
Norway	M			S			S						O		
Portugal				S		O	M			M		S	S		
Singapore	M			S	S	S							S	S	
Spain	M														
Sweden				M	S										
Thailand				M			M								
United Kingdom	(2)			M (3)	M (4)									S (5)	
United States															
Venezuela				M	S				O	O	O		O		

(a) Existing registers of business maintained by the statistical agency or other government agencies. (b) Taxation records, files, or lists. (c) Information held by foreign investment approval or monitoring boards. (d) Central bank records, such as prudential information and lists of entities coming under the central bank's supervision (e.g., lists of registered banks and other deposit-accepting institutions). (e) Information held by other regulatory authorities, such as lists of entities coming under their supervision (e.g., lists of securities brokers, investment managers, investment advisors, and authorized pension or mutual funds). (f) Statutory company reports and company registration details. (g) Records held in foreign exchange controls or international transaction reporting systems (e.g., records identifying the originators or recipients of large portfolio investment flows). (h) Other (please specify). (i) International credit rating agencies' publications (e.g., Moody's, Standard and Poor's). (j) The stock exchange register. (k) Commercial equity registers' information services. (l) Market research reports or services, such as reviews by accounting or brokerage firms. (m) Media reports (newspapers and periodicals). (n) Trade associations and their associated reports and releases. (o) Other (please specify).

(1) Detailed monthly transactions from brokers. (2) Nonfinancial institutions (M); nonbank financial institutions (S). (3) U.K. banks' data collected for statistical purposes. (4) Nonbank financial institutions. (5) Nonbank financial institutions.

- *response log reports*: summary counts of survey forms mailed, received, deleted, and percentage outstanding; response log listing all survey respondents; survey status sorted by name, identification code, and so on.

V. Choosing and Developing a Computer Package to Process the Survey Results

5.25 Choosing the appropriate computer package is important and needs to be considered carefully by national compilers. This section is intended to provide some guidance on how to make this decision.

5.26 The most straightforward approach is to choose the computer package that is already standard in one's own statistical agency. This approach has a number of advantages: staff are already trained in how to use the package, the capabilities of the package are known, and computer support is presumably available if any technical difficulties arise. In addition, only limited time and effort need be spent on deciding on the appropriate package. However, if the survey is a new undertaking, it is worthwhile to consider whether the existing standard package can meet the processing requirements of the survey.

5.27 There are many ways to store information. The volume of data and whether the survey is to be repeated regularly could determine how information is stored. For example, a small aggregate survey could be handled by a commercial spreadsheet program, whereas a large, detailed survey could require a relational database. However, if the survey is to be conducted regularly and reasonably frequently, the data might need to be held in time-series form and therefore require a different type of database. Table 5.2 outlines the systems used by the participants in the 1997 CPIS. This list is provided for information purposes only; the Task Force makes no recommendations. Compilers who approach commercial database vendors will need to judge whether the product meets their needs; Task Force members are prepared to assist countries in their deliberations about which system to use (their names and e-mail addresses are shown at the front of this *Survey Guide).*

VI. Quality Control

5.28 The importance of quality control[57] cannot be overestimated. If, despite all the preparations, survey respondents submit poor-quality data, the value of the whole exercise is undermined.

5.29 All experience suggests that national compilers can expect survey respondents to make mistakes. Those compilers conducting a national survey for the first time need to be especially vigilant in checking the data supplied; the more experience the respondent has in completing the survey form, the less likely that any significant error will be made.[58] Nevertheless, even the most experienced respondents can make mistakes.

5.30 National compilers can conduct quality-control checks on a number of levels in a number of ways. The compilers can include checks in the survey form, cross-check survey data against other reported data, and devise analytical checks. They should also be able to check data received from the domestic custodians or domestic end-investors at a detailed or aggregated level.

5.31 This section provides some guidance on a range of possible checks. Nonetheless, it should be borne in mind that the more the survey form fits the domestic circumstances and the more that survey respondents are consulted about what is required of them, the greater the probability of receiving good-quality data and, perhaps just as important, the greater the likelihood of cooperation if the national compiler needs to question data supplied by the respondent.

5.32 Because one of the purposes of the CPIS is for comparable data to be exchanged among participating countries, national compilers will receive

Box 5.2: Information That Can Be Stored on a Computerized Register

Classification Information

Respondent identification code
Respondent name
Type of respondent (custodian, mutual fund, pension fund, etc.)
Respondent contact person
Address of respondent
Telephone number of respondent
E-mail address
Facsimile number of respondent
Language (of survey form)
Mailing status (yes or no)
Type of media sent to the respondent (survey form, diskette, letter, or other)
Flags to alert for special cases to be handled separately from the automated system

Response Log Details

Response status (mailed, received, in contact, re-mail, exempt, removed, etc.)
Type of media used by the respondent (survey form, tape, diskette, printout)
Type of record layout provided by the respondent (aggregate or detailed data)
Date mailed
Date re-mailed
Date received
Date of first follow-up
Date of second follow-up
Date removed

Some Useful Advice

At the planning stage, it is important to consider which fields will be filled automatically by the computerized system. For example, would the "date mailed" field be updated directly by the mailing program? Be sure to provide sufficient space for addresses and other such information; it may be appropriate to subdivide fields for some items (for example, distinguishing the postal code from the remainder of the address). Take care when assigning default values to fields and (as a safeguard against inputting errors) have an accessible, on-line, separate file that lists those types of input that are currently acceptable for a specified field; that way, unacceptable inputs will be rejected—for instance, if a letter is entered in a field that can "accept" only numbers. It is also useful to have a comment area for each entry.

[57]See Chapter 6 for some practical examples from countries involved in the 1997 CPIS.
[58]The same applies for the compiler: an experienced compiler understands the requirements of the survey better than a novice. Also, when data have been received on an ongoing basis, the compiler is in a position to compare the most recent results with those in earlier returns.

Box 5.3: Information Stored on the Registers of Statistics Canada and Singapore's Department of Statistics

Canada

Information relating to respondents

Status of the respondent (in process, follow-up)
Contact 1—Provider of the information
Contact 2—Subject matter/end-investor
Addresses (postal and e-mail), phone and fax numbers of the respondents and contacts

Response log details

Detailed track record of the discussion with the respondents
Follow-up dates (first and second date mailed received, etc.)

Other

Codes of funds
List of funds of the company
List of funds by provider of information
Fund type (international fund, retail funds, etc.)
Sector of the funds (mutual fund, pension fund, insurance, segregated fund, banking, etc.)
Submission format (Excel, ASCII, etc.)
Manager of the fund
Previous recorded value by fund (used to validate)
Date of previous recorded value of fund
Previous number of funds submitted

Singapore

Information relating to respondents

Respondent identification code
Registry of business number
Respondent name
Respondent address
Respondent contract person/authorized person
Designation of authorized person
Telephone number of respondent
Facsimile number of respondent
Activity code of respondent (i.e., business sector of respondent)
Commencement year of respondent's business
Investment code of respondent (on record whether respondent is involved in overseas direct or portfolio investment or both, or no overseas investment)
Financial period of respondent's business (i.e., accounting period)

Response log details

Response status (accepted, liquidated, untraceable, dormant)
Date mailed—automatically filled by computerized system
Date received
Date due
Date of first and second follow-up
Edit date—case edited

data on their residents' portfolio investment liabilities to nonresidents. Some broad checks on the data received—either by individual counterpart country or on a global basis (i.e., total liabilities to nonresidents)—should be possible. The following subsections focus on the various checks.

A. Quality Control Checks Through the Survey Form

5.33 The sooner errors are spotted and corrected, the better. For this reason, it is recommended that national compilers consider devising a survey form that explicitly includes quality-control checks or requires extra information that can be used as a consistency check. However, if extra information is required, it should be kept to the minimum necessary, and the national compiler should clearly explain the purpose for the collection of those additional data.

(i) Security-by-security survey forms

5.34 In its security-by-security collection from custodians, the United States found that respondents can make a number of errors. These errors include (i) failure to differentiate between long- and short-term securities as well as between securities issued by residents and securities issued by nonresidents; (ii) incorrect currency conversion of foreign currency securities into domestic currency; (iii) use of incorrect prices to arrive at market valuation; (iv) reporting of position date other than the survey date; and (v) problems relating to the reporting of asset-backed securities. Some respondents also reported holdings of debt instruments that had already matured by the survey's reference date.

5.35 A number of additional pieces of information can be requested on a security-by-security survey form to help address such reporting issues. They include the following:

- *The security number.* With the help of a securities database, the security number can help the national compiler to distinguish a domestic from a nonresident security and a long- from a short-term security and denote the currency of the security.
- *The quantity of securities held.* This information can allow the national compiler to derive the implicit market value of each individual security holding and help to detect direct investment relationships.
- *The face or nominal value of the (debt) security.* This again is a check on the implicit price valuation in the report and may highlight securities for which survey respondents are unable to provide market prices.

(ii) Aggregate survey forms

5.36 On an aggregate survey form, a number of checks are possible. In the Australian system, because positions and transactions data are gathered on the same survey form, the reconciliation is done directly by the respondent. But this is a system where collection of position data is ongoing. The national compiler of a first-time national survey might consider requesting that survey respondents provide the value of total security assets held or simply total assets held, against which the reported nonresident holdings could be compared. This would help to identify severe misreporting, such as reporting all security assets as nonresident.

5.37 It is recommended that simple computer-checking procedures be written to process reported aggregate data. For instance, a computer check could be written that sums the individual country data and compares them with the reported total holdings; the difference should be zero. Likewise, a check could be written that highlights zeros or data above a certain size so that any unusual figures can immediately be brought to the national compiler's attention. Many other similar routine checks can be devised.

5.38 More generally, the national compiler could require a senior official of the responding entity to certify that the information provided is complete and accurate; this could help to ensure the data quality and punctuality. Similarly, requesting the name of a contact person helps to ensure that follow-up inquiries are dealt with efficiently.

B. Quality-Control Checks Against Other Reported Data

5.39 Different possibilities exist for checking data against other reported data, especially for assets of financial intermediaries like banks or investment companies, both at the level of the individual respondent and the aggregated level. These financial intermediaries might report separately statistics on portfolio investment position data for supervisory or statistical requirements. Some examples are given below. Verification of the basis for valuation of the assets needs to be ascertained because valuation principles for these other sources may not be at market price. Moreover, it is also necessary to ensure that the data are provided on the residence basis required for the CPIS (as well as the balance of payments and the IIP), since some data sources may be on the entity's global consolidated balance sheet, not just the balance sheet for the domestic economy. It is important to ascertain that the reporting unit is the same and that there is no double counting; for example, one unit within an enterprise group does not report if there is a consolidated report for the whole domestic group.

(i) Central bank (monetary authorities)

5.40 As noted in Chapter 1, the IMF Committee was of the view that reserve assets should be shown separately in global totals and not as part of a country's portfolio investment. Accordingly, a geographical breakdown of securities included in reserves will be collected separately by the IMF in a confidential survey, SEFER (see Chapter 2, Section III).

(ii) Banks

5.41 Position data on investment in securities issued by nonresidents are included in the banking statistics and balance sheets. Furthermore, many reporting central banks provide the Bank for International Settlements (BIS) with information on their commercial banks' investment in securities issued by nonresidents, including a breakdown by country of issuer and by major currency. However, it should be borne in mind when comparing survey results with banking data that the banking data may have been collected for other statistical or other (e.g., supervisory) purposes and that some banks may not record (all) their holdings of securities assets at market prices, especially those held in the "investment account"[59] (which may be held for reserve or capital requirement purposes and be recorded on a different valuation basis).

(iii) Insurance companies and pension funds

5.42 Position data on investment in securities issued by nonresidents should be included on the balance sheets of insurance companies and pension funds. However, when undertaking these types of checks, it is important to remember that definitions of terms may differ according to purpose. For example, for pension funds in the United States, securities issued by nonresidents but trading on U.S. securities markets are categorized as "U.S. securities."

(iv) Investment companies

5.43 Position data on investment in securities issued by nonresidents should be included on the balance sheets of investment companies; in addition, the

[59]As opposed to the "trading book," which is usually marked to market prices on a regular basis.

Table 5.2: Computer Packages Used to Process the 1997 CPIS Results

Countries	Commercial spreadsheet program	Relational database management system	Personal database management system	Large relational database management system	Time-series (temporal) database management system	Was this package already available?	If package was not already available, why was this one chosen?
Argentina	X					X	
Australia	X			X		X	
Austria	X			X		X	
Belgium			X			X	
Bermuda	X					X	
Canada		X				X	
Chile	X	X	X	X	X	X	
Denmark	X		X			X	
Finland	X					X	
France				X		X	
Iceland	X					X	
Indonesia	X					X	
Ireland	X	X					
Israel					X	X	
Italy		X				X	
Japan	X			X		X	
Korea	X					X	
Malaysia				X		X	
Netherlands	X			X		X	
New Zealand	X	X				X	
Norway	X		X			X	
Portugal	X		X			X[1]	
Singapore		X				X[2]	
Spain				X		X	
Sweden			X				3
Thailand	X			X		X	
United Kingdom	X	X[4]			X[5]	X	
United States	X	X	X	X		X[6]	
Venezuela	X					X	

Note: Canada, Ireland, and Israel subsequently moved, or are planning to move, to relational databases.
[1]Although these packages were already available, they were adapted to meet the needs of the users.
[2]Modified from the package developed for previous surveys.
[3]A process and data input system was constructed in SAS.
[4]Database for nonbank institutions.
[5]U.K. banking data held on Bank of England's own time-series database.
[6]Extensive programming was also done in conjunction with a large relational database.

geographical allocation of the individual investment funds may be estimated through knowledge of their published investment strategy.

(v) Nonfinancial economic sectors (such as companies or households)

5.44 Position data on investment in securities issued by nonresidents could be included in corporate balance sheets, but it might be difficult to confirm the data for nonfinancial sectors.

5.45 For those countries where there are no balance of payments transaction data (and, therefore, where the range of analytical checks that can be conducted is limited; see next section), attribution of investments by sector and a comparison with available sector data, as outlined above, is probably the best check that can be made.

C. Quality Control Through Analytical Checks

5.46 The degree to which analytical checks can be developed depends on the availability of comparable data. If data are available, the following checks can be devised.

- If stock data and flow data are independently assembled, an attempt should be made to reconcile these data. To do so requires consideration of effects caused by different prices, exchange rates, other adjustments like write-offs, or thresholds. Checks can be applied at the individual respondent and aggregate data levels. However, it should be noted that some reconciliation may not be possible, depending on data sources. For example, transaction data may be reported by securities dealers, which could involve some securities sold to nonresident custodians. In that case, these securities are unlikely to be recorded if the survey focuses on resident custodians.

- In countries where transaction data are available and the position data are being produced for the first time after a lapse of a number of years, an attempt could be made to reconcile position data that were estimated by accumulating transaction data with reported position data. The method of calculating position data from transaction data is described in paragraphs 740–743 of the IMF's *Balance of Payments Compilation Guide* (Washington, 1995). The degree of deviation of the cumulated transaction and reported position data could depend on the composition of the holdings, the variability of the relevant exchange rates and market prices of securities, and the length of time over which transactions have been cumulated as well as net errors and omissions in the reporting systems. However, if the national compiler judges the discrepancy to be significant, it should be investigated. Given the number of assumptions and potential time frame of observations, this check is probably more appropriate for aggregate data, although it could be developed for checking individual respondent's data. The more frequent the surveys of positions, the more reliable the reconciliation.

5.47 One important piece of information required to develop these analytical checks is the currency composition of the portfolio assets, without which the currency and security price revaluations are, at best, an estimate. Therefore, the national compiler might ask survey respondents to provide a breakdown of investments by currency—although this is not a mandatory requirement of the CPIS. As a second-best option, the national compiler might use data on the currency composition of holdings provided by different financial intermediaries (e.g., banks) as a proxy for the currency composition of all survey respondents' holdings.

5.48 Some compilers will face problems, particularly when checking data for claims vis-à-vis individual countries, if their transactions data are based on the "transactor" principle, as opposed to the debtor/creditor principle used for position data (see *BPM5*, paragraphs 484–488). In other words, it might not be possible to reconcile cumulated transaction data with the position data from the national survey because different principles of geographic allocation are being used.

D. Quality Control from the Viewpoint of the Recipient (Debtor) Country

5.49 Because comparable data are to be exchanged among participating countries (subject to confidentiality constraints), national compilers will receive data on their residents' securitized liabilities to nonresidents. Although quality control is primarily the responsibility of the national compiler in the creditor country, the recipient compiler could be in the position to check the data received. Checks could be carried out on data vis-à-vis a single counterpart (creditor) country or on data vis-à-vis a group of reporting countries.

5.50 Regarding individual counterpart countries, the recipient compiler (debtor country) could check the data received to

- compare the data with those previously published. At present, several countries (e.g., the Netherlands) publish data on their investment in securities issued by nonresidents, which can be used as an approximated range for the position data at end-December 2001 (and beyond, in the event that the survey is repeated or undertaken on a regular basis);
- use information about interest payments vis-à-vis single counterpart countries. From these data, the country attribution of the outstanding volume of domestic securities could be estimated. However, care is needed with this check because the residence of recipients of interest payments on bearer securities may itself be estimated; and
- use data published in the BIS statistics on banks' investments in securities issued by nonresidents. These data give a partial picture of nonresident investment in domestic securities. If information is available on the banks' percentage share of total holdings of securities issued by nonresidents in the creditor economies, some estimate of the country attribution of the nonresident investment in domestic securities could be made from the partial BIS data.

5.51 Each of the aforementioned estimation methods is only a broad check. Moreover, because many data sources (e.g., the balance of payments, possibly the IIP, and some counterparty country liabilities) are derived from the transactor basis, it is not uncommon for the bilateral data to be misleading when compared with data sources (such as the CPIS) that are constructed on the creditor/debtor principle. Nonetheless, these estimates could provide the recipient compiler with a benchmark against which to judge the data received.

5.52 It is also possible to devise checks for the liabilities data. Nonresident investment in domestic securities could be estimated by residual; that is, the outstanding volume of equity and long-term debt securities issued by residents, adjusted for residents' investments and compared against the aggregate data received. Data on the outstanding volume of domestic securities issued could be available from domestic or international publications. Residents' holdings of resident securities may be published by the domestic statistical agency within the framework of the flow of funds and financial assets and liabilities balances outstanding. However, the compilation and estimation techniques used for flow of funds and financial asset and liability balances outstanding should be explored thoroughly to ensure that these methods would produce sufficiently robust results.

6. Experience in Conducting the 1997 CPIS

This chapter focuses primarily on various countries' experience in conducting the 1997 CPIS and, for several countries, their practices since then, since many of these countries have ongoing portfolio investment surveys. For countries undertaking a benchmark survey for the first time, or for countries wishing to extend or improve their approach, knowledge of other countries' experiences may be helpful. The following topics are addressed:

- *coverage (choice of collection method and limitations in approaches to coverage),*
- *separation of direct investment from portfolio investment,*
- *market price valuation,*
- *treatment of accrued interest,*
- *treatment of nominee accounts,*
- *treatment of collective investment schemes,*
- *direct holdings abroad,*
- *edit checks to verify quality,*
- *steps taken to address low coverage or response rate, and*
- *how sector information was obtained, if at all.*

I. Coverage

A. Choice of Collection Method

6.1 Countries' choices of collection method were influenced by a number of factors, such as availability of the data, ease of collection, respondent burden, availability of resources, existing surveys for collecting data for the international investment position (IIP), a country's national circumstances, and its institutional arrangements. What is important is that the choice maximizes the coverage (without double counting) while minimizing the costs to the respondents and remaining within the resources of the compiler.

6.2 Table 6.1 shows the choices made by the 29 jurisdictions that participated in the 1997 CPIS. The aggregate/end-investor-only approach was chosen by 4 countries; 1 country used an aggregate/end-investor and investment managers approach; the aggregate/combination of end-investor and custodian was chosen by 12; the security-by-security/end-investor approach was the choice of 1 only; and the security-by-security/combination of end-investor and custodian was used by 6 countries. Four countries used other combinations, mixing the aggregate approach with the security-by-security approach. Aggregate/custodian-only and security-by-security/custodian-only approaches were not used by any country. One country did not use any of these approaches because it used administrative records.

Austria

6.3 In its preliminary investigations, the Austrian central bank (Oesterreichische Nationalbank, ONB) found that domestic residents held more than 90 percent of their securities issued by nonresidents with domestic custodians. As a result, the ONB introduced a survey primarily targeted at custodians, requiring that they report on a monthly frequency their own holdings of securities issued by nonresidents and those of their clients.

6.4 The reporting population consists of local (or sub-) custodians (those closest to the end-investors, not global custodians) to avoid double counting. In this new survey, domestic custodians have no difficulty in identifying holdings of securities by residents. End-investors report data only if their holdings of securities issued by nonresidents are entrusted directly to nonresident institutions and have a value exceeding 1 million Austrian schillings on the reporting date. As direct investors also use the services of domestic custodians and as domestic custodians cannot determine whether securities are issued by related enterprises abroad, these holdings (which are appropriate for direct rather than portfolio investment) are estimated from data provided

Table 6.1: Type of Survey Used in 1997 CPIS

Countries	Aggregate Approach: End-investors	Aggregate Approach: Custodians	Security-by-Security Approach: End-investors	Security-by-Security Approach: Custodians
Argentina	[1]	—	—	—
Australia	X[2]	—	—	—
Austria	—	—	X	X
Belgium	X	X	—	—
Bermuda	X	X	—	—
Canada	X[3]	—	X	X
Chile	—	X	X	
Denmark	X	X	—	—
Finland	X	X	—	—
France	X[3]	—	—	X
Iceland	X	X	—	—
Indonesia	X	X	—	—
Ireland	X	—	—	—
Israel	X	—	—	X
Italy	—	—	X	X
Japan	X	X	—	—
Korea	X	X	—	—
Malaysia	—	—	X	X
Netherlands	X	X	—	—
New Zealand	X	X	—	—
Norway	X	—	—	—
Portugal	—	—	X	X
Singapore	X	X	—	—
Spain	—	—	X	X
Sweden	X	X	—	—
Thailand	X	—	—	—
United Kingdom	X	—	—	—
United States	—	—	X	X
Venezuela	—	—	X	—

Note: X = Approach used; — = approach not used.
Source: IMF, *Results of the 1997 Coordinated Portfolio Investment Survey* (Washington, 2000).
[1] Mixed, depending on the available information.
[2] Also used investment managers.
[3] Banks.

by direct investors (Section II, below). Data on nonresident ownership of securities issued by residents are also collected from domestic custodians to measure portfolio investment liabilities.

Bermuda

6.5 In its preliminary investigations, Bermuda determined that the bulk of cross-border portfolio investment is held by the financial sector (including the international financial sector) and that most of these holdings are likely to be placed with nonresident custodians. From discussions with the relevant industry associations, it was determined that banks, insurance companies, and mutual funds could provide the required information on an aggregated basis. For these reasons, the aggregate end-investor approach was selected. Reporting by custodians on an aggregated basis was also included to provide a supplementary data source.

Israel

6.6 In its preliminary investigations, the Bank of Israel concluded that, because residents have to report their cross-border portfolio investment under exchange control regulations, data sources based on these regulations ensure a complete coverage of cross-border portfolio investment and can also be compiled with a high frequency. Data were reported by resident custodians (using the security-by-security approach to facilitate quality control and checking on an instrument basis against other data sources) and by end-investors (on an aggregate basis). Reporting by

Figure 6.1: Framework of Data Collection in Japan[1]

Banks	Securities Companies	Institutional Investors
Deposited overseas in respondent's name (1) Own account (2) Held in custody for clients[2]	Deposited overseas in respondent's name (1) Own account (2) Held in custody for clients[2]	Deposited overseas in respondent's name
Deposited in other domestic banks		Deposited in domestic banks
Deposited in domestic securities companies		Deposited in domestic securities companies

[1]To avoid double counting, only the data in the shaded areas are aggregated to produce total Japanese portfolio investments.
[2]Disaggregated into public sector, banking sector, and other sectors.

end-investors comprises those residents who use the services of nonresident custodians or hold securities in self-custody, and includes businesses and households.

6.7 Because this approach was developed to support the compilation of an IIP statement for portfolio investment assets and liabilities, the resulting database compiled by the Bank of Israel's Foreign Exchange Control Department (FECD) covers residents' holdings of cross-border portfolio assets and nonresidents' holdings of securities issued by residents. Resident custodians report the value of securities traded in Israel that are held by nonresidents. Residents' holdings of shares issued by Israeli companies abroad are compiled from information supplied by the issuers. This information is used to derive estimates of nonresidents' holdings of shares issued by Israeli entities abroad.

Japan

6.8 Figure 6.1 illustrates the framework of data collection in Japan. In its preliminary investigations, the Bank of Japan concluded that institutional investors are the only sector likely to use the services of nonresident custodians. Both the nonfinancial corporate sector and households were believed to prefer the services of domestic custodians. For this reason, reporting by resident custodians and institutional investors was concluded to be sufficient to provide a complete coverage for the IIP and CPIS.

6.9 The Foreign Exchange and Foreign Trade Law and related ordinances provide the legal framework for collecting portfolio investment assets and liabilities as part of the IIP. This legal framework (which was in place before the 1997 CPIS) required that a summary breakdown of portfolio investment assets, by the country of residence of the issuer, be reported, and specified that data be reported on an aggregate basis. Banks were required to report both in their capacity as end-investors and custodians. Hence, the legal framework met the requirements of the CPIS.

6.10 For the IIP and CPIS, the Bank of Japan relied mainly on reports submitted by banks (as end-investors and custodians), securities companies, and institutional investors under the framework prescribed by the Foreign Exchange and Foreign Trade Law. This authority to collect statistics has remained in place notwithstanding recent financial deregulation.

6.11 The most important reason for choosing the aggregate approach was to build on the existing reporting system for IIP purposes, and to avoid any additional burden (that would be seen to result from any change of the basis of reporting) on reporters at a time of financial deregulation.

Netherlands

6.12 The Netherlands Central Bank has been conducting an annual survey of portfolio investment assets and liabilities since 1986. From its experience over the years, the national central bank has concluded that, with the exception of institutional investors, residents use the services of domestic custodians. From discussions with custodians, it was concluded that custodians could be relied upon to provide accurately the required information on an aggregate basis. Hence, a combined custodian/end-investor reporting system was selected, with the latter confined to institutional investors and a few important investment companies. For pension funds and insurance companies, total holdings as reported in the CPIS end-investor survey could be checked against data reported in their annual balance sheets. Any differences between these totals and those reported to be held by resident custodians on behalf of pension funds and insurance companies are taken to be securities held with nonresident custodians.

United Kingdom

6.13 In its preliminary investigations, the Office for National Statistics (ONS) concluded that the existing end-investor surveys used to compile portfolio investment assets in the IIP statement could also be used for the CPIS. For this reason, an aggregate end-investor approach was selected. Questions were added to seek information on the country of residence of the issuer.

6.14 This approach had a number of attractions. First, end-investors were already familiar with the enquiry forms and the subject matter. The contact who has responsibility for the total stock of portfolio investment assets would be the best person to complete the geographical breakdown of those assets. Second, the enquiry team in the ONS was already experienced in the subject matter, had established relationships with end-investors, and was in a good position both to encourage the respondents and guide them through the requirements of the survey. Third, the legal basis of the CPIS data collection could be linked to the existing survey, thus avoiding the need to introduce a new legal provision to collect the information. Fourth, the costs to both the end-investor and the ONS could be minimized in that both already had established systems for generating the total stock of portfolio assets. Other economies resulted from using the existing survey design. Fifth, linking the data to the balance sheet returns provided an in-built consistency check. Finally, potential problems of double counting were minimized in that end-investors would only be reporting their own holdings of portfolio assets.

United States

6.15 From its experience in 1994 from conducting a survey similar to the CPIS, the U.S. Treasury concluded that the bulk of residents' holdings of cross-border portfolio investment assets is entrusted with resident custodians. Reporting by custodians was preferred because there are a comparatively small number of custodians as against the very large number of enterprises that are likely to hold cross-border portfolio investment, and because reporting by custodians made it possible to include the household sector and small businesses. The sampling of enterprises was considered but not thought practical, given the prospect of complete reporting by custodians. For institutional investors likely to use the services of nonresident custodians, an end-investor survey was used. The security-by-security approach was used for custodians because experience had shown that initial data received from custodians were frequently inaccurate as regards the country of residence of the issue and the price of securities. It was found that errors could most readily be detected and resolved only by collecting security-level data. Also, by collecting security-level data, more detailed information would be available for analysis.

6.16 Primary custodians who employ the services of domestic global custodians are required only to report the custodian's name and the amount entrusted, and these data are used in the same manner as those of end-investors employing domestic custodians. End-investors are required to report their foreign holdings security-by-security only when they do not utilize a resident custodian. If they use a resident custodian, they are required to report only the custodian's name and the amount entrusted. These amounts are not added to the survey totals, since this would cause double counting, but they are used to verify the accuracy of the data reported by custodians.

B. Limitations in Approaches to Coverage

6.17 Each of the systems faces potential problems of coverage. In the primarily custodian-based systems, such as Austria, the Netherlands, and the United States, the potential weakness was (and in some cases, where there are ongoing surveys, is) that holdings may be missed if residents do not use the services of resident custodians. The Netherlands compilers cover this problem through the use of published annual accounts of the major investing institutions, although they acknowledge problem areas among nonfinancial companies and the household sector. Austria and the United States require large investors who entrust securities directly with foreign-based financial institutions to report their holdings directly to the compiler. Both Austria and the United States consider aggregate holdings by small investors (including the household sector) who hold securities in self-custody or entrust them with nonresident custodians to be relatively small.

6.18 For all of these collection approaches, the risk of missing direct holdings abroad (especially of households) increases as more use is made of on-line trading in securities issued by nonresidents directly with nonresident brokers. There is, as yet, no satisfactory means of addressing this problem.

Austria

6.19 In its preliminary investigations, the ONB found that banks identify securities by using the security codes of either the Austrian numbering agency (Oesterreichische Kontrolbank) or the German numbering agency (Wertpapiersammelstelle Frankfurt). These codes are linked to the International Securities Identification Number (ISIN) code system.[60] By requiring custodians to report a security identification code and the par value for each security held, the Austrian compilers have been able to ensure, with the use of commercial security databases (see Chapter 4), that securities are correctly allocated geographically and revalued to end-period market prices. Also, because the ONB collects security-by-security information on portfolio investment stocks and flows, it can reconcile stocks and transaction data, recalculate historical time-series aggregates, and ensure that data are consistent with international concepts and principles.

6.20 Although the purchase of commercial security databases is costly, the Austrian compilers have found that the benefits of reliable and frequent data outweigh the costs. Commercial databases are mainly used as the preferred source for market prices of securities. Custodians in Austria prefer security-by-security reporting because the central bank bears the costs of the compilation of aggregates and the costs of developing and running the commercial securities database.

Japan

6.21 The Bank of Japan considers the coverage and quality of data reported annually by end-investors and custodians on their holdings of portfolio investment to be high. The reported data are checked against other information, and any apparent irregularities are followed up with the respondent.

Netherlands

6.22 Although experience from other countries suggests that it may be very difficult to collect accurate aggregate data from resident custodians, Netherlands compilers have extensive and in-depth experience in collecting data by this method and are convinced that their data are of good quality. By comparing data reported by resident custodians against data reported in the annual reports of institutional investors, an independent check is being provided for these investors, assuming that the definitional and conceptual approaches are consistent.

United States

6.23 Because the reporting of aggregate data by resident end-investors would result in a heavy response burden, involve an unmanageably large number of respondents in the survey, and also provide potentially unreliable data on the attributes of the issue and the issuer that are needed for the CPIS, data were collected from resident custodians on a security-by-security basis to facilitate checking and verification against data for holdings reported by resident custodians. Commercial data sources were the preferred source for information on individual securities issued by nonresidents required for the CPIS (such as end-of-period market prices and the country of residence of the issuer). To ensure that the securities were correctly valued and allocated geographically, the survey respondents provided a security identification code number for each security reported. Any of the 33 most commonly used coding systems—for instance, ISIN, CUSIP, SEDOL—were used (see the list in Appendix I). It is not unusual for commonly traded securities to have codes allocated by ten different coding systems. Survey respondents were encouraged to use ISIN codes to identify securities, but in the 1997 survey only 26 percent of all securities were so identified.

6.24 To assist in the process of identifying and valuing securities, the U.S. compilers purchased commercial security databases that covered all the commonly used coding systems and provided pricing information on all securities that had traded within the previous year on any of the world's 87 largest non-U.S. securities exchanges. (See Chapter 4 for a discussion of securities databases.) These databases

[60]See Appendix VII for more information on the ISIN code system.

provided key information that was not always supplied by survey respondents; they also helped to resolve conflicting information, and confirmed the information reported. These included: ISIN and other security identification codes; security type; registered or bearer; issue date; maturity date; coupon rate; issuer name; security description; country of issuer; country of guarantor; country where issued; currency; industry sector; price, price type (current, old, estimated); pricing date; default status; American depository receipts (ADRs); ratio of number of ordinary shares per ADR; dividends per share (past twelve months); and nominal amount outstanding for bonds or the number of shares on issue.

6.25 Data from commercial databases are used extensively to help verify and supplement data received from respondents. Verification programs map reported data to the commercial database based on the security identification code. The reported data are then compared field-by-field with the commercial data, and mismatches are specified in an exception report. In addition, data fields left blank in the reported data can frequently be obtained from the commercial database. This process can also help evaluate the overall accuracy of a given reporter's submission on the assumption that a greater or lesser number of errors in items that can be checked is indicative of the accuracy of data items that cannot be so easily verified.

6.26 The use of commercial databases also reduces reporter burden because some data items that may be required or are highly desirable for analytical purposes (such as amount outstanding, a single security identification system, dividends paid, coupon rate, industry sector, and country of guarantor) need not be obtained from the survey respondents.

6.27 Nonetheless, a major problem for the compilers was revaluing to end-of-period market prices those rarely traded securities, particularly equities, that were reported as unpriced by custodians. However, these securities accounted for only a small proportion of the total number of securities reported.

II. Separating Direct Investment from Portfolio Investment

6.28 One of the major statistical concerns for the balance of payments, IIP, and CPIS is the separation of financial investment into functional categories. In particular, within the context of this survey, direct investment should be separated from portfolio investment. However, if data are collected from data sources that are either unaware of this distinction or unable to make the separation (because they have insufficient information), compilers need to have in place mechanisms that will ensure that the data remain as cleanly separate as possible.

6.29 Because resident custodians are unlikely to be able to identify whether securities are issued by parties (direct investment enterprises) related to the issuer (direct investor), other sources of data will be needed to determine such holdings of securities, which should be included under direct investment abroad. It is frequently the case that direct investors keep such securities in self-custody or use the services of nonresident custodians, but practice varies across countries. Most countries conduct end-investor direct investment surveys in conjunction with portfolio investment surveys, and design the surveys to avoid double counting.

Australia

6.30 Australia has an ongoing, integrated collection system, the Survey of International Investment (SII), that collects, inter alia, portfolio and direct investment and integrates flows and balances. Throughout the SII survey forms, respondents are asked to record separately their liabilities to and claims on (i) nonresident direct investors, (ii) direct investment groups abroad, and (iii) other nonresident investors. Only data collected for the third of these categories are relevant to the CPIS. The definition of direct investment is in line with *BPM5*, and an explanatory diagram is drawn from the IMF's *Balance of Payments Textbook* (Washington, 1996). For each instrument, respondents are generally required to record separately particulars for nonresident direct investors, direct investment groups abroad, and other nonresident investors on the same page of the survey forms. This helps to prevent misreporting among these three categories.

Austria

6.31 A sample of resident direct investors (for outward portfolio investment) was taken to determine the proportion of equity held (i) in custody with resident banks, (ii) in custody with nonresident banks, and (iii) elsewhere. The information was checked against security registers in all cases where the value in custody was more than 10 percent of the total outstanding on the company register. A similar approach was undertaken on the liability side by sampling direct investment enterprises. This permitted an estimate of the direct investment component of all reported investment abroad in equities and of all reported inward investment in equities. See Box 3.3.

Israel

6.32 For inward investment, the differentiation between direct and portfolio investment was derived from information provided by the Tel Aviv Stock Exchange and the Israel Securities Authority (ISA).[61]

6.33 For outward investment, the differentiation between direct and portfolio investment was made by comparing holdings of a particular security against total issues outstanding of that security (as reported in FECD's securities database).

Norway

6.34 CPIS data were checked against the results of a survey of outward direct investment, administrated by the central bank. Because this survey was not fully comparable with the CPIS, the definition of direct investment differed. The outward direct investment survey gave an indication of which direct investment enterprises may have had securities that were reported in the CPIS that should have been treated as direct investment, and therefore provided an indication for further investigation. This approach helped to detect some cases of inaccurate reporting, but its usefulness was limited by lack of supplementary information (such as balance sheets for nonfinancial enterprises) that could confirm possible misreporting.

Portugal

6.35 The exclusion of direct investment securities was accomplished by a twofold procedure. First, the guidance notes to the CPIS clearly defined direct and portfolio investment and gave precise instructions to respondents on how to exclude direct investment positions. Second, information was taken from results of the direct investment survey that was conducted at the same time as the CPIS to ensure that there was no double counting.

[61] Parties at interest are required to file a report with the ISA.

III. How Market Price Valuation Was Addressed

6.36 One of the central principles of the CPIS (as with the IIP and the balance of payments) is the use of market price. For regularly traded equities and debt securities, this should not present any problems except that end-investors may not value all their holdings of securities at market prices and resident custodians may not keep records of the market prices of the securities they are holding. End-investors may follow alternative valuation principles, such as par value, acquisition cost, amortized value, or keep separate books for different portfolios of securities. For example, banks may maintain separate trading books (at current market prices) and investment books (at acquisition cost) for debt securities. (On the other hand, institutional investors and collective investment schemes are likely to use market prices for all their holdings of securities to price them on a regular and frequent basis.) Other problems arise in the case of infrequently traded securities. Lastly, where market sources are used for prices, issues arise concerning the treatment of interest accrued, the use of bid or ask prices, and the impact of time zones.

6.37 Following is description of the experience of four countries (Australia, France, Portugal, and the United States) in seeking to ensure for the 1997 CPIS (and any ongoing survey of portfolio investment) that data were either reported on a market price basis or where there were mechanisms in place by the compiler to make adjustments, where necessary. Securities not traded actively or denominated in foreign currencies are particular problems. Not all of these problems were overcome.

Australia

6.38 Respondents to the SII were requested to report stocks at market value and the explanatory notes provided guidelines on possible valuation methods. In measuring the value of equity securities, respondents were asked to adhere to the following principles: (i) For listed enterprises, the market value of the equity positions should be reported using a recent transaction share price; if recent transaction prices were not available, the midpoint of the quoted buy and sell prices of the shares on their main stock exchange on the reference date specified provided a useful approximation. (ii) For unlisted enterprises, if a market value of the shares was not available, the respondent was asked to estimate the market value by one of the following methods (in descending order of preference): a recent transaction price, a director's valuation, or net asset value. For debt securities, survey respondents were asked to report traded price on the date specified. If that value was not available, they were asked to report using, in order of preference, one of the following methods: yield to maturity, discounted present value, face value less written-down value of discount, issue price plus amortization of discount (less amortization of premium), or another mark-to-market basis. The bases upon which debt securities were actually valued are not known.

France

6.39 Valuations were reported at market prices except for the nontrading book of resident banks, which were reported at book values. The latter accounted for about 25 percent of total holdings of long-term debt securities issued by nonresidents. No attempt was made to adjust the latter to market prices. Security-by-security portfolio investment survey data and banking trading portfolio data were collected through separate data-collecting systems.

Portugal

6.40 It was not possible to adjust fully to market prices because of a lack of information and the practice of using unit values and of reporting unit value as a percentage of the nominal value. This led to further discussion with respondents. The Lisbon Stock Exchange's publications were consulted to perform quality checks on unit values of securities reported in the CPIS and to perform consistency checks against the total value of each investment fund. For each investment fund, published data provided information on the portfolio composition (quantity, market price, and currency) for relevant dates. In cases where respondents could not identify a market price, they were asked to use the alternative methods suggested in paragraphs 3.33–3.42.

United States

6.41 Information on market prices was readily available on large frequently traded issues, which make up the majority of debt issues and the vast majority of equity issues. In the event of missing prices, information available from both commercial sources and other reporters were used. When all such sources were exhausted and failed, estimated prices were used for debt securities. For equities, estimated prices were also used, but these securities would probably be undervalued at very low levels and, in any event, represented only a very small percentage of the total.

IV. Treatment of Accrued Interest

6.42 The 1997 CPIS sought, as the 2001 CPIS seeks, market prices of debt securities to include interest accrued but not yet paid (the so-called dirty price).

6.43 In many countries, long-term debt securities are priced on a "clean" basis—that is, excluding accrual of interest; however, some markets include accrual of interest in "dirty" prices. For long-term debt securities held in investment accounts (that is, they are not held for trading purposes—they are usually held for prudential or reserve capital requirements), the valuation is often that of par or acquisition price, and the valuation does not change with market conditions. Where prices for bonds exclude accrued interest, usually the difference between clean and dirty prices is not substantial when coupons are paid frequently. Even though the CPIS seeks information on market prices, respondents frequently will not revalue their "investment book" (as opposed to their "trading book," which is usually marked to market on a frequent basis—daily, weekly, or monthly). In the same manner, they are unlikely to record accrued interest, and it is often difficult for compilers to obtain the data on the required basis.

6.44 However, for zero-coupon or deep-discount bonds, the difference can be substantial because the amount of interest accruing over five years or more can amount to a substantial proportion of the initial principal lent/borrowed, especially when interest rates are high. In these instances, if respondents are reporting on an aggregate basis, it is important to have respondents report their holdings on a dirty price basis as far as possible. If their holdings are reported on a security-by-security basis, the compiler should be able to make the adjustments, especially if a securities database is available.

6.45 In the 1997 CPIS, short-term debt securities were included only on a voluntary basis, so less experience was reported. Most short-term debt securities are issued at a discount—i.e., they are zero-coupon instruments. There are a number of methods used to record money market instruments: at acquisition cost, at amortized value, at par value, or at market price. Respondents may be able to report at market price those securities held for trading purposes, but, as with bonds held for investment purposes, some respondents may use one of the other methods and be unable or unprepared to report on a different basis. However, because of the shortness of time in which interest can accrue, the issue is less important than for zero-coupon, or deep-discount, bonds. Even so, whenever possible, respondents should be encouraged to include accrued interest.

6.46 The experiences of Ireland, Israel, and Portugal in the 1997 CPIS (and any ongoing survey of portfolio investment) are described below.

Ireland

6.47 Respondents were asked to provide positions on a clean price market-value basis, market-priced transactions, and valuation changes. In addition, details of outstanding interest (positions) and movements in interest (flows) were required. For the CPIS, the clean price positions were combined with outstanding interest to obtain the dirty price market values of the stocks.

Israel

6.48 Tel Aviv Stock Exchange market prices include the element of accrued interest (dirty price), and these figures were used for CPIS liabilities in the local market. Israeli debt issued abroad, however, is based on the nominal value of the debt security and accrued interest.

Portugal

6.49 Respondents were requested to include accrued interest in the market price valuation. Where custodians and investors were unable to do so, no adjustments were made. For investment funds that were checked through the publications of the Lisbon Stock Exchange, accrued interest was added to the total stock value.

V. Treatment of Nominee Accounts

6.50 Nominee accounts pose a problem for compilers of the CPIS. Nominee accounts are a means through which securities are held by one party as a nominee on behalf of another party, usually for reasons of administrative convenience or confidentiality. (See the discussion on nominee accounts in Chapter 3.) For the purposes of the CPIS (and for the balance of payments and the IIP), these holdings should be "looked through," that is, treated as though the nominee account had not been used and the beneficial owner is reported as the holder. However, when nonresident nominee accounts and custodians are used, it is not always possible to identify the beneficial owner. For example, if a resident of country A holds securities issued by a resident of country B and uses a nominee account in country C, and the securities are kept in custody in country C, the custodian in country C may not be aware that the ultimate owner is in Country A. In such cases, efforts should be made to encourage the custodian to obtain the residence of the beneficial owner from the nominee. In some countries, this information may be required by the authorities to restrict tax evasion.

6.51 The approaches by Israel, Singapore, and the United Kingdom in the 1997 CPIS (and any ongoing survey of portfolio investment) are described below.

Israel

6.52 Although residents may hold nominee accounts with resident custodians, the names of the beneficial owners must be provided to the custodian, Hence, resident custodians had no difficulty in identifying accounts held by residents. On the liability side, it was not possible to identify the beneficial owner of nominee accounts.

Singapore

6.53 Custodians reported separately securities held in nominee or similar accounts on behalf of nonresidents. They were, therefore, excluded from the CPIS.

United Kingdom

6.54 The ONS conducts periodic sample surveys of all companies listed on the U.K. stock exchange to determine the ownership of their share issues, based on the share registers maintained by companies. Holders were classified according to their institutional sector. About one third of all ordinary traded shares were estimated to be held through nominees (mainly representing unit trusts and pension funds, offshore entities, and other overseas investors). For the most part, it was possible to identify the investor, since this information was known to the reporting enterprise (knowledge of the beneficial owner is required by company law). A residual of undesignated nominee accounts was attributed to beneficial owners, based on the proportions that obtained for nominee holdings for which beneficial owners were identified.

VI. Treatment of Collective Investment Schemes

6.55 Units in collective investment schemes (mutual funds, investment trusts, unit trusts) are classified as equity, regardless of the type of fund or assets that the fund acquires. Thus, for example, if a resident in country A owns units in a collective investment scheme domiciled in country B that holds only bonds issued by the government of country C, the resident of country A should report that he or she holds an equity claim on country B, not a holding in government bonds from country C. It is important that respondents are aware of this classification because they may classify their portfolios on the basis of ultimate risk and may, therefore, "look through" the collective investment scheme—and report holdings of government bonds of country C, as if they did not have units in the mutual fund in country B.

6.56 The residence of a collective investment scheme is determined by its legal domicile. Mutual funds may be legally domiciled in one economy (e.g., a SEIFiC), be managed in a second, be administered in a third, and be listed in a number of jurisdictions. An investor may be interested in where and how funds are invested, and possibly in the ownership of the mutual fund (such as the parent company), but less so in its legal domicile. For this reason, care will need to be taken to identify the legal domicile of mutual funds in an end-investor reporting system, especially if they are registered, listed, managed, and administered in different jurisdictions. It is also worth emphasizing that units in collective investment schemes are unlikely to be held with custodians for safekeeping. Hence, the investing country will have to rely on end-investor reporting.

6.57 How Bermuda, Ireland, Israel, Sweden, and the United States treated collective investment schemes in the 1997 CPIS (and any ongoing survey of portfolio investment) is described below.

Bermuda

6.58 An end-investor reporting system was introduced for all legally domiciled mutual funds. The respondents included mutual funds that were legally domiciled in Bermuda and also administered in Bermuda and a number that were legally domiciled in Bermuda but administered elsewhere—which meant that time had to be allowed for the relevant accounting centers to be contacted. Although reporting by resident custodians was considered, this did not prove practical because Bermuda's mutual funds tended to use the services of nonresident custodians. Respondents were asked to report their gross holdings of cross-border portfolio investment. These could differ from shareholders' values (net asset values) as a result of leveraging by the managers of the funds (such as by borrowing, the use of repos, or the use of financial derivative instruments). However, in the Bermuda experience, leveraging was not a critical issue. On the asset side, only portfolio investments were included (e.g., any marked-to-market holdings of financial derivative instruments on their balance sheets would be excluded). Holdings of units issued by other mutual funds were reported as issued by the country where such funds were legally domiciled.

6.59 Because the survey was conducted on a voluntary basis, a means for grossing up for non-response was needed. This was done by using the net asset values of respondents as a benchmark—which were required to be reported for regulatory purposes.

Ireland

6.60 Data are collected from mutual funds that are legally domiciled and/or administered in the Dublin International Financial Services Center. However, for the purposes of the CPIS, only the cross-border portfolio investment assets of mutual funds legally domiciled in Ireland were included.

Israel and Sweden

6.61 Holdings in mutual funds are categorized as equity investments regardless of the type of fund or assets held by the fund.

United States

6.62 If U.S. residents owned shares in a foreign mutual fund, these were counted as equity holdings in the country in which the mutual fund is legally domiciled. This was so regardless of what type of security the mutual fund purchases or where the mutual fund managers physically reside. U.S.-based mutual funds (or their U.S.-based custodian) reported in detail the securities they owned that were issued by unrelated nonresidents.

VII. Direct Holdings Abroad

6.63 One of the major problem areas identified by the 1997 CPIS was determining the extent to which residents used the services of custodians abroad or held securities in self-custody. For some countries, their inability to find reliable data sources for such holdings by households and small companies (which could not be covered by end-investor surveys) was of serious concern. For others, such investments were considered to be small, and their omission not likely to much affect the results of the survey. The full extent of the problem could not be identified,[62] but it was believed that some countries had more severe problems than others. For example, in countries where there is a history of bypassing resident financial institutions and investing directly abroad, countries did not have mechanisms to collect the information because a direct survey of households is not a feasible proposition. Quite apart from the cost and difficulty of deriving a representative sample (with a bias toward high-wealth individuals), there is the problem of response rate. If the capital has been placed directly abroad to avoid the attention of the country's authorities, it is probable that those individuals will be disinclined to provide the information for a statistical survey, regardless of assurances of confidentiality. The difficulties in obtaining this information and the perception of its importance is related to how information may be obtained from third-party custodians (that is, custodians who hold securities issued by nonresidents on behalf of nonresidents). See Chapter 4, Section V, for discussion of the issues related to third-party holdings.

6.64 The experiences of Argentina, Australia, Israel, and the Netherlands in addressing the issue of direct holdings abroad in the 1997 CPIS (and any ongoing survey of portfolio investment) are outlined below.

[62]An indication of the problem may be persistently large negative net errors and omissions in the balance of payments. Although there are many reasons for errors and omissions, and a low figure may only indicate offsetting errors and omissions, if the number is large and has been growing strongly since any liberalization of capital markets, there is a possibility that measured outflows in portfolio investment are undercounted. In some countries, estimates of cross-border portfolio investment are made on the basis of cumulative flows—but not included in the CPIS because there is no breakdown by the country of residence of the issuer.

Argentina

6.65 The scale of direct holdings abroad by the private sector (households, financial corporations, and nonfinancial corporations) was thought to be significant. Regulatory sources were available for cross-border portfolio investment, including direct holdings abroad, for selected categories of end-investors (banks, insurance companies, pension funds, and mutual funds). For households, an attempt was made to approach nonresident custodians and other intermediaries but this proved unsuccessful. Some attempt was made to estimate households' cross-border portfolio investment through the use of BIS data and partner-country sources (such as the United States).

Australia

6.66 Direct holdings abroad by Australian enterprises are directly covered in the SII collection. The SII targeted all Australian enterprises that were known to have any international investment activity. Although most enterprises channel such activity through investment (fund) managers or the custody system, those enterprises that have direct holdings abroad are asked to report directly on these holdings. Direct holdings abroad by Australian households, on the other hand, are not directly covered by the SII. Households may invest abroad through one of three routes: (i) direct personal holdings of securities issued by nonresidents, (ii) enterprises and legal entities set up by individuals and families to manage their financial affairs (for example, for tax-efficiency reasons), or (iii) superannuation (pension fund) and other collectively managed investment vehicles. While individuals may deal directly with foreign-based brokers, nominee companies, or foreign-based fund managers, such direct holdings are regarded as being relatively insignificant in the Australian context and are not measured in the SII. Since it is considered that the great majority of investment abroad by households passes through either the second or third routes, holdings by households of securities issued by nonresidents were assumed to be adequately covered in Australian statistics.

Israel

6.67 Aggregate data for holdings abroad are compiled quarterly from entities (businesses, nonprofit organizations, and households) with holdings of at

Figure 6.2: Reconciliation of Reporting of IIP and Balance of Payments Data in Australia

(1)	(2)	(3)	(4)	(5)	(6)	(7)
Position at market value at start of period	+ Purchases during period	– Sales during period	+ Market price changes	+ Exchange rate variations	+ Other changes	= Position at market value at end of period

least $5 million (for nonprofit organizations the threshold was $0.5 million). Additionally, large companies (selected by various criteria) and households holding investment portfolios abroad of at least $0.5 million are required to report monthly and yearly, respectively, to the FECD.

Netherlands

6.68 Resident institutional investors, such as pension funds and insurance companies and, to a lesser extent, resident investment institutions, such as mutual funds and unit trusts, are likely to have direct holdings abroad. For institutional investors, total holdings of foreign shares and bonds are known from balance sheet information. In contrast to the figures derived from the custodian survey, they are not broken down by country. As a consequence, direct holdings may be estimated as the difference between these sources, but without a geographical breakdown. Additionally, the most important institutional investors are required to report their direct holdings annually, broken down by country of residence of the issuer. A similar method is used for investment institutions. For the nonfinancial sector, no information on direct holdings is available. It is assumed that households mainly prefer to use the services of resident custodians rather than invest directly abroad, and that the size of direct holdings abroad by households is, therefore, likely to be small.

VIII. Quality Control

6.69 Data received by the compiler should be verified because there is usually no prima facie assumption that respondents will provide the information on the basis required for the survey. Without good-quality data, the usefulness of the CPIS is seriously reduced. These checks can take a variety of forms. Following is an indication of some of the major verification checks that were used by Australia, Belgium, and Ireland (for the aggregate approach) and by Portugal (for the security-by-security approach). Many of the checks used are applicable to whichever approach is used to collect data for the survey. See also Chapter 5, Section VI.

A. Aggregate Approach

Australia

6.70 *Through survey forms.* In Australia, the international investment reporting forms are structured so that there is a full reconciliation for each item between the opening and closing levels of investment and for transactions during the period as illustrated in Figure 6.2.

6.71 In the Australian experience, this approach both educates respondents about the relationships between individual data items and forces them to consider the consistency of the data reported. The Australian Bureau of Statistics (ABS) has found that full data on transactions and other reasons for changes in stocks are usually available when survey respondents provide data on their own accounts or client activity—for example, pension funds investing and managing their own assets, investment (fund) managers managing assets on behalf of other entities, and trading entities managing their own portfolios. These entities will collect all relevant stocks and transactions data at market prices.

6.72 *Through other reported data.* For the nonfinancial corporations sector, independent sources (for instance, published stock or bond price indices or exchange rate movements over the period) are used to judge whether the reported data are accurate. For example, if a 20 percent change in the value of a U.K. asset in Australian dollar terms is explained by a negative entry in the "exchange rate variations" column (implying a decline in the value of sterling relative to the Australian dollar) and it is known that the bilateral rate had not moved in that direction or by that approximate magnitude over the period, then the ABS questions the respondent. Information from share price indices provides a useful check on entries in the "other factors"[63] box, for equity. Anecdotal evidence, such as that derived from market or media comment or contact with other data providers, is also used to confirm data. For example, if there has been evidence that Australian enterprises in general were selling securities in a specific market, but a particular respondent reported a large increase in assets in that market owing to positive net transactions, the respondent is questioned. Comparisons are also made with the general magnitude, type, and direction of data reported by similar entities to see if they are behaving similarly—and providing consistent explanations for movements.

6.73 *Through analytical checks.* Within the ABS, individual analysts are responsible for confirming the reported data. They produce editorial notes that identify and explain all large movements at the aggregate level by reference to the entities contributing significantly to those movements. The computer system edits and checks the arithmetic and compares large changes in levels with the "reconciliation" data at the individual respondent level. All large amounts (approximately $A 100 million or more) reported in the transactions, exchange rate variations, and "other factors" boxes are validated with respondents.

6.74 *Other edit checks.* Survey outputs are verified through (i) data confrontation with results obtained from the ABS's Survey of Financial Information, which collects data on institutional units' balance sheets, transactions, and "other changes," not just transactions and balances with nonresidents (the Survey of Financial Information does not provide geographical detail); (ii) an examination of the comparability of balance of payments and financial account balancing items; (iii) data confrontation with annual reports and Australian Stock Exchange reports (especially for dividends and reinvested earnings); and (d) checking details provided against press clippings and unit profiling checks.

[63]On the ABS form.

Belgium

6.75 The 1997 CPIS was the first such survey conducted in Belgium. The aggregate/combined end-investors and custodians approach was adopted.

6.76 *Units approached.* The end-investors questioned comprised all institutional investors: credit institutions, investment enterprises, collective investment undertakings, holding companies, insurance enterprises, and private provident institutions as well as those other large enterprises that, according to their balance sheet data, had investments to the value of at least BF 200 million. Other end-investors, including the household sector, were not surveyed directly. Through the inclusion of custodians in the survey, securities issued by nonresidents and held by the household sector that had been deposited with resident custodians were incorporated in the results.

6.77 *Survey forms.* There were separate forms for end-investors and custodians.

6.78 End-investors were required to make a return for each type of instrument, broken down by country of issuer and where held (with custodians abroad, with custodians in Belgium, or in own custody).

6.79 Custodians were required to complete a return, by type of instrument, of the securities that they held in custody for residents, distinguishing between securities held on behalf of other resident custodians and other residents. For the latter, this return was broken down by the country of resident of the issuer and where held.

6.80 *Checks on the data collected.* Provision was made for checks at the level of the individual documents, individual respondents, sectors of respondent, and overall. Checks at the level of individual documents consisted of mathematical checks on the accuracy of the forms completed. Checks at the level of individual respondents were made to exclude direct investment (by comparison with the "direct investment" survey that was conducted at the same time). The data on own portfolio investment reported by each credit institution were individually compared with the asset and liability statements that were filed with the National Bank of Belgium by these institutions for other purposes. The latter sources were also broken down by instrument and by the country of residence of the issuer.

6.81 An examination was carried out by custodian and by instrument to check the value of the securities that the end-investors declared that they had deposited with the custodian and the value that the custodian itself declared that it had received from resident end-investors. The latter value must at least be equal to the former. A positive balance was subsequently assigned to the end-investors that had not been surveyed (mainly the household sector).

6.82 A global sectoral check was also carried out for the following four categories of end-investors for which balance sheet data were available in time within the Belgian National Bank: credit institutions, collective investment undertakings, insurance enterprises, and private provident institutions. For investment enterprises, holding companies, and other large enterprises, there were no similar checks owing to the lack of comparably structured material. With a very high response rate (99.7 percent), the global survey results, including the estimated additions, were then compared, instrument by instrument, with the IIP.

6.83 With regard to quality, it was quite frequently necessary to contact respondents to ensure that the forms were completed correctly. The many individual and global checks built into the survey design and data processing system enabled the quality of the data to be ensured. For credit institutions (the largest sector), the checks were based on individual comparisons, and no noteworthy deviations were found.

6.84 Although the quality of the data collected was regarded as satisfactory, the main areas of concern were the correct attribution of market values for the reference date, and the inability of custodians to adjust the value of the securities placed in custody to exclude repos.

6.85 From a comparison of CPIS with IIP data, it was apparent that the CPIS data were lower, by some 15 percent, than the data for holdings of cross-border portfolio investment in the IIP statement. The larger figure in the IIP statement was attributed to the inclusion of cumulative balance of payment flows, for which a breakdown by the country of residence of the holder could not be provided. These flows were believed to include holdings of euro bonds and smaller enterprises that are retained in self-custody or with nonresident custodians. Custodians are not able to adjust the value of the securities placed in custody.

Ireland

6.86 When compiling the positions data for the 1997 CPIS and other data requirements relating to portfolio investment, the Central Statistical Office (CSO) used a number of sources to validate the data for both balance of payments and IIP purposes. No new collection system was needed because the existing collections already required reporting by instrument and by country of residence of the issuer. Data were reported according to these headings: opening position, transactions increases, transactions decreases, valuation, other changes, and closing position, as well as residence of issuer.

6.87 The survey collects balance sheet data by functional category of the balance of payments *(direct investment, portfolio investment, other investment).* In addition to the balance of payments and the international investment position data, holdings by residents of Ireland are also collected (to provide a fuller and more comprehensive set of data).

6.88 This approach to data collection allowed a higher level of quality control on the data supplied by respondents. A primary quality check ensured that the balance sheet balances through the identity: equity capital (plus all reserves) equals total assets less total liabilities excluding equity. This check was applied to both the positions at the beginning and the end of the period. Interperiod checks at the level of instrument and country, by respondent, were also carried out (e.g., that the closing position in Bonds & Notes for the United Kingdom in period 1 was the same as the opening position for Bonds & Notes in the United Kingdom in period 2).

6.89 The second level of validation checks was applied at the survey level. Ten surveys cover different sectors of the economy, and five are particularly significant in terms of portfolio investment. These were (i) Portfolio Investment by Institutional Investors, (ii) Non-IFSC (International Financial Services Centre) Banks, (iii) IFSC Banks, (iv) Portfolio Investment by Irish Registered Collective Investment schemes at IFSC, and (v) Life and Non-Life Insurance Companies at IFSC. The CSO matched the survey results with available independent sources of data. The surveys are described below.

(i) *Portfolio Investment by Institutional Investors.* Institutional investors report position data in this survey. The CSO validates these survey data using the data produced annually by the Irish Association of Investment Managers (IAIM) on portfolio investment by residents. The CSO compares the aggregate and individual company data reported by IAIM with the CPIS data. The main strength of the data is the detail for individual holders. The results of the validation give an indication of the quality of the data, provide a basis for correcting for undercoverage or nonresponse in the CSO survey, and suggest areas for further investigation.

(ii) *Non-IFSC Bank* and (iii) *IFSC Banks.* These data are checked against Central Bank of Ireland data for the banking sector, which includes data on banks' cross-border holdings of portfolio investment.

(iv) *Portfolio Investment by Irish Registered Collective Investment Schemes at the IFSC.* In the IFSC in Dublin, a large number of collective investment schemes invest predominantly in securities issued by nonresidents and whose units are held almost entirely by nonresident investors. Those collective investment schemes that are legally domiciled in Ireland are treated as resident for the purposes of the CPIS. The CSO validated the data against the summary data collected by the Central Bank of Ireland for regulatory purposes.

(v) *Life and Non-Life Insurance Companies at the IFSC.* The CSO uses data collected by the insurance regulator (the Department of Enterprise and Employment) to validate the data reported to the CSO. The analysis of the assets of life and general insurance companies is comprehensive and includes instrument detail.

B. Security-by-Security Approach

Portugal

6.90 Through security-by-security forms, respondents were asked to provide the security identification number, quantity of securities held, and face or nominal value of each security. Methodological explanations and definitions, in line with those in the 1997 *Survey Guide,* were included in the instructions. Checks were also made to ensure that reported data contained an ISIN code, and that the information was consistent with the Ufficio Italiano dei Cambi (UIC) securities database.

6.91 For banks, data reported in the CPIS survey were compared with information reported in money and banking surveys. For investment companies, data reported in the CPIS survey were checked against data provided by the Lisbon Stock Exchange.

6.92 In the case of some nonfinancial corporations, the accounting reports were used to check the reported information.

6.93 Using a breakdown of portfolio assets by the currency in which issues are denominated, a reconciliation between flows and stocks was performed

6.94 In the event of misreporting (such as of market values or units of values), respondents were asked to provide corrected values. For some banks, the reported value was replaced by that derived from money and banking statistics sources.

6.95 A comparison between the investment funds (aggregate values) and the data provided by the Lisbon Stock Exchange was made. Checks were also made at the aggregate and detailed level of data reported by each custodian. Double counting was minimized by the fact that the CPIS was conducted primarily on a custodian basis, and the requirement that end-investors reported only their holdings of securities held in self-custody or with nonresident custodians.

IX. Steps Taken to Address Low Coverage or Low Response Rates

6.96 In some instances, there may be a need to gross up results, either because the survey did not cover all units in the potential universe or because of a low response rate. The latter problem often arises in situations where a survey is not obligatory. The experiences of Bermuda, Belgium (for coverage of households), and the United Kingdom in the 1997 CPIS are summarized below.

Bermuda

6.97 Because the CPIS was conducted on a voluntary basis, there was extensive reliance on estimation procedures to account for assets held by nonrespondents. The techniques used differed, depending on the sector classification of respondents and the available information. For collective investment schemes and insurance companies, supervisory sources provided some indication of cross-border holdings of portfolio investment, but did not provide a breakdown by the country of residence of the issuer. The CPIS data provided the

Table 6.2: Unadjusted 1997 and 1998 CPIS Results for Belgium
(Billions of Belgian francs)

Investor →	End-investors		Households		Subtotal	
Type ↓	1997	1998	1997	1998	1997	1998
Equity securities	754	1,036	917	1,165	1,671	2,201
Debt securities, <1 year	288	226	110	85	398	311
Debt securities, >1 year	2,606	3,046	392	492	2,998	3,538
Total	3,648	4,308	1,419	1,742	5,067	6,050

latter information, but there was a substantial element of nonresponse. The totals reported by each sector were aggregated, and a calculation was made for the securities held in each country as a percentage of the total assets reported. It was assumed that these percentages also held for the assets of nonrespondents. The respective percentages were applied to the totals reported for supervisory purposes to derive an estimate for portfolio investment in each country. These estimation techniques assumed that the breakdown by the country of residence of the issuer, as reported by CPIS respondents in that sector, was representative of all companies within that sector (i.e., including those that did not complete the CPIS questionnaire).

Belgium

6.98 Bearer securities are important in Belgium and are frequently held with nonresident custodians or in self-custody. In order to mitigate this gap, an attempt was made to find other sources offering sufficient guarantees of accuracy and reliability. Where possible, these data were wholly or partly incorporated in the survey results.

6.99 Table 6.2 summarizes the survey results prior to estimated additions. The figures in the households column result from the difference between the value of the securities that custodians declared to have received from residents and the amounts that end-investors declared to have entrusted to resident custodians. The difference is attributed to the household sector.

6.100 Adjustments based on global comparisons with other sources could not be used owing to their limitations, such as the choice of breakdown, and the level of detail. Adjustments based on information obtained on Belgian holdings of securities issued in Luxembourg seemed to be very reliable and contained the necessary breakdowns for the survey. These data were added only where it was sufficiently certain that the securities concerned were held by residents. The adjustments were confined to units of a *société d'investissement à capital variable* (SICAVs), insurance notes, and bank cash certificates of Luxembourg issuers, which, according to external sources, are the property of Belgian residents and were added to the basic holdings.

6.101 Units of SICAVs were added to the equity securities issued by Luxembourg issuers insofar as they were not yet included in the declarations of end-investors and custodians, on the assumption that all equity securities mentioned under the country "Luxembourg" were SICAVs. This represented a very cautious approximation, but is clearly an underestimate because the survey results presumably also include investments in Luxembourg shares other than SICAVs.

6.102 Insurance bonds and bank cash certificates were added in full to the long-term debt instruments issued by Luxembourg issuers, because these, unlike SICAVs, always give entitlement to coupons and will consequently, for tax reasons, be less quickly deposited in custody with resident custodians.

6.103 The share of the household sector in the CPIS results was about 40 percent of the adjusted total. The underlying figure could well be higher, on the assumption that cross-border holdings of portfolio investment assets compiled on the basis of cumulative flows, as reported in the IIP, mostly comprises portfolio investment by households.

United Kingdom

6.104 An aggregate end-investor survey was conducted for banks by the Bank of England and a separate survey for all other institutions by the ONS. For nonbanks, the CPIS was conducted on a statutory basis. However, as this was a one-off survey, it was not possible to force any respondent to respond. In the event of nonresponse, respondents were reminded by telephone and written reminder. For banks, a specific CPIS survey form was not required because existing survey forms were used. Nonresponse was not a problem for banks.

6.105 In the ONS survey, nonrespondents were assumed to have a pattern of holdings that was the same for those that did respond and therefore were included in the grossing up. The method of grossing was ratio estimation, using the same auxiliary value as used for the other surveys to financial institutions. Since the ONS had separate samples for insurance companies, pension funds, trusts, securities dealers, and nonfinancial companies, grossing up was done for each group separately.

X. Sectoral Information

6.106 Sectoral information about the holder is valuable additional information, but it is only an encouraged item in the CPIS. Information regarding the sector of the holder can be very useful, especially for counterpart liability analysis, because holders of portfolio investments may behave in different ways, especially during periods of financial crisis. However, obtaining this information is not always easy. Sector of holder is straightforward for an end-investor survey (the sectoral information is self-defining), but for a custodian survey it may be very difficult and expensive for the custodian to identify his or her customers' sectors. However, the experience in this respect of Portugal and the United States is useful in having custodians identify the sector for which they hold the securities.

6.107 Identification of the sector of issuer is usually straightforward when using a security-by-security approach.

Portugal

6.108 The CPIS included appropriate fields in order to obtain the institutional sector of the holder and the issuer. The latter information was provided by custodians, and the former obtained indirectly through other data available to the Banco de Portugal.

United States

6.109 Sectoral information was collected with respect to both the sector of the domestic investor and the sector of the issuer. For the holder, custodians were asked to report record-by-record which of the following sectors they were reporting for: (i) own portfolio, (ii) custody for mutual fund, (iii) custody for pension fund, (iv) custody for insurance company, (v) custody for other. However, determining the sector for many investments proved to be difficult.

Appendix 1: Model Form for a Mixed Custodian/ End-Investor Security-by-Security Survey

Survey of Portfolio Investment: Holdings of Equities and Debt Securities Issued by Unrelated Nonresidents as at December 31, 2001

Purpose of Collection

This survey collects information on holdings of residents of **[name of country]** in equities and debt securities issued by unrelated nonresidents as at December 31, 2001. The data from the survey will be used in the compilation of the balance of payments and international investment position statistics of **[name of country].** These statistics are published by **[name of compiling agency].** The survey is being conducted in coordination with other countries to facilitate international data comparability.

Collection Authority

The information requested is collected under the authority of **[state legal authority]**. ***[Delete if voluntary]***

Confidentiality

The completed forms will remain confidential to the **[name of compiling agency]**.

What to Report

The survey should be completed in accordance with the reporting instructions provided. If there are any questions regarding these instructions, please contact **[name of member of the survey staff]** at **[name of compiling agency]**.

When and Where to Report

Please provide the results of this survey by **March 31, 2002** to:

[Postal and e-mail addresses, telephone, and fax numbers of compiler]

Respondents unable to meet the reporting deadline should contact **[name of member of the survey staff]** at **[name of compiling agency]** to request an extension.

How to Report

Data may be submitted on diskettes, electronic mail, or paper forms. Please keep a copy for your records.

[Name of compiling agency and date]

Notes

Note 1. Who must report

(a) Custodians, resident in **[name of country],** who, as at close of business on December 31, 2001, manage the safekeeping of securities issued by nonresidents on behalf of residents of **[name of country],** or on their own account. Resident custodians are defined as entities located in **[name of country]** who manage the safekeeping of securities for investors; and

(b) Investors that are resident in **[name of country]** and own equities or debt securities issued by unrelated nonresidents of **[name of country]** as at the close of business on December 31, 2001 and that do not entrust the safekeeping of any or all of these securities to **resident** custodians. This includes both those who invest for their own account as well as those who invest on behalf of asset pools, such as the managers of mutual funds, insurance companies, and pension funds.

All entities that receive a copy of the survey forms must reply. Those that do not fall into either of the above two categories need only complete the identification information on Form 1a and mark the box indicating that they are exempt from completing Forms 2 and 3.

Note 2. What must be reported

All entities who receive either Form 2 or Form 3 must return the respondent identification section (Form 1a) **within 30 days** of receipt of the form, even those entities indicating that they are exempt from completing Form 1a.

Those respondents meeting the criteria above (see Note 1) must return the completed survey forms (Forms 1b, 2, and 3) by **March 31, 2002.** Respondents unable to meet the reporting schedule should contact **[name of compiling agency]** indicated on the first page of this form to request an extension.

Reporters can file a consolidated report for all related entities that are resident in **[name of country]**, or each resident entity may file independently. If two or more entities are filing separately, please contact the member of the survey staff indicated on the first page of this form at **[name of compiling agency]** for additional identification numbers. If a consolidated report is being supplied for two or more entities, do not supply separate reports for the same entities.

Form 2: Detailed Holdings is used to report detailed information on holdings of securities issued by unrelated nonresidents. Such information must be provided by:

(a) **resident custodians** in respect of securities issued by nonresidents that they manage the safekeeping of, for residents or on own account. Securities issued by nonresidents that are entrusted to other resident custodians and those that are managed for nonresidents are excluded from Form 2: they should be included on Form 3; and

(b) **investors** in respect of securities that are issued by unrelated nonresidents that are not entrusted to the safekeeping of resident custodians. (See Note 6 to determine whether an entity is related. Securities issued by unrelated nonresidents and entrusted to the custody of a resident custodian should be reported on Form 3.)

Form 3: Summary of Holdings Entrusted to Custodians is to show the total value and custodian information. Such information must be provided by:

(a) **resident custodians** in respect of securities that are issued by nonresidents and that are entrusted to the safekeeping of other resident custodians; and

(b) **investors** in respect of securities that are issued by nonresidents and that are entrusted to the safekeeping of resident custodians.

These holdings of securities should not be reported in detail on Form 2. Instead, only the total amounts entrusted to resident custodians should be reported, along with the name and address of the resident custodian.

Some respondents will need to complete both Form 2 and Form 3.

Note 3. Residence

The reporting unit for this form is a **resident of [name of country]**, that is, an individual, enterprise, or other organization domiciled in **[name of country]**. It includes branches and subsidiaries of nonresident enterprises if the branches or subsidiaries are domiciled in **[name of country]**. Domicile is defined as the center of economic interest of the entity, for instance, where an enterprise engages in production. Corporations legally registered in **[name of country]** are considered to be resident even if they have no "physical presence." **A nonresident** of **[name of country]** is any individual, enterprise, or other organization domiciled in a country other than **[name of country]**. Branches and subsidiaries of **[name of country]** enterprises domiciled in other jurisdictions are regarded as nonresidents of **[name of country]**.

The securities are classified by the jurisdiction of **residence of the issuer of the securities**. The residence of an enterprise can be taken to be where it is legally incorporated or, in the absence of legal incorporation, where it is legally domiciled. The country of residence of the issuer may differ from the currency of issue, the place of issue, or the country of the guarantor of the security. (Some securities are guaranteed by another party (such as the parent company or a government), and the guarantee may be either explicit or implicit. Even where the funds raised are for use by the guarantor, the residence of the **issuer** of the security should be used, **not** the residence of the guarantor.) Securities issued by international organizations should be shown under the separate code for international organizations (XX), not included under the country in which the organization is located.

[If one or more international organization is/are located in your country: **[Specify the name(s) of these international organizations]** should **not** be considered to be resident(s) in **[name of country]** and their holdings should not be reported in this return. However, **pension funds** for employees of these international organization(s) are considered to be resident in **[name of country]**. ***(If not relevant, delete this paragraph.***]

Note 4. Definition of equities and long- and short-term debt securities

A **security** is defined as an instrument that is traded or tradable. Examples of equities, long-term debt securities, and short-term debt securities are given below. This survey covers only securities issued by **unrelated** nonresident entities. See Note 6 to determine whether an entity is related. If you have any questions about how to classify an instrument, please contact the member of staff indicated on the first page of this form at **[name of compiling agency]**.

Equity securities cover all instruments and records acknowledging, after the claims of all creditors have been met, claims to the residual values of enterprises.

Include in equities:
- ordinary shares;
- stocks;
- participating preference shares;
- depository receipts (e.g., American depository receipts) denoting ownership of equity securities issued by nonresidents (see Note 8);
- shares/units in mutual funds and investment trusts;
- equity securities that have been sold under repurchase agreements (see Note 7); and
- equity securities that have been "lent" under a securities lending arrangement (see Note 7).

Exclude from equities:
- nonparticipating preference shares (but include these instruments under long-term debt securities);

- rights, options, warrants, and other derivative instruments;
- equity securities that have been bought under repurchase agreements (see Note 7); and
- equity securities that have been acquired under a securities lending arrangement (see Note 7).

Long-term debt securities cover bonds, debentures, and notes that usually give the holder the unconditional right to a fixed cash flow or contractually determined variable money income and have *an original term to maturity of more than one year.*

Include in long-term debt securities:
- bonds such as treasury, zero-coupon, stripped (see Note 9), deep-discounted, currency-linked (e.g., dual-currency), floating-rate, equity-related (e.g., convertible bonds), and Eurobonds;
- asset-backed securities such as mortgage-backed bonds and collateralized mortgage obligations (CMOs);
- index-linked securities (e.g., property index certificates);
- nonparticipating preference shares;
- floating-rate notes (FRN) such as perpetual-rate notes (PRN), variable-rate notes (VRN), structured FRN, reverse FRN, collared FRN, step-up recovery FRN (SURF), and range/corridor/accrual notes;
- euro medium-term notes (EMTN);
- Schuldscheine (German) notes;
- bonds with optional maturity dates, the last of which is more than one year after issue;
- debentures;
- negotiable certificates of deposits with contractual maturity of more than one year;
- other long-term debt securities;
- bearer depository receipts denoting ownership of debt securities issued by nonresidents (see Note 8);
- debt securities that have been sold under repurchase agreements (see Note 7); and
- debt securities that have been "lent" under a securities lending arrangement (see Note 7).

Exclude from long-term debt securities:
- derivative instruments;
- loans;
- trade credit and accounts receivable;
- money market instruments (e.g., treasury notes, bankers' acceptances, negotiable certificates of deposit with contractual maturity of one year or less, note issuance facilities, revolving underwriting facilities, and promissory notes), including short-term debt securities;
- debt securities that have been bought under repurchase agreements (see Note 7); and
- debt securities that have been acquired under a securities lending arrangement (see Note 7).

Short-term debt securities cover only market instruments, such as bills, commercial paper, and bankers' acceptances, that usually give the holder the unconditional right to receive a stated, fixed sum of money on a specified date and have an *original term to maturity of one year or less.*

Include in short-term debt securities:
- treasury bills and notes;
- bankers' acceptances;
- commercial and financial paper;
- certificates of deposit with contractual maturity of one year or less;
- short-term notes issued under note issuance facilities or revolving underwriting facilities and promissory notes (such short-term notes are included even though the underlying facility [the contingency] may be for more than one year because the notes themselves are of a short-term nature);
- debt securities that have been sold under repurchase agreements (see Note 7); and
- debt securities that have been "lent" under a securities lending arrangement (see Note 7).

Exclude from short-term debt securities:

- bonds such as treasury, zero-coupon, stripped (see Note 9), deep-discounted, currency-linked (e.g., dual-currency), floating-rate, equity-related (e.g., convertible bonds), and Eurobonds;
- asset-backed securities such as mortgage-backed bonds, and collateralized mortgage obligations (CMOs);
- index-linked securities (e.g., property index certificates);
- nonparticipating preference shares;
- floating-rate notes (FRN) such as perpetual-rate notes (PRN), variable-rate notes (VRN), structured FRN, reverse FRN, collared FRN, step-up recovery FRN (SURF), and range/corridor/accrual notes;
- euro medium-term notes (EMTN);
- Schuldscheine (German) notes;
- bonds with optional maturity dates, the latest of which is more than one year after issue;
- debentures;
- negotiable certificates of deposits with contractual maturity of more than one year;
- other long-term debt securities;
- bearer depository receipts denoting ownership of debt securities issued by nonresidents (see Note 8);
- debt securities that have been bought under repurchase agreements (see Note 7);
- debt securities that have been acquired under a securities lending arrangement (see Note 7);
- derivative instruments;
- loans; and
- trade credit and accounts receivable.

Financial derivatives are **not** to be reported because they are not classified as securities, but as a separate type of instrument. Record the value of the underlying security separately from any derivative that may be held in relation to it; however, if a security has an **embedded derivative,** do not attempt to separate the security from the embedded security. Include the value of such a security, including the embedded financial derivative, in your submission.

If you have any questions about how to classify an instrument, please contact the survey staff member indicated on the first page of this form at **[name of compiling agency]**.

Note 5. Valuation

Market value should be used to report all holdings of securities. Do **not** report the face value of the security as the market value.

Equity securities should be reported at market prices converted to [**domestic currency**] using the exchange rate prevailing at the close of business on December 31, 2001.

For enterprises listed on a stock exchange, the market value of your holding of their equity securities should be calculated using the market price on their main stock exchange prevailing at the close of business on December 31, 2001.

For unlisted enterprises, if a market value is not available at the close of business on December 31, 2001, estimate the market value of your holding of equity securities by using one of the following:

- a recent transaction price;
- directors' valuation; or
- net asset value (net asset value is equal to total assets, including intangibles, less nonequity liabilities and the paid-up value of nonvoting shares; assets and liabilities should be recorded at current, rather than historical, value).

Debt securities should be recorded using one of the market valuation methods listed below in descending order of preference and converted to **[domestic currency]**, using the exchange rate prevailing at the close of business on December 31, 2001:

- a quoted traded market price at the close of business on December 31, 2001;
- the present value of the expected stream of future payments or receipts associated with the securities;

- for unlisted securities, the price used to value securities for accounting or regulatory purposes;
- for deep-discount or zero-coupon securities, the issue price plus amortization of the discount; or
- for debt instruments issued at a premium, the issue price less the amortization of the premium.

Note 6. Exclusion of securities issued by related enterprises

Securities (whether equities or debt) issued by a nonresident enterprise that is related to the resident owner of those securities **should be excluded** from this report. Related nonresident enterprises are enterprises in which an enterprise **group** has an equity interest of 10 percent or more or where a nonresident has more than 10 percent or more holdings in your group. Ownership is measured in terms of ordinary shares or voting stock of incorporated enterprises or equivalent beneficial interest in unincorporated enterprises. Where such a relationship exists, exclude all securities (debt and equities).

The only exception is if the nonresident entity that issued the security and the resident owner of the security are affiliated financial intermediaries—banks, for instance. In these circumstances, securities issued by related enterprises, other than equity or permanent debt, should be included in this report.

Note 7. Treatment of securities involved in repurchase and securities lending arrangements

A **repurchase agreement**[1] (repo) is an arrangement involving the sale of securities at a specified price with a commitment[2] to repurchase the same or similar securities at a fixed price on a specified future date. A reverse repo is the same transaction seen from the other side; that is, an agreement whereby a security is purchased at a specified price with a commitment to resell the same or similar securities at a fixed price on a specified future date. **Securities (or stock or bond) lending** is an arrangement whereby the ownership of a security is transferred in return for collateral, usually another security, under the condition that the security or similar securities will revert to its original owner at a specified future date.

- Securities acquired under reverse repos or securities borrowing arrangements are to be *excluded* from the form.
- Securities sold under repos or "lent" under securities lending arrangements are to be *included* in the form.
- Securities acquired under reverse repos or securities borrowing arrangements and subsequently sold to a third party should be reported as a *negative* holding—namely, a short position. (See Form 2, item 10.)
- Valuations of securities under repos or securities lending arrangements should be at *market value* as at the close of business on December 31, 2001.

Note 8. Treatment of depository receipts

Depository receipts, which denote ownership of equity or debt securities issued by nonresidents—for instance, American depository receipts (ADRs) or bearer depository receipts (BDRs)—should be attributed to the country of residence of the issuer of the security underlying the depository receipt. Financial intermediaries should not report holdings of any securities against which depository receipts have been issued and sold; however, if a depository receipt has been issued before the financial institution arranging the issue has acquired the underlying securities, that financial institution should report a negative holding in the underlying security. (See Form 2, item 10.)

Note 9. Treatment of stripped securities

Stripped securities (strips) are securities that have been transformed from a principal amount with periodic interest coupons into a series of zero-coupon securities, with the range of maturities matching the coupon payment dates and the redemption date of the principal amount.

[1]Also included are sale/buy backs, carries, bond or stock lending with cash collateral, and similar transactions that involve the sale of a security with a commitment to repurchase it at a fixed price on a specified date or on demand.

[2]If there is no commitment to repurchase the securities, the transaction should be regarded as a straight sale of the security and should not be classified as a repo.

- If strips remain the direct obligation of the original issuer, then the residence of the issuer of the strips remains the same as for the original security. Dealers who request that a settlement house or clearing house create strips from an existing security issued by a nonresident should not report ownership of the underlying security after the strips have been created.
- If strips have been created and issued by an entity in its own name, then the security should be classified according to the residence of the issuer of the strips. In turn, such an issuer of strips should report its ownership of the underlying securities if they were issued by a nonresident.

Strips with an original maturity of less than one year are classified as money market instruments and thus, if identifiable, should be reported as short-term debt securities.

Note 10. Asset-backed securities

In reporting the market value of holdings of asset-backed securities, the respondent must be aware of the possibility of early partial redemption of principal. The market value of the principal amount outstanding at close of business on December 31, 2001, should be reported; if principal has been repaid, this market value will **not** be the same as the original face value revalued at end-period market prices.

If there are any questions regarding these instructions, please contact the survey staff member at [name of compiling agency] indicated on the front of this form.

SURVEY OF PORTFOLIO INVESTMENT—DECEMBER 31, 2001

FORM 1a: RESPONDENT IDENTIFICATION
To be returned within 30 days

1. Identification number: Enter the identification number from the mailing label on this survey. [ ]

2. Company name: ____________________

3. Street address: ____________________

4. City: ____________ 5. State: ________ 6. Postal code: ________

7. Reporting status   Form 2 ☐   Form 3 ☐   Exempt ☐

Form 2: Detailed Holdings is used to report detailed information on holdings of securities issued by unrelated nonresidents. Such information must be provided by:
(a) **resident custodians** in respect of securities issued by unrelated nonresidents that they manage the safekeeping of, for residents or on own account. Securities that are entrusted to other resident custodians and those that are managed for nonresidents are excluded; and
(b) **investors** in respect of securities that are issued by unrelated nonresidents that are not entrusted to the safekeeping of resident custodians.

Form 3: Summary of Holdings Entrusted to Custodians is used to report the total value of securities and custodian information. Such information must be provided by:
(a) **resident custodians** in respect of securities that are issued by nonresidents and that are entrusted to the safekeeping of other resident custodians; and
(b) **investors** in respect of securities that are issued by nonresidents and that are entrusted to the safekeeping of resident custodians.
These holdings of securities should not be reported in detail on Form 3. Instead, only the total amounts entrusted to resident custodians should be reported, along with the name and address of the resident custodian.

Some respondents will need to complete both Form 2 and Form 3.

Respondents with **no holdings of securities** issued by unrelated nonresidents **should check "exempt."**

8. In the event of a query, the national compiler may contact: ____________________

9. Tel. no.: ____________ 10. Fax no.: ____________ 11. E-mail address: ____________

By signing the certification line, the Certifier acknowledges that:
- He or she has read and understood the reporting requirements of this survey,
- He or she is aware of any penalties that may be imposed for filing an inaccurate report, ***[Delete if voluntary]*** and
- He or she certifies that he or she is sufficiently knowledgeable about the activities of the reporting organization that he or she can knowingly and with reasonable confidence certify that the information provided in this report is both accurate and complete.

Certifier's signature: ____________________

12. Certifier's name and title: ____________________

13. Certifier's telephone number: ____________ 14. Date signed: ____________

Official use only Logged in:	Data entered	Amendments

Form 1b Instructions

This form must be completed by all organizations that receive these survey forms that are not exempt. It is used to:

- provide basic identifying information;
- provide summaries of data reported on Form 2 and Form 3.

Notes on selected items

Item 1: **Identification number**—Enter the identification number from the top right-hand corner of the address label to these survey forms. If your number is unknown, please contact the member of the survey staff indicated on the first page of this form at **[name of compiling agency]**.

Item 9: **Number of Form 2 records reported**—Enter the total number of Form 2 records submitted with your report, whether they are submitted on paper, tape, or diskette.

Item 10: **Number of Form 3 records reported—**Enter the total number of Form 3 records submitted.

Item 11: **Total [domestic currency] value of all priced equities—**For all equity securities (Form 2, item 7, type 1) for which prices are known, enter the total domestic currency value (Form 2, item 10) of all such records.

Item 12: **Total [domestic currency] value of all priced long-term debt securities—**For all long-term debt securities (Form 2, item 7, type 2) for which prices are known, enter the total domestic currency value (Form 2, item 10) of all such records.

Item 13: **Total [domestic currency] value of all priced short-term debt securities—**For all short-term debt securities (Form 2, item 7, type 3) for which prices are known, enter the total domestic currency value (Form 2, item 10) of all such records.

Item 14: **Total number of shares of unpriced equity—**For all equity securities (Form 2, item 7, type 1) for which prices are unknown, enter the total number of shares (Form 2, item 12) of all such records.

Item 15: **Total face value of all unpriced long-term debt securities—**For all long-term securities (Form 2, item 7, type 2) for which prices are unknown, enter the total face value (Form 2, item 12) of all such records.

Item 16: **Total face value of all unpriced short-term debt securities—**For all short-term securities (Form 2, item 7, type 3) for which prices are unknown, enter the total face value (Form 2, item 12) of all such records.

SURVEY OF PORTFOLIO INVESTMENT—DECEMBER 31, 2001

FORM 1b: RESPONDENT IDENTIFICATION
To be returned with completed Forms 2 and/or 3 by March 31, 2002

1. Identification number: ______________________________

2. Company name: ______________________________

3. Street address: ______________________________

4. City: ____________________ 5. State: __________ 6. Postal code: ______________

7. In the event of a query, the national compiler may contact: ______________________

8. Tel. no.: ______________ 9. Fax no.:______________ 10. E-mail address: ______________

SUMMARY OF FORM 2 AND FORM 3 INFORMATION

9. Number of Form 2 records reported	
10. Number of Form 3 records reported	
11. Total value of all priced equities in [millions of domestic currency]	
12. Total value of all priced long-term debt in [millions of domestic currency] .	
13. Total value of all priced short-term debt in [millions of domestic currency] .	
14. Total number of shares of unpriced equity	
15. Total face value of all unpriced long-term debt	
16. Total face value of all unpriced short-term debt	

CERTIFICATION

By signing the certification line, the Certifier acknowledges that:

- He or she has read and understood the reporting requirements of this survey,
- He or she is aware of any penalties that may be imposed for filing an inaccurate report, ***[Delete if voluntary]*** and
- He or she certifies that he or she is sufficiently knowledgeable about the activities of the reporting organization that he or she can knowingly and with reasonable confidence certify that the information provided in this report is both accurate and complete.

Certifier's signature: ______________________________

17. Certifier's name and title: ______________________________

18. Certifier's telephone number: ______________________ 19. Date signed: ______________________

Official use only **Logged in:**	Data entered	Amendments

Form 2 Instructions

This form should be used by:

(a) **resident custodians** to report their custody holdings for resident clients of securities issued by nonresidents (if these securities have not in turn been entrusted to other resident custodians), and

(b) **resident investors** who own such securities but who have not entrusted the safekeeping of these securities to resident custodians (i.e., include any securities that have been entrusted to nonresident custodians). Own account holdings that have not been entrusted to other custodians should also be included.

Securities issued by entities related to the investor should **not** be reported (see Note 6 to the survey, above, for more information on securities issued by related enterprises).

Resident custodians who entrust their holdings of securities issued by unrelated nonresidents to other resident custodians should report these holdings on Form 3, not on Form 2. Only the custodian who arranges for the safekeeping of securities abroad (either directly or through a foreign local subcustodian) should report its holdings on Form 2.

However, securities entrusted by custodians directly to central securities depositories, such as Depository Trust Company, Euroclear, and Clearstream, or other nonresident custodians, should be reported on Form 2 by the custodian who entrusted the securities to the central depository.

Notes on Form 2

Item 1: **Identification number**—Enter the identification number from Form 1b, item 1.

Item 2: **Sequence number**—Starting at 1, sequentially number each record. The last record should have the same sequence number as the total number of records reported on Form 1b, item 9.

Item 3: **Security identification code**—Enter the security identification code used to identify this record. Use either an International Securities Identification Number (ISIN) code or a code issued by a national or international numbering agency, such as a SEDOL, CUSIP, or common code. **Do not use internally created codes unless this security has not been assigned a code by any recognized numbering agency.**

Item 4: **Security identification coding system**—From Annex A, select the two-digit code that corresponds to the security identification coding system that allocated the code reported in item 3.

Item 5: **Name of other ID coding system**—If the security identification code entered in item 3 above was issued by a security identification coding system not listed in Annex A, enter the name of that organization or system here.

Item 6: **Ownership code**—Indicate whether the security is held on (1) own account or (2) on behalf of a client.

Item 7: **Security type**—Indicate whether the security is (1) equity, (2) long-term debt, or (3) short-term debt.

Item 8: **Name of issuer**—Enter the name of the organization that issued this security.

Item 9: **Security description**—Provide pertinent descriptive information.

Item 10: **[National currency] value of security held**—Enter the total national currency value (price times quantity) of your holdings of this security. If reporting a negative position in the security, enter "S" before the value (see also Note 7 to the survey, above, on repurchase and securities lending arrangements and Note 8, on depository receipts).

For equity securities (Form 2, item 7, type 1), enter the national currency price equivalent (Form 2, item 11) of this security multiplied by the number of shares held (Form 2, item 12).

For long-term debt securities (Form 2, item 7, type 2), enter the product of the price (Form 2, item 11) of this security and its face value (Form 2, item 12) in the currency of denomination multiplied by the exchange rate (Form 2, item 14).

For short-term debt securities (Form 2, item 7, type 3), enter the product of the price (Form 2, item 11) of this security and its face value (Form 2, item 12) in the currency of denomination multiplied by the exchange rate (Form 2, item 14).

***Item 11*: Market price**—See Note 5 to the survey (on valuation), above, for further information on market prices.

For equity securities, enter your best estimate of the price per share in national currency.

For both long-term and short-term debt securities, enter the price as a percentage of the security's original face value. Thus, if a security is trading at 90 percent of its original value, enter .900 in this field. In the case of long-term zero-coupon or deep-discount issues, which trade when issued at a small percentage of their face value at maturity, enter the percentage of their face value at maturity that they are worth as at December 31, 2001. Thus, if a zero coupon bond were originally issued at a value equal to 17 percent of its face value at maturity and has—by December 31, 2001—appreciated to 43 percent of its face value at maturity, enter .430 in this field.

Note: Custodians must provide prices for securities in a manner consistent with their normal business practices for providing prices to their customers. Thus, if a firm typically provides prices to its customers for all securities for which prices are commercially available, the same practice should be followed when reporting on the survey.

***Item 12*: Face value or number of shares held**—For equity securities, enter the number of shares held, rounded to the nearest share. For both long-term and short-term debt securities, enter the face value held **in the currency of denomination**. For asset-backed securities, for which principal is repaid over time, enter the **remaining**, unrepaid face value of principal outstanding for this security as at close of business on December 31, 2001.

***Item 13*: Original face value for asset-backed securities only**—Pertaining to the amount entered in item 12 above, enter the original face value of principal that would have been outstanding if no principal had been repaid.

For example, if $1,000,000 of an asset-backed security were bought at date of issue, and 30 percent of the principal of this security had been repaid as at close of business on December 31, 2001, $700,000 should be entered in item 12, and $1,000,000 should be entered in item 13. The ratio between the amounts entered in item 12 and item 13 (700,000/1,000,000 = .700) should equal the "factor value" for this security.

***Item 14*: Exchange rate used**—Enter the exchange rate used to convert the currency of denomination into national currency. This rate should be that prevailing at the close of business on December 31, 2001, and should be expressed as the national currency value of one unit of the currency of denomination.

***Item 15*: Currency of denomination**—Enter the three-digit code corresponding to the currency used in item 14 from the list provided in Annex C. If the currency used in item 14 is not listed in Annex C, please contact the member of the survey staff at [**name of compiling agency**] indicated on the front page of this form.

***Item 16*: Amount on loan**—Of the total amount held of this security as reported in item 12, indicate how much of this position was on loan as at December 31, 2001.

***Item 17*: Country of issuer of security**—Enter the two-digit country code from the list provided in Annex B that corresponds to the country of domicile of the entity issuing the security. Holdings of issues of international organizations (such as the World Bank or United Nations) should be entered as country code XX, not as issues of the countries in which they are physically located.

SURVEY OF PORTFOLIO INVESTMENT—DECEMBER 31, 2001

FORM 2: DETAILED RECORD OF HOLDINGS

This form should be used by: (a) resident custodians who manage the safekeeping of securities, as well as (b) investors that own securities issued by unrelated entities and that do not entrust them to the safekeeping of resident custodians.

1. Identification number: Enter the identification number from Form 1a, item 1

2. Sequence no.: From 1 to the number of detailed records submitted

3. Security identification code:

4. Security identification coding system: Enter the relevant code from Annex A.

5. Name of the other security ID coding system: If the security identification code is not issued by an agency listed in Annex A, enter the name of that organization or system that allocated it:

6. Ownership code:
   1. Own portfolio
   2. Custody for other

7. Security type:
   1. Equity
   2. Long-term debt securities
   3. Short-term debt securities

8. Name of issuer:

9. Security description:

10. [National currency] value of security held: Value (price times quantity) of your holdings of this security. For equity, enter the [national currency] price (Form 2, item 11) times the number of shares held for this security. For debt, enter the price (Form 2, item 11) multiplied by the face value (Form 2, item 12) multiplied by the exchange rate (Form 2, item 14). If reporting a negative position in the security, enter "S" in the first (separate) box.

11. Market price: For equity, enter the price per share in [national currency]. For debt, enter the price as a percentage of the security's original face value.

12. Face value or number of shares held: For equity, enter the number of shares held, rounded to the nearest share. For debt, enter the face value held in the currency of denomination. For asset-backed securities, enter the remaining face value of principal still outstanding.

Item 13 applies to asset-backed securities only

13. Original face value for asset-backed security: Pertaining to the amount entered in item 12, enter the face value of principal which would have been outstanding if no principal had been repaid.

14. Exchange rate used: Enter the exchange rate used to convert the price in item 10 into national currency, if known.

15. Currency of denomination: Enter the code from Annex C for the currency used in item 14 (see also Notes on Form 2, item 15).

16. Amount on loan: Of the total national currency value held (as reported in item 10), enter the amount of this position that was on loan as at December 31, 1997.

17. Country of issuer: Enter the code from Annex A for the country of residence of the entity issuing the security.

SURVEY OF PORTFOLIO INVESTMENT—DECEMBER 31, 2001

FORM 3: SUMMARY OF HOLDINGS ENTRUSTED TO CUSTODIANS

This form should be used by: (a) **investors** that own securities issued by unrelated nonresidents and that entrust the safekeeping of securities to resident custodians, **as well as** (b) **custodians** who have entrusted the safekeeping of securities entrusted to them to other *resident* custodians. In item 1, starting at number 1, sequentially number each record. The last record should have the same sequence number as the total number of records reported on Form 1b, item 10. Indicate the names and addresses of the domestic custodian to whom the securities have been entrusted, as well as the total estimated market value, as at December 31, 2001, in item 7.

Identification number: Include the identification number for this entity on each page

1. Sequence number:
2. Name of custodian:
3. Street address of custodian:
4. City / 5. State / 6. Postal Code
7. Total [**domestic currency**] market value of equities and debt securities issued by nonresidents entrusted to this custodian as at December 31, 2001, rounded to the [nearest million].

1. Sequence number:
2. Name of custodian:
3. Street address of custodian:
4. City / 5. State / 6. Postal Code
7. Total [**domestic currency**] market value of equities and debt securities issued by nonresidents entrusted to this custodian as at December 31, 2001, rounded to the [nearest million].

1. Sequence number:
2. Name of custodian:
3. Street address of custodian:
4. City / 5. State / 6. Postal Code
7. Total [**domestic currency**] market value of equities and debt securities issued by nonresidents entrusted to this custodian as at December 31, 2001, rounded to the [nearest million].

ANNEX A: SECURITY IDENTIFICATION CODING SYSTEMS

SYSTEM CODE	ISSUING COUNTRY/AGENCY	SECURITY IDENTIFICATION CODING SYSTEM
01	Association of National Numbering Agencies (ANNA)	ISIN (International Security Identification Number)
02	Cedel	Cedel Code
03	Euroclear	Euroclear Code
04	Euroclear/Clearstream	Common Code
05	Australia	ASX Security Code (Australian Stock Exchange)
06	Austria	WPK Nummer (Wertpapierkenn-Nummer)
07	Belgium	SVM Code (Secrétariat des Valeurs Mobilières)
08	Brazil	National Stock Exchange Association (Comissao Nacional de Bolsas de Valores)
09	Brazil	Rio de Janeiro Stock Exchange
10	Brazil	São Paulo Stock Exchange
11	Denmark	Fondskode
12	France	SICOVAM (Société Interprofessionnelle pour la Compensation des Valeurs Mobilières)
13	Germany	WKN (Wertpapierkenn-Nummer)
14	Hong Kong SAR	Stock Exchange of Hong Kong Code
15	Italy	UIC (Ufficio Italiano dei Cambi)
16	Italy	ABI Code (Codice Associazione Bancaria Italiana)
17	Japan	SICC Code (Securities Identification Code Conference)
18	Japan	TSE Code (Tokyo Stock Exchange Code) (Toushou Code)
19	Korea, Republic of	Clearing Code (Korean Stock Exchange)
20	Mexico	Mexican Stock Exchange Code (Clave de Pizarra de la Bolsa Mexicana de Valores)
21	Netherlands	Clearingcode (Amsterdam Stock Exchange)
22	New Zealand	New Zealand Stock Exchange Code
23	Norway	Modified ISIN (Verdipapirsentralen) (VPS)
24	Portugal	Lisbon Stock Exchange Code
25	Portugal	Oporto Stock Exchange Code
26	South Africa	Clearing House Code (Johannesburg Stock Exchange)
27	Spain	CNMV Code (Comisión Nacional del Mercado de Valores)
28	Sweden	VPC Number
29	Switzerland	VALOR (Valorennummer)
30	Thailand	Stock Exchange of Thailand
31	United Kingdom	SEDOL (Stock Exchange Daily Official List)
32	United States	CUSIP Number (for North American Securities)
33	United States	CINS (CUSIP International Number System: for Non-North American Securities)

ANNEX B: JURISDICTION CODES

JURISDICTION	CODE
Afghanistan, I.S. of	AF
Albania	AL
American Samoa	AS
Algeria	DZ
Andorra	AD
Angola	AO
Anguilla	AI
Antigua and Barbuda	AG
Argentina	AR
Armenia	AM
Aruba	AW
Australia	AU
Austria	AT
Azerbaijan	AZ
Bahamas, The	BS
Bahrain	BH
Bangladesh	BD
Barbados	BB
Belarus	BY
Belgium	BE
Belize	BZ
Benin	BJ
Bermuda	BM
Bhutan	BT
Bolivia	BO
Bosnia and Herzegovina	BA
Botswana	BW
Bouvet Island	BV
Brazil	BR
British Virgin Islands	VG
Brunei Darussalam	BN
Bulgaria	BG
Burkina Faso	BF
Burundi	BI
Cambodia	KH
Cameroon	CM
Canada	CA
Cape Verde	CV
Cayman Islands	KY
Central African Republic	CF
Chad	TD
Chile	CL
China, People's Republic of	CN
Christmas Island	CX
Cocos (Keeling) Islands	CC
Colombia	CO
Comoros	KM
Congo, Democratic Republic of	CD
Congo, Republic of	CG

JURISDICTION	CODE
Cook Islands	CK
Costa Rica	CR
Côte d'Ivoire	CI
Croatia	HR
Cuba	CU
Cyprus	CY
Czech Republic	CZ
Denmark	DK
Djibouti	DJ
Dominica	DM
Dominican Republic	DO
East Timor	TP
Ecuador	EC
Egypt	EG
El Salvador	SV
Equatorial Guinea	GQ
Eritrea	ER
Estonia	EE
Ethiopia	ET
Faeroe Islands	FO
Falkland Islands	FK
Fiji	FJ
Finland	FI
France	FR
French Guiana	GF
French Polynesia	PF
French Southern Territories	TF
Gabon	GA
Gambia, The	GM
Georgia	GE
Germany	DE
Ghana	GH
Gibraltar	GI
Greece	GR
Greenland	GL
Grenada	GD
Guadeloupe	GP
Guam	GU
Guatemala	GT
Guernsey, C.I.	GG
Guinea	GN
Guinea-Bissau	GW
Guyana	GY
Haiti	HT
Heard and McDonald Islands	HM
Honduras	HN
Hong Kong SAR	HK
Hungary	HU
Iceland	IS

ANNEX B *(continued)*

JURISDICTION	CODE	JURISDICTION	CODE
India	IN	Myanmar	MM
Indonesia	ID	Namibia	NA
Iran, Islamic Republic of	IR	Nauru	NR
Iraq	IQ	Nepal	NP
Ireland	IE	Netherlands	NL
Isle of Man	IM	Netherlands Antilles	AN
Israel	IL	New Caledonia	NC
Italy	IT	New Zealand	NZ
Jamaica	JM	Nicaragua	NI
Japan	JP	Niger	NE
Jersey, C.I.	JE	Nigeria	NG
Jordan	JO	Niue Island	NU
Kazakhstan	KZ	Norfolk Island	NF
Kenya	KE	Northern Mariana Islands	MP
Kiribati	KI	Norway	NO
Korea, Democratic People's Republic of (North)	KP	Oman	OM
Korea, Republic of (South)	KR	Pakistan	PK
Kuwait	KW	Palau	PW
Kyrgyz Republic	KG	Panama	PA
Lao, P.D.R.	LA	Papua New Guinea	PG
Latvia	LV	Paraguay	PY
Lebanon	LB	Peru	PE
Lesotho	LS	Philippines	PH
Liberia	LR	Pitcairn Island	PN
Libya	LY	Poland	PL
Liechtenstein	LI	Portugal	PT
Lithuania	LT	Puerto Rico	PR
Luxembourg	LU	Qatar	QA
Macao SAR	MO	Reunion	RE
Macedonia, FYR of	MK	Romania	RO
Madagascar	MG	Russian Federation	RU
Malawi	MW	Rwanda	RW
Malaysia	MY	St. Helena	SH
Maldives	MV	St. Kitts and Nevis	KN
Mali	ML	St. Lucia	LC
Malta	MT	St. Pierre and Miquelon	PM
Marshall Islands	MH	St. Vincent and the Grenadines	VC
Martinique	MQ	Samoa	WS
Mauritania	MR	San Marino	SM
Mauritius	MU	São Tomé and Príncipe	ST
Mayotte	YT	Saudi Arabia	SA
Mexico	MX	Senegal	SN
Micronesia, Fed. States of	FM	Seychelles	SC
Moldova	MD	Sierra Leone	SL
Monaco	MC	Singapore	SG
Mongolia	MN	Slovak Republic	SK
Montserrat	MS	Slovenia	SI
Morocco	MA	Solomon Islands	SB
Mozambique	MZ	Somalia	SO

ANNEX B *(concluded)*

JURISDICTION	CODE	JURISDICTION	CODE
South Africa	ZA	Uganda	UG
South Georgia and Sandwich Island	GS	Ukraine	UA
Spain	ES	United Arab Emirates	AE
Sri Lanka	LK	United Kingdom	GB
Sudan	SD	United States	US
Suriname	SR	United States Pacific Islands	UM
Svalbard and Jan Mayen Islands	SJ	United States Virgin Islands	VI
Swaziland	SZ	Uruguay	UY
Sweden	SE	Uzbekistan	UZ
Switzerland	CH	Vanuatu	VU
Syrian Arab Republic	SY	Vatican City State	VA
Taiwan Province of China	TW	Venezuela, Rep. Bol. de	VE
Tajikistan	TJ	Vietnam	VN
Tanzania	TZ	Wallis and Futuna Islands	WF
Thailand	TH	West Bank and Gaza	PS
Togo	TG	Western Sahara	EH
Tokelau Islands	TK	Yemen, Republic of	YE
Tonga	TO	Yugoslavia, Fed. Rep. of	YU
Trinidad and Tobago	TT	Zambia	ZM
Tunisia	TN	Zimbabwe	ZW
Turkey	TR	Other (please specify)	
Turkmenistan	TM	Other (please specify)	
Turks and Caicos Islands	TC	Other (please specify)	
Tuvalu	TV	International Organizations	XX

ANNEX C: CURRENCY CODES

JURISDICTION	CURRENCY	CURRENCY CODE
Afghanistan, I.S. of	Afghani	AFA
Albania	Lek	ALL
Algeria	Algerian dinar	DZD
Andorra	Andorran peseta	ADP
Angola	Kwanza	AOA
Anguilla	East Caribbean dollar	XCD
Antigua and Barbuda	East Caribbean dollar	XCD
Argentina	Peso	ARS
Armenia	Dram	AMD
Aruba	Aruban guilder/florin	AWG
Australia	Australian dollar	AUD
Austria	Schilling	ATS
Austria	Euro	EUR
Azerbaijan	Manat	AZM
Bahamas, The	Bahamian dollar	BSD
Bahrain	Bahraini dinar	BHD
Bangladesh	Taka	BDT
Bank of Central African States	CFA franc BEAC	XAF
Barbados	Barbados dollar	BBD
Belarus	Belarusian rubel	BYR
Belgium	Belgium franc	BEF
Belgium	Euro	EUR
Belize	Belize dollar	BZD
Benin	CFA franc BCEAO	XOF
Bermuda	Bermuda dollar	BMD
Bhutan	Ngultrum	BTN
Bolivia	Boliviano	BOB
Bosnia and Herzegovina	Convertible marka	BAM
Botswana	Pula	BWP
Brazil	Real	BRL
Brunei Darussalam	Brunei dollar	BND
Bulgaria	Lev	BGL
Burkina Faso	CFA franc BCEAO	XOF
Burundi	Burundi franc	BIF
Cambodia	Riel	KHR
Cameroon	CFA franc BEAC	XAF
Canada	Canadian dollar	CAD
Cape Verde	Cape Verde escudo	CVE
Cayman Islands	Cayman Islands dollar	KYD
Central African Republic	CFA franc BEAC	XAF
Central Bank of West African States	CFA franc BCEAO	XOF
Chad	CFA franc BEAC	XAF
Chile	Chilean peso	CLP
China, People's Republic of	Yuan	CNY
Colombia	Colombian peso	COP

ANNEX C *(continued)*

JURISDICTION	CURRENCY	CURRENCY CODE
Comoros	Comorian franc	KMF
Congo, Democratic Republic of	Franc congolais	CDF
Congo, Republic of	Congo franc	XAF
Costa Rica	Costa Rican colon	CRC
Côte d'Ivoire	CFA Franc BCEAO	XOF
Croatia	Kuna	HRK
Cuba	Cuban peso	CUP
Cyprus	Cyprus pound	CYP
Czech Republic	Czech koruna	CZK
Denmark	Danish krone	DKK
Djibouti	Djibouti franc	DJF
Dominica	East Caribbean dollar	XCD
Dominican Republic	Dominican peso	DOP
East Carribbean	East Caribbean dollar	XCD
East Timor	Timor escudo	TPE
Egypt	Egyptian pound	EGP
El Salvador	El Salvador colon	SVC
Equatorial Guinea	CFA franc BEAC	XAF
Eritrea	Nafka	ERN
Estonia	Estonian kroon	EEK
Ethiopia	Ethiopian birr	ETB
Falkland Islands	Falkland Islands pound	FKP
Fiji	Fiji dollar	FJD
Finland	Markka	FIM
Finland	Euro	EUR
France	French franc	FRF
France	Euro	EUR
French Polynesia	CPF franc	XPF
Gabon	CFA franc BEAC	XAF
Gambia, The	Dalasi	GMD
Georgia	Lari	GEL
Germany	Deutsche mark	DEM
Germany	Euro	EUR
Ghana	Cedi	GHC
Gibraltar	Gibraltar pound	GIP
Greece	Drachma	GDR
Greece	Euro	EUR
Grenada	East Caribbean dollar	XCD
Guatemala	Quetzal	GTQ
Guernsey, C. I.	Guernsey pound	GGP
Guinea	Guinean franc	GNF
Guinea-Bissau	CFA franc BCEAO	XOF
Guyana	Guyana dollar	GYD
Haiti	Gourde	HTG
Honduras	Lempira	HNL
Hong Kong SAR	Hong Kong dollar	HKD

ANNEX C *(continued)*

JURISDICTION	CURRENCY	CURRENCY CODE
Hungary	Forint	HUF
Iceland	Icelandic krona	ISK
India	Indian rupee	INR
Indonesia	Rupiah	IDR
Iran, Islamic Republic of	Iranian rial	IRR
Iraq	Iraqi dinar	IQD
Ireland	Irish pound	IEP
Ireland	Euro	EUR
Isle of Man	Manx pound	IMP
Israel	New shekel	ILS
Italy	Italian lira	ITL
Italy	Euro	EUR
Jamaica	Jamaican dollar	JMD
Japan	Yen	JPY
Jersey, C. I.	Jersey pound	JEP
Jordan	Jordanian dinar	JOD
Kazakhstan	Tenge	KZT
Kenya	Kenya shilling	KES
Korea, Democratic People's Republic of (North)	DPRK won	KPW
Korea, Republic of (South)	Republic of Korea won	KRW
Kuwait	Kuwaiti dinar	KWD
Kyrgyz Republic	Som	KGS
Lao, P.D.R	Kip	LAK
Latvia	Lats	LVL
Lebanon	Lebanese pound	LBP
Lesotho	Loti	LSL
Liberia	Liberian dollar	LRD
Libya	Libyan dinar	LYD
Lithuania	Litas	LTL
Luxembourg	Luxembourg franc	LUF
Luxembourg	Euro	EUR
Macao SAR	Pataca	MOP
Macedonia, FYR of	Denar	MKD
Madagascar	Malagasy franc	MGF
Malawi	Kwacha	MWK
Malaysia	Malaysian ringgit	MYR
Maldives	Rufiyan	MVR
Mali	CFA franc BCEAO	XOF
Malta	Maltese lira	MTL
Mauritania	Ouguiya	MRO
Mauritius	Mauritian rupee	MUR
Mexico	Mexican peso	MXN
Moldova	Leu	MDL
Mongolia	Togrog	MNT
Montserrat	East Caribbean dollar	XCD
Morocco	Moroccan dirham	MAD

ANNEX C *(continued)*

JURISDICTION	CURRENCY	CURRENCY CODE
Mozambique	Metical	MZM
Myanmar	Kyat	MMK
Namibia	Namibia dollar	NAD
Nepal	Nepalese rupee	NPR
Netherlands	Netherlands guilder	NLG
Netherlands	Euro	EUR
Netherlands Antilles	Netherlands Antillean guilder	ANG
New Caledonia	CFP franc	XPF
New Zealand	New Zealand dollar	NZD
Nicaragua	Cordoba	NIC
Niger	CFA franc BCEAO	XOF
Nigeria	Naira	NGN
Norway	Norwegian krone	NOK
Oman	Rial Omani	OMR
Pakistan	Pakistan rupee	PKR
Panama	Balboa	PAB
Papua New Guinea	Kina	PGK
Paraguay	Guarani	PYG
Peru	New sol	PEN
Philippines	Philippines peso	PHP
Poland	Zloty	PLN
Portugal	Portuguese escudo	PTE
Portugal	Euro	EUR
Qatar	Qatar riyal	QAR
Romania	Leu	ROL
Russian Federation	Ruble	RUB
Rwanda	Rwanda franc	RWF
St. Helena	St. Helena pound	SHP
St. Kitts and Nevis	East Caribbean dollar	XCD
St. Lucia	East Caribbean dollar	XCD
St. Vincent and the Grenadines	East Caribbean dollar	XCD
Samoa	Tala	WST
São Tomé and Príncipe	Dobra	STD
Saudi Arabia	Saudi Arabian riyal	SAR
Senegal	CFA franc BCEAO	XOF
Seychelles	Seychelles rupee	SCR
Sierra Leone	Leone	SLL
Singapore	Singapore dollar	SGD
Slovak Republic	Slovak koruna	SKK
Slovenia	Tolar	SIT
Solomon Islands	Solomon Islands dollar	SBD
Somalia	Somali shilling	SOS
South Africa	Rand	ZAR
Spain	Spanish peseta	ESP
Spain	Euro	EUR

ANNEX C *(concluded)*

JURISDICTION	CURRENCY	CURRENCY CODE
Sri Lanka	Sri Lanka rupee	LKR
Sudan	Sudanese dinar	SDD
Suriname	Suriname guilder	SRG
Swaziland	Lilangeni	SZL
Sweden	Swedish krona	SEK
Switzerland	Swiss franc	CHF
Syrian Arab Republic	Syrian pound	SYP
Taiwan Province of China	New Taiwan dollar	TWD
Tajikistan	Somoni	TJS
Tanzania	Tanzanian shilling	TZS
Thailand	Baht	THB
Togo	CFA franc BCEAO	XOF
Tonga	Pa'anga	TOP
Trinidad and Tobago	Trinidad and Tobago dollar	TTD
Tunisia	Tunisian dinar	TND
Turkey	Turkish lira	TRL
Turkmenistan	Manat	TMM
Uganda	Uganda shilling	UGX
Ukraine	Hryvnia	UAH
United Arab Emirates	Dirham	AED
United Kingdom	Pound sterling	GBP
United States	United States dollar	USD
Uruguay	Uruguayan peso	UYS
Uzbekistan	Uzbek sum	UZS
Vanuatu	Vatu	VUV
Venezuela, Rep. Bol. de	Bolivar	VEB
Vietnam	Dong	VND
Wallis and Futuna Islands	CFP franc	XPF
Yemen, Republic of	Yemeni rial	YER
Yugoslavia, Fed. Rep. of	Yugoslav dinar	YUM
Zambia	Kwacha	ZMK
Zimbabwe	Zimbabwe dollar	ZWD

Appendix II: Model Form for an End-Investor Survey on an Aggregate Basis

Survey of Portfolio Investment: Holdings of Equities and Debt Securities Issued by Unrelated Nonresidents as at December 31, 2001

Purpose of Collection

This survey collects information on holdings of residents of **[name of country]** in equities and debt securities issued by unrelated nonresidents as at December 31, 2001. The data from the survey will be used in the compilation of the balance of payments and international investment position statistics of **[name of country]**. These statistics are published by **[name of compiling agency]**. The survey is being conducted in coordination with other countries to facilitate international data comparability.

Collection Authority

The information requested is collected under the authority of **[state legal authority]**. ***[Delete if voluntary]***

Confidentiality

The completed forms will remain confidential to the **[name of compiling agency]**.

What to Report

The survey should be completed in accordance with the reporting instructions provided. If there are any questions regarding these instructions, please contact **[name of member of the survey staff]** at **[name of compiling agency]**.

When and Where to Report

Please provide the results of this survey by March 31, 2002 to:

[Postal and e-mail addresses, telephone, and fax numbers of compiler]

Respondents unable to meet the reporting deadline should contact **[name of member of the survey staff]** at **[name of compiling agency]** to request an extension.

How to Report

Data may be submitted on diskettes, electronic mail, or paper forms. Please keep a copy for your records.

[Name of compiling agency and date]

Notes

Note 1. Who must report

Entities that are resident in **[name of country]** and that own equities or debt securities issued by unrelated nonresidents of **[name of country]** as at the close of business on December 31, 2001.

Note 2. What must be reported

All entities that receive a copy of the forms must return the respondent identification section (Form 1) **within 30 days** of receipt of the forms, even those entities indicating that they are exempt from completing Form 1.

Those respondents meeting the criteria above (see Note 1) must return the completed survey forms (Form 2) by **March 31, 2002.** Respondents unable to meet the reporting schedule should contact **[name of compiling agency]** indicated on the first page of this form to request an extension.

Reporters can file a consolidated report for all related entities that are resident in **[name of country]**, or each resident entity may file independently. If two or more entities are filing separately, please contact the member of the survey staff indicated on the first page of this form at **[name of compiling agency]** for additional identification numbers. If a consolidated report is being supplied for two or more entities, do not supply separate reports for the same entities.

Note 3. Residence

The reporting unit for this form is a **resident of [name of country]**, that is, an individual, enterprise, or other organization domiciled in **[name of country]**. It includes branches and subsidiaries of nonresident enterprises if the branches or subsidiaries are domiciled in **[name of country]**. Domicile is defined as the center of economic interest of the entity, for instance, where an enterprise engages in production. Corporations legally registered in **[name of country]** are considered to be resident even if they have no "physical presence." A **nonresident** of **[name of country]** is any individual, enterprise, or other organization domiciled in a country other than **[name of country]**. Branches and subsidiaries of **[name of country]** enterprises domiciled in other jurisdictions are regarded as nonresidents of **[name of country]**.

The securities are classified by the jurisdiction of **residence of the issuer of the securities**. The residence of an enterprise can be taken to be where it is legally incorporated or, in the absence of legal incorporation, where it is legally domiciled. The country of residence of the issuer may differ from the currency of issue, the place of issue, or the country of the guarantor of the security. (Some securities are guaranteed by another party (such as the parent company or a government), and the guarantee may be either explicit or implicit. Even where the funds raised are for use by the guarantor, the residence of the **issuer** of the security should be used, **not** the residence of the guarantor.) Securities issued by international organizations should be shown under the separate code for international organizations (XX), not included under the country in which the organization is located.

Note 4. Definition of equities and long- and short-term debt securities

A **security** is defined as an instrument that is traded or tradable. Examples of equities, long-term debt securities, and short-term debt securities are given below. This survey covers only securities issued by **unrelated** nonresident entities. See Note 6 to determine whether an entity is related. If you have any questions about how to classify an instrument, please contact the member of staff indicated on the first page of this form at **[name of compiling agency]**.

Equity securities cover all instruments and records acknowledging, after the claims of all creditors have been met, claims to the residual values of enterprises.

Include in equities:

- ordinary shares;
- stocks;
- participating preference shares;
- depository receipts (e.g., American depository receipts) denoting ownership of equity securities issued by nonresidents (see Note 8);
- shares/units in mutual funds and investment trusts;
- equity securities that have been sold under repurchase agreements (see Note 7); and
- equity securities that have been "lent" under a securities lending arrangement (see Note 7).

Exclude from equities:

- nonparticipating preference shares (but include these instruments under long-term debt securities);
- rights, options, warrants, and other derivative instruments;
- equity securities that have been bought under repurchase agreements (see Note 7); and
- equity securities that have been acquired under a securities lending arrangement (see Note 7).

Long-term debt securities cover bonds, debentures, and notes that usually give the holder the unconditional right to a fixed cash flow or contractually determined variable money income and have *an original term to maturity of more than one year.*

Include in long-term debt securities:

- bonds such as treasury, zero-coupon, stripped (see Note 9), deep-discounted, currency-linked (e.g., dual-currency), floating-rate, equity-related (e.g., convertible bonds), and Eurobonds;
- asset-backed securities such as mortgage backed bonds and collateralized mortgage obligations (CMOs);
- index-linked securities (e.g., property index certificates);
- nonparticipating preference shares;
- floating-rate notes (FRN) such as perpetual-rate notes (PRN), variable-rate notes (VRN), structured FRN, reverse FRN, collared FRN, step-up recovery FRN (SURF), and range/corridor/accrual notes;
- euro medium-term notes (EMTN);
- Schuldscheine (German) notes;
- bonds with optional maturity dates, the last of which is more than one year after issue;
- debentures;
- negotiable certificates of deposits with contractual maturity of more than one year;
- other long-term debt securities;
- bearer depository receipts denoting ownership of debt securities issued by nonresidents (see Note 8);
- debt securities that have been sold under repurchase agreements (see Note 7); and
- debt securities that have been "lent" under a securities lending arrangement (see Note 7).

Exclude from long-term debt securities:

- derivative instruments;
- loans;
- trade credit and accounts receivable;
- money market instruments (e.g., treasury notes, bankers' acceptances, negotiable certificates of deposit with contractual maturity of one year or less, note issuance facilities, revolving underwriting facilities, and promissory notes), including short-term debt securities;
- debt securities that have been bought under repurchase agreements (see Note 7); and
- debt securities that have been acquired under a securities lending arrangement (see Note 7).

Short-term debt securities cover only market instruments, such as bills, commercial paper, and bankers' acceptances that usually give the holder the unconditional right to receive a stated, fixed sum of money on a specified date and have an *original term to maturity of one year or less.*

Include in short-term debt securities:
- treasury bills and notes;
- bankers' acceptances;
- commercial and financial paper;
- certificates of deposit with contractual maturity of one year or less;
- short-term notes issued under note issuance facilities or revolving underwriting facilities and promissory notes (such short-term notes are included even though the underlying facility [the contingency] may be for more than one year because the notes themselves are of a short-term nature);
- debt securities that have been sold under repurchase agreements (see Note 7); and
- debt securities that have been "lent" under a securities lending arrangement (see Note 7).

Exclude from short-term debt securities:
- bonds such as treasury, zero-coupon, stripped (see Note 9), deep-discounted, currency linked (e.g., dual-currency), floating-rate, equity-related (e.g., convertible bonds), and Eurobonds;
- asset-backed securities such as mortgage-backed bonds, and collateralized mortgage obligations (CMOs);
- index-linked securities (e.g., property index certificates);
- nonparticipating preference shares;
- floating-rate notes (FRN) such as perpetual-rate notes (PRN), variable rate notes (VRN), structured FRN, reverse FRN, collared FRN, step up recovery FRN (SURF), and range/corridor/accrual notes;
- euro medium-term notes (EMTN);
- Schuldscheine (German) notes;
- bonds with optional maturity dates, the latest of which is more than one year after issue;
- debentures;
- negotiable certificates of deposits with contractual maturity of more than one year;
- other long-term debt securities;
- bearer depository receipts denoting ownership of debt securities issued by nonresidents (see Note 8);
- debt securities that have been bought under repurchase agreements (see Note 7);
- debt securities that have been acquired under a securities lending arrangement (see Note 7);
- derivative instruments;
- loans; and
- trade credit and accounts receivable.

Financial derivatives are **not** to be reported because they are not classified as securities, but as a separate type of instrument. Record the value of the underlying security separately from any derivative that may be held in relation to it; however, if a security has an **embedded derivative,** do not attempt to separate the security from the embedded security. Include the value of such a security, including the embedded financial derivative in your submission.

If you have any questions about how to classify an instrument, please contact the survey staff member indicated on the first page of this form at **[name of compiling agency]**.

Note 5. Valuation

Market value should be used to report all holdings of securities. Do **not** report the face value of the security as the market value.

Equity securities should be reported at market prices converted to **[domestic currency]** using the exchange rate prevailing at December 31, 2001.

For enterprises listed on a stock exchange, the market value of your holding of their equity securities should be calculated using the market price on their main stock exchange prevailing at December 31, 2001.

For unlisted enterprises, if a market value is not available at December 31, 2001, estimate the market value of your holding of equity securities by using one of the following:

- a recent transaction price;
- directors' valuation; or
- net asset value (net asset value is equal to total assets, including intangibles, less nonequity liabilities and the paid-up value of nonvoting shares; assets and liabilities should be recorded at current, rather than historical, value).

Debt securities should be recorded using one of the market valuation methods listed below in descending order of preference and converted to **[domestic currency]**, using the exchange rate prevailing at December 31, 2001:

- a quoted traded market price at December 31, 2001;
- the present value of the expected stream of future payments or receipts associated with the securities;
- for unlisted securities, the price used to value securities for accounting or regulatory purposes;
- for deep-discount or zero-coupon securities, the issue price plus amortization of the discount; or
- for debt instruments issued at a premium, the issue price less the amortization of the premium.

Note 6. Exclusion of securities issued by related enterprises

Securities (whether equities or debt) issued by a nonresident enterprise that is related to the resident owner of those securities **should be excluded** from this report. Related nonresident enterprises are enterprises in which an enterprise **group** has an equity interest of 10 percent or more or where a nonresident has more than 10 percent or more holdings in your group. Ownership is measured in terms of ordinary shares or voting stock of incorporated enterprises or equivalent beneficial interest in unincorporated enterprises. Where such a relationship exists, exclude all securities (debt and equities).

The only exception is if the nonresident entity that issued the security and the resident owner of the security are affiliated financial intermediaries—banks, for instance. In these circumstances, securities issued by related enterprises, other than equity or permanent debt, should be included in this report.

Note 7. Treatment of securities involved in repurchase and securities lending arrangements

A **repurchase agreement**[1] (repo) is an arrangement involving the sale of securities at a specified price with a commitment[2] to repurchase the same or similar securities at a fixed price on a specified future date. A reverse repo is the same transaction seen from the other side; that is, an agreement whereby a security is purchased at a specified price with a commitment to resell the same or similar securities at a fixed price on a specified future date. **Securities (or stock or bond) lending** is an arrangement whereby the ownership of a security is transferred in return for collateral, usually another security, under the condition that the security or similar securities will revert to its original owner at a specified future date.

- Securities acquired under reverse repos or securities borrowing arrangements are to be *excluded* from the form.
- Securities sold under repos or "lent" under securities lending arrangements are to be *included* in the form.
- Securities acquired under reverse repo or securities borrowing arrangements and subsequently sold to a third party should be reported as a *negative* holding—namely, a short position.
- Valuations of securities under repurchase or securities lending arrangements should be at *market value* as at December 31, 2001.

Note 8. Treatment of depository receipts

Depository receipts, which denote ownership of equity or debt securities issued by nonresidents—for instance, American depository receipts (ADRs) or bearer depository receipts (BDRs)—should be attributed to the coun-

[1]Also included are sale/buy backs, carries, bond or stock lending with cash collateral, and similar transactions that involve the sale of a security with a commitment to repurchase it at a fixed price on a specified date or on demand.

[2]If there is no commitment to repurchase the securities, the transaction should be regarded as a straight sale of the security and should not be classified as a repo.

try of residence of the issuer of the security underlying the depository receipt. Financial intermediaries should not report holdings of any securities against which depository receipts have been issued and sold; however, if a depository receipt has been issued before the financial institution arranging the issue has acquired the underlying securities, that financial institution should report a negative holding in the underlying security.

Note 9. Treatment of stripped securities

Stripped securities (strips) are securities that have been transformed from a principal amount with periodic interest coupons into a series of zero-coupon securities, with the range of maturities matching the coupon payment dates and the redemption date of the principal amount.

- If strips remain the direct obligation of the original issuer, then the residence of the issuer of the strips remains the same as for the original security. Dealers who request that a settlement house or clearing house create strips from an existing security issued by a nonresident should not report ownership of the underlying security after the strips have been created.
- If strips have been created and issued by an entity in its own name, then the security should be classified according to the residence of the issuer of the strips. In turn, such an issuer of strips should report its ownership of the underlying securities if they were issued by a nonresident.

Strips with an original maturity of less than one year are classified as money market instruments and thus, if identifiable, should be reported as short-term debt securities.

Note 10. Asset-backed securities

In reporting the market value of holdings of asset-backed securities, the respondent must be aware of the possibility of early partial redemption of principal. The market value of the principal amount outstanding at December 31, 2001, should be reported; if principal has been repaid, this market value will **not** be the same as the original face value revalued at end-period market prices.

If there are any questions regarding these instructions, please contact the survey staff member at [name of compiling agency] indicated on the front of this form.

SURVEY OF PORTFOLIO INVESTMENT—DECEMBER 31, 2001

FORM 1: RESPONDENT IDENTIFICATION
To be returned within 30 days

1. Identification number: Enter the identification number from the mailing label on this survey. ☐

2. Company name : ______________________

3. Street address: ______________________

4. City: ____________ 5. State: ________ 6. Postal code: ________

7. Reporting status Form 2 ☐ Exempt ☐

Respondents with **no holdings of securities** issued by unrelated nonresidents **should check "exempt."**

8. In the event of a query, the national compiler may contact: ______________

9. Tel. no.: ________ 10. Fax no.:________ 11. E-mail address: ________

By signing the certification line, the Certifier acknowledges that:

- He or she has read and understood the reporting requirements of this survey,
- He or she is aware of any penalties that may be imposed for filing an inaccurate report, ***[Delete if voluntary]*** and
- He or she certifies that he or she is sufficiently knowledgeable about the activities of the reporting organization that he or she can knowingly and with reasonable confidence certify that the information provided in this report is both accurate and complete.

Certifier's signature: ______________________

12. Certifier's name and title: ______________________

13. Certifier's telephone number: ________ 14. Date signed: ________

Official use only **Logged in:**	Data entered	Amendments

SURVEY OF PORTFOLIO INVESTMENT—DECEMBER 31, 2001

FORM 2: HOLDINGS OF SECURITIES ISSUED BY UNRELATED NONRESIDENTS

[Delete own jurisdiction if it is included on this list] [Add appropriate currency and units]					
		Market value of securities as at December 31, 2001 [Currency - millions]			
Jurisdiction of issuer	Code	EQUITIES (1)	LONG-TERM DEBT SECURITIES (2)	SHORT-TERM DEBT SECURITIES (3)	Office use only
Afghanistan, I.S. of	AF				
….	..				
….	..				
Zimbabwe	ZW				
Other (please specify)					
International Organizations	XX				
Total Value of Securities Reported					

For presentation, only the first and last countries on the list are shown here. The complete list of countries is shown in Annex B of Appendix I.

Appendix III: Model Form for a Mixed Custodian/ End-Investor Survey on an Aggregate Basis

Survey of Portfolio Investment: Holdings of Equities and Debt Securities Issued by Unrelated Nonresidents as at December 31, 2001

Purpose of Collection

This survey collects information on holdings of residents of **[name of country]** in equities and debt securities issued by unrelated nonresidents as at December 31, 2001. The data from the survey will be used in the compilation of the balance of payments and international investment position statistics of **[name of country]**. These statistics are published by **[name of compiling agency]**. The survey is being conducted in coordination with other countries to facilitate international data comparability.

Collection Authority

The information requested is collected under the authority of **[state legal authority]**. ***[Delete if voluntary]***

Confidentiality

The completed forms will remain confidential to the **[name of compiling agency]**.

What to Report

The survey should be completed in accordance with the reporting instructions provided. If there are any questions regarding these instructions, please contact **[name of member of the survey staff]** at **[name of compiling agency]**.

When and Where to Report

Please provide the results of this survey by **March 31, 2002** to:

[Postal and e-mail addresses, telephone, and fax numbers of compiler]

Respondents unable to meet the reporting deadline should contact **[name of member of the survey staff]** at **[name of compiling agency]** to request an extension.

How to Report

Data may be submitted on diskette, electronic mail, or paper forms. Please keep a copy for your records.

[Name of compiling agency and date]

Notes

Note 1. Who must report

(a) **Custodians**, resident in **[name of country]**, who, as at December 31, 2001, manage the safekeeping of securities issued by nonresidents on behalf of residents of **[name of country]**, or **on their own account**. Resident custodians are defined as entities located in **[name of country]** who manage the safekeeping of securities for investors; and

(b) **Investors** that are resident in **[name of country]** and that own equities or debt securities issued by unrelated nonresidents of **[name of country]** as at December 31, 2001 and that do not entrust the safekeeping of any or all of these securities to **resident** custodians. This includes both those who invest for their own account as well as those who invest on behalf of asset pools, such as the managers of mutual funds, insurance companies, and pension funds.

All entities that receive a copy of the survey forms must reply. Those that do not fall into either of the above two categories need only complete the identification information on Form 1 and mark the box indicating that they are exempt from completing Forms 2a, 2b, 2c (for end-investors) and Form 2d (for custodians).

Note 2. What must be reported

All entities that receive a copy of the survey forms must complete the **respondent identification section** of Form 1 and return a copy to the **[name of compiling agency] within 30 days** of receipt of the survey forms.

All entities that receive a copy of the survey forms must submit their survey responses by **March 31, 2001,** to **[name of compiling agency]**, whose address is listed in the key information section of Form 1. Respondents unable to meet the reporting schedule should contact **[name of member of the survey staff shown on the front of this form]** at **[name of compiling agency]** to request an extension.

End-Investors

Resident end-investors of **[name of country]** should complete Form 1 and Form 2a (for equity holdings), Form 2b (for long-term debt securities holdings), and Form 2c (for short-term debt securities holdings) in respect of securities issued by unrelated nonresidents:

(a) held on their own account (i.e., not entrusted to a custodian) (column 1), and

(b) entrusted to a nonresident custodian (column 2),

as at December 31, 2001.

Securities entrusted to resident custodians should be excluded from this form because they will be reported by the custodians.

Custodians' own account holdings should be included in Forms 2a, 2b, or 2c, as appropriate.

Reporters can file a consolidated report for all related entities that are resident in **[name of country]**, or each resident entity may file independently. If two or more entities are filing separately, please contact the member of the survey staff indicated on the first page of this form at **[name of compiling agency]** for additional identification numbers. Do **not** file both a consolidated report for the entire resident organization **and** for the separate units.

Custodians

In addition to Form 1, **all** custodians of **[name of country]** should complete Form 2d in respect of securities issued by nonresidents and which were held as at December 31, 2001 on behalf of residents of **[name of country]**. Report the holdings of equities in column 1, long-term debt securities in column 2, and short-term debt securities in column 3.

Do not include own account holdings in Form 2d; these should be reported on Forms 2a, 2b, and 2c, as appropriate.

Securities issued by entities that are related to the investor should **not** be reported (see Note 6 on exclusion of securities issued by related enterprises).

Where securities have been entrusted by a resident of **[name of country]** to a custodian who is a resident of **[name of country]**, and that custodian has passed the securities to another custodian, the **first** custodian should report the holding. The second (or subsequent) custodian in that chain of custody should **not** report holdings of securities issued by nonresidents held on behalf of another custodian.

All entities who receive any of the above forms must return the respondent identification section (Form 1) **within 30 days** of receipt of the forms, even those entities indicating that they are exempt from completing Form 1.

Those respondents meeting the criteria above (see Note 1) must return the completed survey forms (for end-investors: Forms 2a, 2b, and 2c; for custodians: Form 2d) by **March 31, 2002.**

Respondents unable to meet the reporting schedule should contact **[name of compiling agency]** indicated on the first page of this form to request an extension.

Note 3. Residence

The reporting unit for this form is a **resident of [name of country]**, that is, an individual, enterprise, or other organization domiciled in **[name of country]**. It includes branches and subsidiaries of nonresident enterprises if the branches or subsidiaries are domiciled in **[name of country]**. Domicile is defined as the center of economic interest of the entity, for instance, where an enterprise engages in production. Corporations legally registered in **[name of country]** are considered to be resident even if they have no "physical presence." A **nonresident** of **[name of country]** is any individual, enterprise, or other organization domiciled in a country other than **[name of country]**. Branches and subsidiaries of **[name of country]** enterprises domiciled in other jurisdictions are regarded as nonresidents of **[name of country]**.

The securities are classified by the jurisdiction of **residence of the issuer of the securities** . The residence of an enterprise can be taken to be where it is legally incorporated or, in the absence of legal incorporation, where it is legally domiciled. The country of residence of the issuer may differ from the currency of issue, the place of issue, or the country of the guarantor of the security. (Some securities are guaranteed by another party (such as the parent company or a government), and the guarantee may be either explicit or implicit. Even where the funds raised are for use by the guarantor, the residence of the **issuer** of the security should be used, **not** the residence of the guarantor.) Securities issued by international organizations should be shown under the separate code for international organizations (XX), not included under the country in which the organization is located.

[If one or more international organization is/are located in your country: **[Specify the name(s) of these international organizations]** should **not** be considered to be resident(s) in **[name of country]** and their holdings should not be reported in this return. However, **pension funds** for employees of these international organization(s) are considered to resident in **[name of country]. *(If not relevant, delete this paragraph.*]**

Note 4. Definition of equities and long- and short-term debt securities

A **security** is defined as an instrument that is traded or tradable. Examples of equities, long-term debt securities, and short-term debt securities are given below. This survey covers only securities issued by **unrelated** nonresident entities. See Note 6 to determine whether an entity is related. If you have any questions about how to classify an instrument, please contact the member of staff indicated on the first page of this form at **[name of compiling agency]**.

Equity securities cover all instruments and records acknowledging, after the claims of all creditors have been met, claims to the residual values of enterprises.

Include in equities:
- ordinary shares;
- stocks;
- participating preference shares;
- depository receipts (e.g., American depository receipts) denoting ownership of equity securities issued by nonresidents (see Note 8);
- shares/units in mutual funds and investment trusts;
- equity securities that have been sold under repurchase agreements (see Note 7); and
- equity securities that have been "lent" under a securities lending arrangement (see Note 7).

Exclude from equities:
- nonparticipating preference shares (but include these instruments under long-term debt securities);
- rights, options, warrants, and other derivative instruments;
- equity securities that have been bought under repurchase agreements (see Note 7); and
- equity securities that have been acquired under a securities lending arrangement (see Note 7).

Long-term debt securities cover bonds, debentures, and notes that usually give the holder the unconditional right to a fixed cash flow or contractually determined variable money income and have *an original term to maturity of more than one year.*

Include in long-term debt securities:
- bonds such as treasury, zero-coupon, stripped (see Note 9), deep-discounted, currency-linked (e.g., dual-currency), floating-rate, equity-related (e.g., convertible bonds), and Eurobonds;
- asset-backed securities such as mortgage backed bonds and collateralized mortgage obligations (CMOs);
- index-linked securities (e.g., property index certificates);
- nonparticipating preference shares;
- floating-rate notes (FRN) such as perpetual-rate notes (PRN), variable-rate notes (VRN), structured FRN, reverse FRN, collared FRN, step-up recovery FRN (SURF), and range/corridor/accrual notes;
- euro medium-term notes (EMTN);
- Schuldscheine (German) notes;
- bonds with optional maturity dates, the last of which is more than one year after issue;
- debentures;
- negotiable certificates of deposits with contractual maturity of more than one year;
- other long-term debt securities;
- bearer depository receipts denoting ownership of debt securities issued by nonresidents (see Note 8);
- debt securities that have been sold under repurchase agreements (see Note 7); and
- debt securities that have been "lent" under a securities lending arrangement (see Note 7).

Exclude from long-term debt securities:
- derivative instruments;
- loans;
- trade credit and accounts receivable;

- money market instruments (e.g., treasury notes, banker's acceptances, negotiable certificates of deposit with contractual maturity of one year or less, note issuance facilities, revolving underwriting facilities, and promissory notes), including short-term debt securities;
- debt securities that have been bought under repurchase agreements (see Note 7); and
- debt securities that have been acquired under a securities lending arrangement (see Note 7).

Short-term debt securities cover only market instruments, such as bills, commercial paper, and bankers' acceptances that usually give the holder the unconditional right to receive a stated, fixed sum of money on a specified date and have an *original term to maturity of one year or less.*

Include in short-term debt securities:
- treasury bills and notes;
- bankers' acceptances;
- commercial and financial paper;
- certificates of deposit with contractual maturity of one year or less;
- short-term notes issued under note issuance facilities or revolving underwriting facilities and promissory notes (such short-term notes are included even though the underlying facility [the contingency] may be for more than one year because the notes themselves are of a short-term nature);
- debt securities that have been sold under repurchase agreements (see Note 7); and
- debt securities that have been "lent" under a securities lending arrangement (see Note 7).

Exclude from short-term debt securities:
- bonds such as treasury, zero-coupon, stripped (see Note 9), deep-discounted, currency-linked (e.g., dual-currency), floating-rate, equity-related (e.g., convertible bonds), and Eurobonds;
- asset-backed securities such as mortgage-backed bonds, and collateralized mortgage obligations (CMOs);
- index-linked securities (e.g., property index certificates);
- nonparticipating preference shares;
- floating-rate notes (FRN) such as perpetual-rate notes (PRN), variable rate notes (VRN), structured FRN, reverse FRN, collared FRN, step up recovery FRN (SURF), and range/corridor/accrual notes;
- euro medium-term notes (EMTN);
- Schuldscheine (German) notes;
- bonds with optional maturity dates, the latest of which is more than one year after issue;
- debentures;
- negotiable certificates of deposits with contractual maturity of more than one year;
- other long-term debt securities;
- bearer depository receipts denoting ownership of debt securities issued by nonresidents (see Note 8);
- debt securities that have been bought under repurchase agreements (see Note 7);
- debt securities that have been acquired under a securities lending arrangement (see Note 7);
- derivative instruments;
- loans; and
- trade credit and accounts receivable.

Financial derivatives are **not** to be reported because they are not classified as securities, but as a separate type of instrument. Record the value of the underlying security separately from any derivative that may be held in relation to it; however, if a security has an **embedded derivative,** do not attempt to separate the security from the embedded security. Include the value of such a security, including the embedded financial derivative, in your submission.

If you have any questions about how to classify an instrument, please contact the survey staff member indicated on the first page of this form at **[name of compiling agency]**.

Note 5. Valuation

Market value should be used to report all holdings of securities. Do **not** report the face value of the security as the market value.

Equity securities should be reported at market prices converted to **[domestic currency]** using the exchange rate prevailing at December 31, 2001.

For enterprises listed on a stock exchange, the market value of your holding of their equity securities should be calculated using the market price on their main stock exchange prevailing at December 31, 2001.

For unlisted enterprises, if a market value is not available at December 31, 2001, estimate the market value of your holding of equity securities by using one of the following:
- a recent transaction price;
- directors' valuation; or
- net asset value (net asset value is equal to total assets, including intangibles, less nonequity liabilities and the paid-up value of nonvoting shares; assets and liabilities should be recorded at current, rather than historical, value).

Debt securities should be recorded using one of the market valuation methods listed below in descending order of preference and converted to **[domestic currency]**, using the exchange rate prevailing at December 31, 2001:
- a quoted traded market price at December 31, 2001;
- the present value of the expected stream of future payments or receipts associated with the securities;
- for unlisted securities, the price used to value securities for accounting or regulatory purposes;
- for deep-discount or zero-coupon securities, the issue price plus amortization of the discount; or
- for debt instruments issued at a premium, the issue price less the amortization of the premium.

Note 6. *Exclusion of securities issued by related enterprises*

Securities (whether equities or debt) issued by a nonresident enterprise that is related to the resident owner of those securities **should be excluded** from this report. Related nonresident enterprises are enterprises in which an enterprise **group** has an equity interest of 10 percent or more or where a nonresident has more than 10 percent or more holdings in your group. Ownership is measured in terms of ordinary shares or voting stock of incorporated enterprises or equivalent beneficial interest in unincorporated enterprises. Where such a relationship exists, exclude all securities (debt and equities).

The only exception is if the nonresident entity that issued the security and the resident owner of the security are affiliated financial intermediaries—banks, for instance. In these circumstances, securities issued by related enterprises, other than equity or permanent debt, should be included in this report.

Note 7. *Treatment of securities involved in repurchase and securities lending arrangements*

A **repurchase agreement**[1] (repo) is an arrangement involving the sale of securities at a specified price with a commitment[2] to repurchase the same or similar securities at a fixed price on a specified future date. A reverse repo is the same transaction seen from the other side; that is, an agreement whereby a security is purchased at a specified price with a commitment to resell the same or similar securities at a fixed price on a specified future date. **Securities (or stock or bond) lending** is an arrangement whereby the ownership of a security is transferred in return for collateral, usually another security, under the condition that the security or similar securities will revert to its original owner at a specified future date.
- Securities acquired under reverse repos or securities borrowing arrangements are to be *excluded* from the form.
- Securities sold under repos or "lent" under securities lending arrangements are to be *included* in the form.
- Securities acquired under reverse repo or securities borrowing arrangements and subsequently sold to a third party should be reported as a *negative* holding—namely, a short position (see Form 2, item 10).

---

[1]Also included are sale/buy backs, carries, bond or stock lending with cash collateral, and similar transactions that involve the sale of a security with a commitment to repurchase it at a fixed price on a specified date or on demand.

[2]If there is no commitment to repurchase the securities, the transaction should be regarded as a straight sale of the security and should not be classified as a repo.

- Valuations of securities under repurchase or securities lending arrangements should be at *market value* as at December 31, 2001.

Note 8. Treatment of depository receipts

Depository receipts, which denote ownership of equity or debt securities issued by nonresidents—for instance, American depository receipts (ADRs) or bearer depository receipts (BDRs)—should be attributed to the country of residence of the issuer of the security underlying the depository receipt. Financial intermediaries should not report holdings of any securities against which depository receipts have been issued and sold; however, if a depository receipt has been issued before the financial institution arranging the issue has acquired the underlying securities, that financial institution should report a negative holding in the underlying security.

Note 9. Treatment of stripped securities

Stripped securities (strips) are securities that have been transformed from a principal amount with periodic interest coupons into a series of zero-coupon securities, with the range of maturities matching the coupon payment dates and the redemption date of the principal amount.

- If strips remain the direct obligation of the original issuer, then the residence of the issuer of the strips remains the same as for the original security. Dealers who request that a settlement house or clearing house create strips from an existing security issued by a nonresident should not report ownership of the underlying security after the strips have been created.
- If strips have been created and issued by an entity in its own name, then the security should be classified according to the residence of the issuer of the strips. In turn, such an issuer of strips should report its ownership of the underlying securities if they were issued by a nonresident.

Strips with an original maturity of less than one year are classified as money market instruments and thus, if identifiable, should be reported as short-term debt securities.

Note 10. Asset-backed securities

In reporting the market value of holdings of asset-backed securities, the respondent must be aware of the possibility of early partial redemption of principal. The market value of the principal amount outstanding at December 31, 2001, should be reported; if principal has been repaid, this market value will **not** be the same as the original face value revalued at end-period market prices.

If there are any questions regarding these instructions, please contact the survey staff member at [name of compiling agency] indicated on the front of this form.

SURVEY OF PORTFOLIO INVESTMENT—DECEMBER 31, 2001

FORM 1: RESPONDENT IDENTIFICATION
To be returned within 30 days

1. Identification number: Enter the identification number from the mailing label on this survey. ☐

2. Company name: ______________________________

3. Street address: ______________________________

4. City: ____________ 5. State: ____________ 6. Postal code: ____________

7. Reporting status   Holding securities issued by nonresidents ☐   Exempt ☐

Respondents with **no holdings of securities** issued by unrelated nonresidents **should check "exempt."**

8. In the event of a query, the national compiler may contact: ______________________________

9. Tel. no.: ____________ 10. Fax no.:____________ 11. E-mail address: ____________

By signing the certification line, the Certifier acknowledges that:

- He or she has read and understood the reporting requirements of this survey,
- He or she is aware of any penalties that may be imposed for filing an inaccurate report, ***[Delete if voluntary]*** and
- He or she certifies that he or she is sufficiently knowledgeable about the activities of the reporting organization that he or she can knowingly and with reasonable confidence certify that the information provided in this report is both accurate and complete.

Certifier's signature: ______________________________

12. Certifier's name and title: ______________________________

13. Certifier's telephone number: ____________ 14. Date signed: ____________

Official use only **Logged in:**	Data entered	Amendments

SURVEY OF PORTFOLIO INVESTMENT—DECEMBER 31, 2001

FORM 2a: HOLDINGS OF END-INVESTOR OF EQUITY SECURITIES ISSUED BY UNRELATED NONRESIDENTS

[Delete own jurisdiction if it is included on this list] [Add appropriate currency and units]				
		Market value of equity securities as at December 31, 2001 [Currency - millions]		
Jurisdiction of issuer	Code	HELD IN OWN CUSTODY (1)	HELD WITH NONRESIDENT CUSTODIAN (2)	Office use only
Afghanistan, I.S. of	AF			
….	..			
….	..			
Zimbabwe	ZW			
Other (please specify)				
International Organizations	XX			
Total Value of Equity Securities Reported				

For presentation, only the first and last countries on the list are shown here. The complete list of countries is shown in Annex B of Appendix I.

SURVEY OF PORTFOLIO INVESTMENT—DECEMBER 31, 2001

FORM 2b: HOLDINGS OF END-INVESTOR LONG-TERM DEBT SECURITIES ISSUED BY UNRELATED NONRESIDENTS

[Delete own jurisdiction if it is included on this list]
[Add appropriate currency and units]

		Market value of long-term debt securities as at December 31, 2001 [Currency - millions]		
Jurisdiction of issuer	Code	HELD IN OWN CUSTODY (1)	HELD WITH NONRESIDENT CUSTODIAN (2)	Office use only
Afghanistan, I.S. of	AF			
....	..			
....	..			
Zimbabwe	ZW			
Other (please specify)				
International Organizations	XX			
Total Value of Long-Term Debt Securities Reported				

For presentation, only the first and last countries on the list are shown here. The complete list of countries is shown in Annex B of Appendix I.

SURVEY OF PORTFOLIO INVESTMENT—DECEMBER 31, 2001

FORM 2c: HOLDINGS OF END-INVESTOR OF SHORT-TERM DEBT SECURITIES ISSUED BY UNRELATED NONRESIDENTS

[Delete own jurisdiction if it is included on this list] [Add appropriate currency and units]				
		Market value of short-term debt securities as at December 31, 2001 [Currency - millions]		
Jurisdiction of issuer	Code	HELD IN OWN CUSTODY (1)	HELD WITH NONRESIDENT CUSTODIAN (2)	Office use only
Afghanistan, I.S. of	AF			
....	..			
....	..			
Zimbabwe	ZW			
Other (please specify)				
International Organizations	XX			
Total Value of Short-Term Debt Securities Reported				

For presentation, only the first and last countries on the list are shown here. The complete list of countries is shown in Annex B of Appendix I.

SURVEY OF PORTFOLIO INVESTMENT—DECEMBER 31, 2001

FORM 2d: HOLDINGS OF CUSTODIAN ON BEHALF OF RESIDENTS OF [NAME OF COUNTRY] OF SECURITIES ISSUED BY NONRESIDENTS

[Delete own jurisdiction if it is included on this list]
[Add appropriate currency and units]

		Market value of securities as at December 31, 2001 [Currency - millions]			
Jurisdiction of issuer	Code	EQUITIES (1)	LONG-TERM DEBT SECURITIES (2)	SHORT-TERM DEBT SECURITIES (3)	Office use only
Afghanistan, I.S. of	AF				
....	..				
....	..				
Zimbabwe	ZW				
Other (please specify)					
International Organizations	XX				
Total Value of Securities Reported					

For presentation, only the first and last countries on the list are shown here. The complete list of countries is shown in Annex B of Appendix I.

Appendix IV: Model Form for an End-Investor Survey on an Aggregate Basis for a Small Economy with an International Financial Center (SEIFiC)

Survey of Portfolio Investment: Holdings of Equities and Debt Securities Issued by Unrelated Nonresidents as at December 31, 2001

Purpose of Collection

This survey collects information on holdings of residents of **[name of jurisdiction]** in equities and debt securities issued by unrelated nonresidents as at December 31, 2001. The data from the survey will be used in the compilation of the balance of payments and international investment position statistics of **[name of jurisdiction]**. These statistics are published by **[name of compiling agency]**. The survey is being conducted in coordination with other countries to facilitate international data comparability.

Collection Authority

The information requested is collected under the authority of **[state legal authority]**. ***[Delete if voluntary]***

Confidentiality

The completed forms will remain confidential to the **[name of compiling agency]**.

What to Report

The survey should be completed in accordance with the reporting instructions provided. If there are any questions regarding these instructions, please contact **[name of member of the survey staff]** at **[name of compiling agency]**.

When and Where to Report

Please provide the results of this survey by **March 31, 2002** to:

[Postal and e-mail addresses, telephone, and fax numbers of compiler]

Respondents unable to meet the reporting deadline should contact **[name of member of the survey staff]** at **[name of compiling agency]** to request an extension.

How to Report

Data may be submitted on diskettes, electronic mail, or paper forms. Please keep a copy for your records.

[Name of compiling agency and date]

Notes

Note 1. Who must report

Entities that are resident in **[name of jurisdiction]** and that own equities or debt securities issued by unrelated nonresidents of **[name of jurisdiction]** as at the close of business on December 31, 2001.

Note 2. What must be reported

All entities that receive a copy of the forms must return the respondent identification section (Form 1) **within 30 days** of receipt of the forms, even those entities indicating that they are exempt from completing Form 1.

Those respondents meeting the criteria above (see Note 1) must return the completed survey forms (Form 2) by **March 31, 2002.** Respondents unable to meet the reporting schedule should contact **[name of compiling agency]** indicated on the first page of this form to request an extension.

Reporters can file a consolidated report for all related entities that are resident in **[name of jurisdiction]**, or each resident entity may file independently. If two or more entities are filing separately, please contact the member of the survey staff indicated on the first page of this form at **[name of compiling agency]** for additional identification numbers. If a consolidated report is being supplied for two or more entities, do **not** supply separate reports for the same entities.

Note 3. Residence

The reporting unit for this form is a **resident of [name of jurisdiction]**, that is, an individual, enterprise, or other organization domiciled in **[name of jurisdiction]**. It includes branches and subsidiaries of nonresident enterprises if the branches or subsidiaries are domiciled in **[name of jurisdiction]**. Domicile is defined as the center of economic interest of the entity, for instance, where an enterprise engages in production. Corporations legally registered in **[name of jurisdiction]** are considered to be resident even if they have no "physical presence." A **nonresident** of **[name of jurisdiction]** is any individual, enterprise, or other organization domiciled in a jurisdiction other than **[name of jurisdiction]**. Branches and subsidiaries of **[name of jurisdiction]** enterprises domiciled in other jurisdictions are regarded as nonresidents of **[name of jurisdiction]**.

The securities are classified by the jurisdiction of **residence of the issuer of the securities**. The residence of an enterprise can be taken to be where it is legally incorporated or, in the absence of legal incorporation, where it is legally domiciled. The jurisdiction of residence of the issuer may differ from the currency of issue, the place of issue, or the jurisdiction of the guarantor of the security. (Some securities are guaranteed by another party (such as the parent company or a government), and the guarantee may be either explicit or implicit. Even where the funds raised are for use by the guarantor, the residence of the **issuer** of the security should be used, **not** the residence of the guarantor.) Securities issued by international organizations should be shown under the separate code for international organizations (XX), not included under the jurisdiction in which the organization is located.

Note 4. Definition of equities and long- and short-term debt securities

A **security** is defined as an instrument that is traded or tradable. Examples of equities, long-term debt securities, and short-term debt securities are given below. This survey covers only securities issued by **unrelated** nonresident entities. See Note 6 to determine whether an entity is related. If you have any questions about how to classify an instrument, please contact the member of staff indicated on the first page of this form at **[name of compiling agency]**.

Equity securities cover all instruments and records acknowledging, after the claims of all creditors have been met, claims to the residual values of enterprises.

Include in equities:
- ordinary shares;
- stocks;
- participating preference shares;
- depository receipts (e.g., American depository receipts) denoting ownership of equity securities issued by nonresidents (see Note 8);
- shares/units in mutual funds and investment trusts;
- equity securities that have been sold under repurchase agreements (see Note 7); and
- equity securities that have been "lent" under a securities lending arrangement (see Note 7).

Exclude from equities:
- nonparticipating preference shares (but include these instruments under long-term debt securities);
- rights, options, warrants, and other derivative instruments;
- equity securities that have been bought under repurchase agreements (see Note 7); and
- equity securities that have been acquired under a securities lending arrangement (see Note 7).

Long-term debt securities cover bonds, debentures, and notes that usually give the holder the unconditional right to a fixed cash flow or contractually determined variable money income and have *an original term to maturity of more than one year.*

Include in long-term debt securities:
- bonds such as treasury, zero-coupon, stripped (see Note 9), deep-discounted, currency-linked (e.g., dual-currency), floating-rate, equity-related (e.g., convertible bonds), and Eurobonds;
- asset-backed securities such as mortgage backed bonds and collateralized mortgage obligations (CMOs);
- index-linked securities (e.g., property index certificates);
- nonparticipating preference shares;
- floating-rate notes (FRN) such as perpetual-rate notes (PRN), variable-rate notes (VRN), structured FRN, reverse FRN, collared FRN, step-up recovery FRN (SURF), and range/corridor/accrual notes;
- euro medium-term notes (EMTN);
- Schuldscheine (German) notes;
- bonds with optional maturity dates, the last of which is more than one year after issue;
- debentures;
- negotiable certificates of deposits with contractual maturity of more than one year;
- other long-term debt securities;
- bearer depository receipts denoting ownership of debt securities issued by nonresidents (see Note 8);
- debt securities that have been sold under repurchase agreements (see Note 7); and
- debt securities that have been "lent" under a securities lending arrangement (see Note 7).

Exclude from long-term debt securities:
- derivative instruments;
- loans;
- trade credit and accounts receivable;
- money market instruments (e.g., treasury notes, bankers' acceptances, negotiable certificates of deposit with contractual maturity of one year or less, note issuance facilities, revolving underwriting facilities, and promissory notes), including short-term debt securities;
- debt securities that have been bought under repurchase agreements (see Note 7); and
- debt securities that have been acquired under a securities lending arrangement (see Note 7).

Short-term debt securities cover only market instruments, such as bills, commercial paper, and bankers' acceptances that usually give the holder the unconditional right to receive a stated, fixed sum of money on a specified date and have an *original term to maturity of one year or less.*

Include in short-term debt securities:
- treasury bills and notes;
- bankers' acceptances;
- commercial and financial paper;
- certificates of deposit with contractual maturity of one year or less;
- short-term notes issued under note issuance facilities or revolving underwriting facilities and promissory notes (such short-term notes are included even though the underlying facility [the contingency] may be for more than one year because the notes themselves are of a short-term nature);
- debt securities that have been sold under repurchase agreements (see Note 7); and
- debt securities that have been "lent" under a securities lending arrangement (see Note 7).

Exclude from short-term debt securities:
- bonds such as treasury, zero-coupon, stripped (see Note 9), deep-discounted, currency-linked (e.g., dual-currency), floating-rate, equity-related (e.g., convertible bonds), and Eurobonds;
- asset-backed securities such as mortgage-backed bonds, and collateralized mortgage obligations (CMOs);
- index-linked securities (e.g., property index certificates);
- nonparticipating preference shares;
- floating-rate notes (FRN) such as perpetual-rate notes (PRN), variable-rate notes (VRN), structured FRN, reverse FRN, collared FRN, step up recovery FRN (SURF), and range/corridor/accrual notes;
- euro medium-term notes (EMTN);
- Schuldscheine (German) notes;
- bonds with optional maturity dates, the latest of which is more than one year after issue;
- debentures;
- negotiable certificates of deposits with contractual maturity of more than one year;
- other long-term debt securities;
- bearer depository receipts denoting ownership of debt securities issued by nonresidents (see Note 8);
- debt securities that have been bought under repurchase agreements (see Note 7);
- debt securities that have been acquired under a securities lending arrangement (see Note 7);
- derivative instruments;
- loans; and
- trade credit and accounts receivable.

Financial derivatives are **not** to be reported because they are not classified as securities but as a separate type of instrument. Record the value of the underlying security separately from any derivative that may be held in relation to it; however, if a security has an **embedded derivative,** do not attempt to separate the security from the embedded security. Include the value of such a security, including the embedded financial derivative in your submission.

If you have any questions about how to classify an instrument, please contact the survey staff member indicated on the first page of this form at **[name of compiling agency]**.

Note 5. Valuation

Market value should be used to report all holdings of securities. Do **not** report the face value of the security as the market value.

Equity securities should be reported at market prices converted to **[domestic currency]** using the exchange rate prevailing at December 31, 2001.

For enterprises listed on a stock exchange, the market value of your holding of their equity securities should be calculated using the market price on their main stock exchange prevailing at December 31, 2001.

For unlisted enterprises, if a market value is not available at December 31, 2001, estimate the market value of your holding of equity securities by using one of the following:
- a recent transaction price;
- directors' valuation; or
- net asset value (net asset value is equal to total assets, including intangibles, less nonequity liabilities and the paid-up value of nonvoting shares; assets and liabilities should be recorded at current, rather than historical, value).

Debt securities should be recorded using one of the market valuation methods listed below in descending order of preference and converted to **[domestic currency]**, using the exchange rate prevailing at December 31, 2001:
- a quoted traded market price at December 31, 2001;
- the present value of the expected stream of future payments or receipts associated with the securities;
- for unlisted securities, the price used to value securities for accounting or regulatory purposes;
- for deep-discount or zero-coupon securities, the issue price plus amortization of the discount; or
- for debt instruments issued at a premium, the issue price less the amortization of the premium.

Note 6. *Exclusion of securities issued by related enterprises*

Securities (whether equities or debt) issued by a nonresident enterprise that is related to the resident owner of those securities **should be excluded** from this report. Related nonresident enterprises are enterprises in which an enterprise **group** has an equity interest of 10 percent or more or where a nonresident has more than 10 percent or more holdings in your group. Ownership is measured in terms of ordinary shares or voting stock of incorporated enterprises or equivalent beneficial interest in unincorporated enterprises. Where such a relationship exists, exclude all securities (debt and equities).

The only exception is if the nonresident entity that issued the security and the resident owner of the security are affiliated financial intermediaries—banks, for instance. In these circumstances, securities issued by related enterprises, other than equity or permanent debt, should be included in this report.

Note 7. *Treatment of securities involved in repurchase and securities lending arrangements*

A **repurchase agreement**[1] (repo) is an arrangement involving the sale of securities at a specified price with a commitment[2] to repurchase the same or similar securities at a fixed price on a specified future date. A reverse repo is the same transaction seen from the other side; that is, an agreement whereby a security is purchased at a specified price with a commitment to resell the same or similar securities at a fixed price on a specified future date. **Securities (or stock or bond) lending** is an arrangement whereby the ownership of a security is transferred in return for collateral, usually another security, under the condition that the security or similar securities will revert to its original owner at a specified future date.
- Securities acquired under reverse repos or securities borrowing arrangements are to be *excluded* from the form.
- Securities sold under repos or "lent" under securities lending arrangements are to be *included* in the form.
- Securities acquired under reverse repo or securities borrowing arrangements and subsequently sold to a third party should be reported as a *negative* holding—namely, a short position.
- Valuations of securities under repurchase or securities lending arrangements should be at *market value* as at December 31, 2001.

Note 8. *Treatment of depository receipts*

Depository receipts, which denote ownership of equity or debt securities issued by nonresidents—for instance, American depository receipts (ADRs) or bearer depository receipts (BDRs)—should be attributed to the jurisdiction of residence of the issuer of the security underlying the depository receipt. Financial intermediaries

[1] Also included are sale/buy backs, carries, bond or stock lending with cash collateral, and similar transactions that involve the sale of a security with a commitment to repurchase it at a fixed price on a specified date or on demand.

[2] If there is no commitment to repurchase the securities, the transaction should be regarded as a straight sale of the security and should not be classified as a repo.

should not report holdings of any securities against which depository receipts have been issued and sold; however, if a depository receipt has been issued before the financial institution arranging the issue has acquired the underlying securities, that financial institution should report a negative holding in the underlying security.

Note 9. Treatment of stripped securities

Stripped securities (strips) are securities that have been transformed from a principal amount with periodic interest coupons into a series of zero-coupon securities, with the range of maturities matching the coupon payment dates and the redemption date of the principal amount.

- If strips remain the direct obligation of the original issuer, then the residence of the issuer of the strips remains the same as for the original security. Dealers who request that a settlement house or clearing house create strips from an existing security issued by a nonresident should not report ownership of the underlying security after the strips have been created.
- If strips have been created and issued by an entity in its own name, then the security should be classified according to the residence of the issuer of the strips. In turn, such an issuer of strips should report its ownership of the underlying securities if they were issued by a nonresident.

Strips with an original maturity of less than one year are classified as money market instruments and thus, if identifiable, should be reported as short-term debt securities.

Note 10. Asset-backed securities

In reporting the market value of holdings of asset-backed securities, the respondent must be aware of the possibility of early partial redemption of principal. The market value of the principal amount outstanding at December 31, 2001, should be reported; if principal has been repaid, this market value will **not** be the same as the original face value revalued at end-period market prices.

If there are any questions regarding these instructions, please contact the survey staff member at [name of compiling agency] indicated on the front of this form.

SURVEY OF PORTFOLIO INVESTMENT—DECEMBER 31, 2001

FORM 1: RESPONDENT IDENTIFICATION
To be returned within 30 days

1. Identification number: Enter the identification number from the mailing label on this survey. ☐

2. Company name: ______________________

3. Street address: ______________________

4. City: ____________ 5. State: ________ 6. Postal code: __________

7. Reporting status Holding securities issued by nonresidents ☐ Exempt ☐

Respondents with **no holdings of securities** issued by unrelated nonresidents **should check "exempt."**

8. In the event of a query, the national compiler may contact: ______________

9. Tel. no.: __________ 10. Fax no.:__________ 11. E-mail address: __________

By signing the certification line, the Certifier acknowledges that:

- He or she has read and understood the reporting requirements of this survey,
- He or she is aware of any penalties that may be imposed for filing an inaccurate report, ***[Delete if voluntary]*** and
- He or she certifies that he or she is sufficiently knowledgeable about the activities of the reporting organization that he or she can knowingly and with reasonable confidence certify that the information provided in this report is both accurate and complete.

Certifier's signature: ______________________

12. Certifier's name and title: ______________________

13. Certifier's telephone number: __________ 14. Date signed: __________

Official use only **Logged in:**	Data entered	Amendments

SURVEY OF PORTFOLIO INVESTMENT—DECEMBER 31, 2001

FORM 2: HOLDINGS OF SECURITIES ISSUED BY UNRELATED NONRESIDENTS

[Delete own jurisdiction if it is included on this list]
[Add other countries that are important in your jurisdiction]
[Add appropriate currency and units]

		Market value of securities assets as at December 31, 2001 [Currency - millions]			
Jurisdiction of issuer	Code	EQUITIES (1)	LONG-TERM DEBT SECURITIES (2)	SHORT-TERM DEBT SECURITIES (3)	Office use only
Argentina	AR				
Australia	AU				
Brazil	BR				
Canada	CA				
Cayman Islands	KY				
France	FR				
Germany	DE				
Hong Kong SAR	HK				
Italy	IT				
Japan	JP				
Korea, Republic of (South)	KR				
Netherlands	NL				
Spain	ES				
Sweden	SE				
Switzerland	CH				
United Kingdom (excluding Guernsey, Jersey, and Isle of Man)	GB				
United States	US				
Other (please specify)					
International Organizations	XX				
Total Value of Securities Reported					

Appendix V: Model Form for a Mixed Custodian/ End-Investor Survey on an Aggregate Basis for a Small Economy with an International Financial Center (SEIFiC)

Survey of Portfolio Investment: Holdings of Equities and Debt Securities Issued by Unrelated Nonresidents as at December 31, 2001

Purpose of Collection

This survey collects information on holdings of residents of **[name of jurisdiction]** in equities and debt securities issued by unrelated nonresidents as at December 31, 2001. The data from the survey will be used in the compilation of the balance of payments and international investment position statistics of **[name of jurisdiction]**. These statistics are published by **[name of compiling agency]**. The survey is being conducted in coordination with other countries to facilitate international data comparability.

Collection Authority

The information requested is collected under the authority of **[state legal authority]**. ***[Delete if voluntary]***

Confidentiality

The completed forms will remain confidential to the **[name of compiling agency]**.

What to Report

The survey should be completed in accordance with the reporting instructions provided. If there are any questions regarding these instructions, please contact **[name of member of the survey staff]** at **[name of compiling agency]**.

When and Where to Report

Please provide the results of this survey by **March 31, 2002** to:

[Postal and e-mail addresses, telephone, and fax numbers of compiler]

Respondents unable to meet the reporting deadline should contact **[name of member of the survey staff]** at **[name of compiling agency]** to request an extension.

How to Report

Data may be submitted on diskettes, electronic mail, or paper forms. Please keep a copy for your records.

[Name of compiling agency and date]

Notes

Note 1. Who must report

(a) **Custodians**, resident in **[name of jurisdiction]**, who, as at December 31, 2001, manage the safekeeping of securities issued by nonresidents on behalf of residents of **[name of jurisdiction]**, or **on their own account**. Resident custodians are defined as entities located in **[name of jurisdiction]** who manage the safekeeping of securities for investors; and

(b) **Investors** that are resident in **[name of jurisdiction]**and that own equities or debt securities issued by unrelated nonresidents of **[name of jurisdiction]** as at December 31, 2001 and that do not entrust the safekeeping of any or all of these securities to **resident** custodians. This includes both those who invest for their own account as well as those who invest on behalf of asset pools, such as the managers of mutual funds, insurance companies, and pension funds.

All entities that receive a copy of the survey forms must reply. Those that do not fall into either of the above two categories need only complete the identification information on Form 1 and mark the box indicating that they are exempt from completing Forms 2a, 2b, 2c (for end-investors), and Form 2d (for custodians).

Note 2. What must be reported

All entities that receive a copy of the survey forms must complete the **respondent identification section** of Form 1 and return a copy to the **[name of compiling agency] within 30 days** of receipt of the survey forms.

All entities that receive a copy of the survey forms must submit their survey responses by **March 31, 2001,** to **[name of compiling agency]**, whose address is listed in the key information section of Form 1. Respondents unable to meet the reporting schedule should contact **[name of member of the survey staff shown on the front of this form]** at **[name of compiling agency]** to request an extension.

End-Investors

Resident end-investors of **[name of jurisdiction]** should complete Form 1 and Form 2a (for equity holdings), Form 2b (for long-term debt securities holdings), and Form 2c (for short-term debt securities holdings) in respect of securities issued by unrelated nonresidents:

(a) held on their own account (i.e., not entrusted to a custodian) (column 1), and

(b) entrusted to a nonresident custodian (column 2),

as at December 31, 2001.

Securities entrusted to resident custodians should be excluded from this form as they will be reported by the custodians.

Custodians' own account holdings should be included in Forms 2a, 2b, and 2c, as appropriate.

Reporters can file a consolidated report for all related entities that are resident in **[name of jurisdiction]**, or each resident entity may file independently. If two or more entities are filing separately, please contact the member of the survey staff indicated on the first page of this form at **[name of compiling agency]** for additional identification numbers. Do **not** file both a consolidated report for the entire resident organization **and** for the separate units.

Custodians

In addition to Form 1, **all** custodians of **[name of country]** should complete Form 2d in respect of securities issued by nonresidents and which were held as at December 31, 2001 on behalf of residents of **[name of country]**. Report the holdings of equities in column 1, long-term debt securities in column 2, and short-term debt securities in column 3.

Do not include own account holdings in Form 2d; these should be reported on Forms 2a, 2b, and 2c, as appropriate.

Securities issued by entities that are related to the investor should **not** be reported (see Note 6 on exclusion of securities issued by related enterprises).

Where securities have been entrusted by a resident of **[name of jurisdiction]** to a custodian who is resident of **[name of jurisdiction]**, and that custodian has passed the securities to another custodian, the **first** custodian should report the holding. The second (or subsequent) custodian in that chain of custody should **not** report holdings of securities issued by nonresidents held on behalf of another custodian.

All entities who receive any of the above forms must return the respondent identification section (Form 1) **within 30 days** of receipt of the forms, even those entities indicating that they are exempt from completing Form 1.

Those respondents meeting the criteria above (see Note 1) must return the completed survey forms (for end-investors: Forms 2a, 2b, and 2c; for custodians: Form 2d) by **March 31, 2002.**

Respondents unable to meet the reporting schedule should contact **[name of compiling agency]** indicated on the first page of this form to request an extension.

Note 3. Residence

The reporting unit for this form is a **resident of [name of jurisdiction]**, that is, an individual, enterprise, or other organization domiciled in **[name of jurisdiction]**. It includes branches and subsidiaries of nonresident enterprises if the branches or subsidiaries are domiciled in **[name of jurisdiction]**. Domicile is defined as the center of economic interest of the entity, for instance, where an enterprise engages in production. Corporations legally registered in **[name of jurisdiction]** are considered to be resident even if they have no "physical presence." A **nonresident** of **[name of jurisdiction]** is any individual, enterprise, or other organization domiciled in a jurisdiction other than **[name of jurisdiction]**. Branches and subsidiaries of **[name of jurisdiction]** enterprises domiciled in other jurisdictions are regarded as nonresidents of **[name of jurisdiction]**.

The securities are classified by the jurisdiction of **residence of the issuer of the securities**. The residence of an enterprise can be taken to be where it is legally incorporated or, in the absence of legal incorporation, where it is legally domiciled. The jurisdiction of residence of the issuer may differ from the currency of issue, the place of issue, or the jurisdiction of the guarantor of the security. (Some securities are guaranteed by another party (such as the parent company or a government), and the guarantee may be either explicit or implicit. Even where the funds raised are for use by the guarantor, the residence of the **issuer** of the security should be used, **not** the residence of the guarantor.) Securities issued by international organizations should be shown under the separate code for international organizations (XX), not included under the jurisdiction in which the organization is located.

[If one or more international organization is/are located in your country: **[Specify the name(s) of these international organizations]** should **not** be considered to be resident(s) in **[name of country]** and their holdings should not be reported in this return. However, **pension funds** for employees of these international organization(s) are considered to resident in **[name of country]**. ***[If not relevant, delete this paragraph.]***

Note 4. Definition of equities and long- and short-term debt securities

A **security** is defined as an instrument that is traded or tradable. Examples of equities, long-term debt securities, and short-term debt securities are given below. This survey covers only securities issued by **unrelated** nonresident entities. See Note 6 to determine whether an entity is related. If you have any questions about how to classify an instrument, please contact the member of staff indicated on the first page of this form at **[name of compiling agency]**.

Equity securities cover all instruments and records acknowledging, after the claims of all creditors have been met, claims to the residual values of enterprises.

Include in equities:
- ordinary shares;
- stocks;
- participating preference shares;
- depository receipts (e.g., American depository receipts) denoting ownership of equity securities issued by nonresidents (see Note 8);
- shares/units in mutual funds and investment trusts;
- equity securities that have been sold under repurchase agreements (see Note 7); and
- equity securities that have been "lent" under a securities lending arrangement (see Note 7).

Exclude from equities:
- nonparticipating preference shares (but include these instruments under long-term debt securities);
- rights, options, warrants, and other derivative instruments;
- equity securities that have been bought under repurchase agreements (see Note 7); and
- equity securities that have been acquired under a securities lending arrangement (see Note 7).

Long-term debt securities cover bonds, debentures, and notes that usually give the holder the unconditional right to a fixed cash flow or contractually determined variable money income and have *an original term to maturity of more than one year.*

Include in long-term debt securities:
- bonds such as treasury, zero-coupon, stripped (see Note 9), deep-discounted, currency-linked (e.g., dual-currency), floating-rate, equity-related (e.g., convertible bonds), and Eurobonds;
- asset-backed securities such as mortgage backed bonds and collateralized mortgage obligations (CMOs);
- index-linked securities (e.g., property index certificates);
- nonparticipating preference shares;
- floating-rate notes (FRN) such as perpetual-rate notes (PRN), variable-rate notes (VRN), structured FRN, reverse FRN, collared FRN, step-up recovery FRN (SURF), and range/corridor/accrual notes;
- euro medium-term notes (EMTN);
- Schuldscheine (German) notes;
- bonds with optional maturity dates, the last of which is more than one year after issue;
- debentures;
- negotiable certificates of deposits with contractual maturity of more than one year;
- other long-term debt securities;
- bearer depository receipts denoting ownership of debt securities issued by nonresidents (see Note 8);
- debt securities that have been sold under repurchase agreements (see Note 7); and
- debt securities that have been "lent" under a securities lending arrangement (see Note 7).

Exclude from long-term debt securities:
- derivative instruments;
- loans;
- trade credit and accounts receivable;

- money market instruments (e.g., treasury notes, bankers' acceptances, negotiable certificates of deposit with contractual maturity of one year or less, note issuance facilities, revolving underwriting facilities, and promissory notes), including short-term debt securities;
- debt securities that have been bought under repurchase agreements (see Note 7); and
- debt securities that have been acquired under a securities lending arrangement (see Note 7).

Short-term debt securities cover only market instruments, such as bills, commercial paper, and bankers' acceptances that usually give the holder the unconditional right to receive a stated, fixed sum of money on a specified date and have an *original term to maturity of one year or less.*

Include in short-term debt securities:
- treasury bills and notes;
- bankers' acceptances;
- commercial and financial paper;
- certificates of deposit with contractual maturity of one year or less;
- short-term notes issued under note issuance facilities or revolving underwriting facilities and promissory notes (such short-term notes are included even though the underlying facility [the contingency] may be for more than one year because the notes themselves are of a short-term nature);
- debt securities that have been sold under repurchase agreements (see Note 7); and
- debt securities that have been "lent" under a securities lending arrangement (see Note 7).

Exclude from short-term debt securities:
- bonds such as treasury, zero-coupon, stripped (see Note 9), deep-discounted, currency-linked (e.g., dual-currency), floating-rate, equity-related (e.g., convertible bonds), and Eurobonds;
- asset-backed securities such as mortgage-backed bonds, and collateralized mortgage obligations (CMOs);
- index-linked securities (e.g., property index certificates);
- nonparticipating preference shares;
- floating-rate notes (FRN) such as perpetual-rate notes (PRN), variable-rate notes (VRN), structured FRN, reverse FRN, collared FRN, step up recovery FRN (SURF), and range/corridor/accrual notes;
- euro medium-term notes (EMTN);
- Schuldscheine (German) notes;
- bonds with optional maturity dates, the latest of which is more than one year after issue;
- debentures;
- negotiable certificates of deposits with contractual maturity of more than one year;
- other long-term debt securities;
- bearer depository receipts denoting ownership of debt securities issued by nonresidents (see Note 8);
- debt securities that have been bought under repurchase agreements (see Note 7);
- debt securities that have been acquired under a securities lending arrangement (see Note 7);
- derivative instruments;
- loans; and
- trade credit and accounts receivable.

Financial derivatives are **not** to be reported because they are not classified as securities, but as a separate type of instrument. Record the value of the underlying security separately from any derivative that may be held in relation to it; however, if a security has an **embedded derivative,** do not attempt to separate the security from the embedded security. Include the value of such a security, including the embedded financial derivative, in your submission.

If you have any questions about how to classify an instrument, please contact the survey staff member indicated on the first page of this form at **[name of compiling agency]**.

Note 5. Valuation

Market value should be used to report all holdings of securities. Do **not** report the face value of the security as the market value.

Equity securities should be reported at market prices converted to **[domestic currency]** using the exchange rate prevailing at December 31, 2001.

For enterprises listed on a stock exchange, the market value of your holding of their equity securities should be calculated using the market price on their main stock exchange prevailing at December 31, 2001.

For unlisted enterprises, if a market value is not available at December 31, 2001, estimate the market value of your holding of equity securities by using one of the following:
- a recent transaction price;
- directors' valuation; or
- net asset value (net asset value is equal to total assets, including intangibles, less nonequity liabilities and the paid-up value of nonvoting shares; assets and liabilities should be recorded at current, rather than historical, value).

Debt securities should be recorded using one of the market valuation methods listed below in descending order of preference and converted to **[domestic currency]**, using the exchange rate prevailing at December 31, 2001:
- a quoted traded market price at December 31, 2001;
- the present value of the expected stream of future payments or receipts associated with the securities;
- for unlisted securities, the price used to value securities for accounting or regulatory purposes;
- for deep-discount or zero-coupon securities, the issue price plus amortization of the discount; or
- for debt instruments issued at a premium, the issue price less the amortization of the premium.

Note 6. Exclusion of securities issued by related enterprises

Securities (whether equities or debt) issued by a nonresident enterprise that is related to the resident owner of those securities **should be excluded** from this report. Related nonresident enterprises are enterprises in which an enterprise **group** has an equity interest of 10 percent or more or where a nonresident has more than 10 percent or more holdings in your group. Ownership is measured in terms of ordinary shares or voting stock of incorporated enterprises or equivalent beneficial interest in unincorporated enterprises. Where such a relationship exists, exclude all securities (debt and equities).

The only exception is if the nonresident entity that issued the security and the resident owner of the security are affiliated financial intermediaries—banks, for instance. In these circumstances, securities issued by related enterprises, other than equity or permanent debt, should be included in this report.

Note 7. Treatment of securities involved in repurchase and securities lending arrangements

A **repurchase agreement**[1] (repo) is an arrangement involving the sale of securities at a specified price with a commitment[2] to repurchase the same or similar securities at a fixed price on a specified future date. A reverse repo is the same transaction seen from the other side; that is, an agreement whereby a security is purchased at a specified price with a commitment to resell the same or similar securities at a fixed price on a specified future date. **Securities (or stock or bond) lending** is an arrangement whereby the ownership of a security is transferred in return for collateral, usually another security, under the condition that the security or similar securities will revert to its original owner at a specified future date.

[1]Also included are sale/buy backs, carries, bond or stock lending with cash collateral, and similar transactions that involve the sale of a security with a commitment to repurchase it at a fixed price on a specified date or on demand.

[2]If there is no commitment to repurchase the securities, the transaction should be regarded as a straight sale of the security and should not be classified as a repo.

- Securities acquired under reverse repos or securities borrowing arrangements are to be *excluded* from the form.
- Securities sold under repos or "lent" under securities lending arrangements are to be *included* in the form.
- Securities acquired under reverse repo or securities borrowing arrangements and subsequently sold to a third party should be reported as a *negative* holding—namely, a short position (see Form 2, item 10).
- Valuations of securities under repurchase or securities lending arrangements should be at *market value* as at December 31, 2001.

Note 8. Treatment of depository receipts

Depository receipts, which denote ownership of equity or debt securities issued by nonresidents—for instance, American depository receipts (ADRs) or bearer depository receipts (BDRs)—should be attributed to the jurisdiction of residence of the issuer of the security underlying the depository receipt. Financial intermediaries should not report holdings of any securities against which depository receipts have been issued and sold; however, if a depository receipt has been issued before the financial institution arranging the issue has acquired the underlying securities, that financial institution should report a negative holding in the underlying security.

Note 9. Treatment of stripped securities

Stripped securities (strips) are securities that have been transformed from a principal amount with periodic interest coupons into a series of zero-coupon securities, with the range of maturities matching the coupon payment dates and the redemption date of the principal amount.

- If strips remain the direct obligation of the original issuer, then the residence of the issuer of the strips remains the same as for the original security. Dealers who request that a settlement house or clearing house create strips from an existing security issued by a nonresident should not report ownership of the underlying security after the strips have been created.
- If strips have been created and issued by an entity in its own name, then the security should be classified according to the residence of the issuer of the strips. In turn, such an issuer of strips should report its ownership of the underlying securities if they were issued by a nonresident.

Strips with an original maturity of less than one year are classified as money market instruments and thus, if identifiable, should be reported as short-term debt securities.

Note 10. Asset-backed securities

In reporting the market value of holdings of asset-backed securities, the respondent must be aware of the possibility of early partial redemption of principal. The market value of the principal amount outstanding at December 31, 2001, should be reported; if principal has been repaid, this market value will **not** be the same as the original face value revalued at end-period market prices.

If there are any questions regarding these instructions, please contact the survey staff member at [name of compiling agency] indicated on the front of this form.

SURVEY OF PORTFOLIO INVESTMENT—DECEMBER 31, 2001

FORM 1: RESPONDENT IDENTIFICATION
To be returned within 30 days

1. Identification number: Enter the identification number from the mailing label on this survey. [ ]

2. Company name: ____________________

3. Street address: ____________________

4. City: ____________ 5. State: ____________ 6. Postal code: ____________

7. Reporting status Holding securities issued by nonresidents ☐ Exempt ☐

Respondents with **no holdings of securities** issued by unrelated nonresidents **should check "exempt."**

8. In the event of a query, the national compiler may contact: ____________________

9. Tel. no.: ____________ 10. Fax no.:____________ 11. E-mail address: ____________

By signing the certification line, the Certifier acknowledges that:

- He or she has read and understood the reporting requirements of this survey,
- He or she is aware of any penalties that may be imposed for filing an inaccurate report, ***[Delete if voluntary]*** and
- He or she certifies that he or she is sufficiently knowledgeable about the activities of the reporting organization that he or she can knowingly and with reasonable confidence certify that the information provided in this report is both accurate and complete.

Certifier's signature: ____________________

12. Certifier's name and title: ____________________

13. Certifier's telephone number: ____________ 14. Date signed: ____________

Official use only **Logged in:**	Data entered	Amendments

SURVEY OF PORTFOLIO INVESTMENT—DECEMBER 31, 2001

FORM 2a: HOLDINGS OF END-INVESTOR OF EQUITY SECURITIES ISSUED BY UNRELATED NONRESIDENTS

[Delete own jurisdiction if it is included on this list] [Add appropriate currency and units]				
		Market value of equity securities as at December 31, 2001 [Currency - millions]		
Jurisdiction of issuer	Code	HELD IN OWN CUSTODY (1)	HELD WITH NONRESIDENT CUSTODIAN (2)	Office use only
Argentina	AR			
Australia	AU			
Brazil	BR			
Canada	CA			
Cayman Islands	KY			
France	FR			
Germany	DE			
Hong Kong SAR	HK			
Italy	IT			
Japan	JP			
Korea, Republic of (South)	KR			
Netherlands	NL			
Spain	ES			
Sweden	SE			
Switzerland	CH			
United Kingdom (excluding Guernsey, Jersey, and Isle of Man)	GB			
United States	US			
Other (please specify)				
International Organizations	XX			
Total Value of Equity Securities Reported				

SURVEY OF PORTFOLIO INVESTMENT—DECEMBER 31, 2001

FORM 2b: HOLDINGS OF END-INVESTOR LONG-TERM DEBT SECURITIES ISSUED BY UNRELATED NONRESIDENTS

[Delete own jurisdiction if it is included on this list] [Add appropriate currency and units]				
		Market value of long-term debt securities as at December 31, 2001 [Currency - millions]		
Jurisdiction of issuer	Code	HELD IN OWN CUSTODY (1)	HELD WITH NONRESIDENT CUSTODIAN (2)	Office use only
Argentina	AR			
Australia	AU			
Brazil	BR			
Canada	CA			
Cayman Islands	KY			
France	FR			
Germany	DE			
Hong Kong SAR	HK			
Italy	IT			
Japan	JP			
Korea, Republic of (South)	KR			
Netherlands	NL			
Spain	ES			
Sweden	SE			
Switzerland	CH			
United Kingdom (excluding Guernsey, Jersey, and Isle of Man)	GB			
United States	US			
Other (please specify)				
International Organizations	XX			
Total Value of Long-Term Debt Securities Reported				

SURVEY OF PORTFOLIO INVESTMENT—DECEMBER 31, 2001

FORM 2c: HOLDINGS OF END-INVESTOR OF SHORT-TERM DEBT SECURITIES ISSUED BY UNRELATED NONRESIDENTS

[Delete own jurisdiction if it is included on this list] [Add appropriate currency and units]				
		Market value of short-term debt securities as at December 31, 2001 [Currency - millions]		
Jurisdiction of issuer	Code	HELD IN OWN CUSTODY (1)	HELD WITH NONRESIDENT CUSTODIAN (2)	Office use only
Argentina	AR			
Australia	AU			
Brazil	BR			
Canada	CA			
Cayman Islands	KY			
France	FR			
Germany	DE			
Hong Kong SAR	HK			
Italy	IT			
Japan	JP			
Korea, Republic of (South)	KR			
Netherlands	NL			
Spain	ES			
Sweden	SE			
Switzerland	CH			
United Kingdom (excluding Guernsey, Jersey, and Isle of Man)	GB			
United States	US			
Other (please specify)				
International Organizations	XX			
Total Value of Short-Term Debt Securities Reported				

SURVEY OF PORTFOLIO INVESTMENT—DECEMBER 31, 2001

FORM 2d: HOLDINGS OF CUSTODIAN ON BEHALF OF RESIDENTS OF [NAME OF JURISDICTION] OF SECURITIES ISSUED BY NONRESIDENTS

[Delete own jurisdiction if it is included on this list] [Add appropriate currency and units]					
		Market value of securities as at December 31, 2001 [Currency - millions]			
Jurisdiction of issuer	Code	EQUITIES (1)	LONG-TERM DEBT SECURITIES (2)	SHORT-TERM DEBT SECURITIES (3)	Office use only
Argentina	AR				
Australia	AU				
Brazil	BR				
Canada	CA				
Cayman Islands	KY				
France	FR				
Germany	DE				
Hong Kong SAR	HK				
Italy	IT				
Japan	JP				
Korea, Republic of (South)	KR				
Netherlands	NL				
Spain	ES				
Sweden	SE				
Switzerland	CH				
United Kingdom (excluding Guernsey, Jersey, and Isle of Man)	GB				
United States	US				
Other (please specify)					
International Organizations	XX				
Total Value of Securities Reported					

Appendix VI: Definition and Description of Instruments

Equity Instruments

Ordinary Share

Ownership share with full voting rights, commonly known as "equities." Ordinary shares are usually issued in registered form.

Preference Share

Part of the share capital of a company that ranks after secured creditors but before ordinary shareholders in the event of liquidation. Preference rights are defined in the articles of association of the relevant company but may relate to dividend, voting rights, or distribution of surplus assets. (Issued in registered form.)

Participating Preference Share

These preference shares have further rights that are normally linked to the relevant company's profits or dividend payment on ordinary shares. (Issued in registered form.)

Other Preference Shares

These will have the rights of standard preference shares but may also be:

- cumulative (i.e., income arrears are carried forward to the next payment date),
- convertible (into ordinary shares),
- redeemable (at a fixed date or contingent on a special event), or
- permanent (not redeemable except at issuer's option). (Issued in registered form.)

Preferred Stock

Stock that pays a stipulated dividend to the holder. Preferred stock has a claim prior to that of common stock upon the earnings of a corporation and upon the assets of the corporation in the event of its liquidation. Frequently without voting rights. (Registered; may be held in book-entry form.)

Callable Preferred Stock

Callable preferred stock can be repurchased by its issuer at a specified price. (Registered; may be held in book-entry form.)

Convertible Preferred Stock

Convertible into a fixed amount of common stock at the option of the owner. (Registered; may be held in book-entry form.)

Protected Preferred Stock

Protected stock has its dividend guaranteed in the event that the corporation does not earn a profit in a certain year. A special fund established from previous corporate earnings pays the dividend when it is due. (Registered; may be held in book-entry form.)

Cumulative Preferred Stock

Cumulative preferred stock is entitled to receive at a later date those dividends that accumulate during profitless years (dividends in arrears). During such years, common stock and regular preferred stock are generally paid no dividends. (Registered; may be held in book-entry form.)

Participating Preferred Stock

Participating preferred stock allows its holders to receive dividends in addition to the fixed amount in years in which the common stock dividend exceeds a specified level. (Registered; may be held in book-entry form.)

Prior Preferred Stock

A class of preferred stock that has senior rights over other classes of preferred stock. (Registered; may be held in book-entry form.)

Investment Trust Share

A share of a company bound by a trust deed, formed to invest in specific types of securities. Shares in an investment trust can usually be bought and sold only through the stock exchange. Sometimes referred to as a "closed-end" fund. (Issued in registered form.)

Unit Trust and OEIC (Open-Ended Investment Company)

A unit of an open-end fund or an open-ended investment company (OEIC) governed by a trust deed or memorandum with specific investment objectives. The funds are pooled under management, and the price of units is based on net asset value. Purchases and sales are largely directed through the managers. (Issued in registered form; the units may be certificate or dematerialized.)

Share Action d'une Société d'Investissement à Capital Variable (SICAV)

Share representing one part of ownership in an open-ended investment company (OEIC) with a variable capital (SICAV). Certain companies issue capitalization and distribution shares. (Issued in bearer or registered form; may also be held in book-entry form.)

Share Action d'une Société d'Investissement à Capital Fixe (SICAF)

Share representing one part of ownership in a fixed capital investment company. (Issued in bearer or registered form; may also be held in book-entry form.)

Unit Trust Part d'un Fonds Commun de Placement

Participation unit in a mutual fund ("unit trust"). A unit trust can issue capitalization and distribution units. (Issued in registered or bearer form; may be held in book-entry form.)

Debt Instruments

Due to the increasing internationalization of debt instruments, they are defined by market, interest, maturity, currency, borrower, amount issued, collateral, convertibility, and subordination.

Defined by the Market

The matrix below helps to classify a debt instrument by market, taking into account the other main elements of the instrument. Many (domestic) sovereign bonds are now traded intensively on international markets. Nevertheless, they still remain domestic instruments: Their form, tax, and custody aspects are fixed under specific rules, which all are different, depending on the market.

Market	Currency	Issuer	Main market
Domestic	Domestic	Domestic	Domestic
Foreign	Domestic	Foreign	Domestic
International	Domestic and basket	Any	International and domestic
Euro	Eurocurrency	Any	International
Global	Eurocurrency	Any	International and domestic

International Bond

Bond issued by a borrower in a foreign country. International bonds include foreign bonds, parallel bonds, and Eurobonds.

Global Bond

International issue placed at the same time in the Euro and one or more domestic markets with securities fungible between the markets.

Eurobond

Bond issued by a borrower in a foreign country, denominated in a Eurocurrency (e.g., U.S. dollar, Canadian dollar, yen, euro, French franc, etc.), underwritten and sold by an international syndicate of financial institutions.

Foreign Bond

Securities—for example, Yankee, Samurai, Shogun, Shibosai, Bulldog, Matador, and Daimyo bonds—issued by a borrower in a domestic capital market other than its own, usually denominated in the currency of that market, underwritten and sold by a national underwriting and selling group of the lenders' country. (Usually issued in bearer or registered form.)

Defined by Interest

Fixed-Rate Bond

A fixed-rate, interest-bearing debt security.

Bull and Bear Bond

Fixed-interest bond whose value at maturity is dependent on the performance of a stock market index. The issue is divided into two parts: a bull bond and a bear bond. The bull bond's redemption value rises if the market index increases and declines if the index decreases. Conversely, the bear bond has a higher redemption value if the stock market weakens and a lower value if stock prices rise.

Step-Up or Step-Down Bond (or Note)

Rate will go up or down as indicated in the terms and conditions of the notes.

Zero-Coupon Bond

Bond without a coupon providing interest payments. Zero-coupon bonds have an issue price well below 100 percent, with repayment on maturity at face value or par. The investor's return is the difference between the issue price and redemption value. Variants of zero-coupon bonds include the following:

Capital Growth Bond

Issue price of par (100 percent) with redemption at a multiple of that amount.

Deep-Discount Bond

A bond with issue price significantly below maturity price because of a lack of coupon or a coupon below market rate.

Liquid Yield Option Note (LYON)

A LYON combines the features of a zero-coupon bond with those of a convertible bond. The zero-coupon bond pays no interest until it is redeemed at or before maturity; the difference between the issue price and the redemption price represents the accrued interest. In addition, the LYON bond may be converted by the holder into stock of the issuing corporation within a specified period and at a specified conversion price.

Floating-Rate Notes (FRNs)

FRNs are medium- to long-term debt obligations with variable interest rates that are adjusted periodically (typically every one, three, or six months). The interest rate is usually fixed at a specified spread over one of the following specified deposit rates:
- London interbank offered rate (LIBOR),
- London interbank bid rate (LIBID), or
- London interbank mean rate (LIMEAN) (average of LIBOR and LIBID)

FRNs may also use short-term obligations of the U.S. government (Treasury bills) to establish their interest rate. Interest is payable at the end of each interest period.

Variants of FRN are:

Drop-Lock Bond

The drop-lock bond (DL bond) combines the features of both floating- and fixed-rate securities. The DL bond is issued with a floating-rate interest that is reset semiannually at a specified margin above a base rate, such as six months LIBOR. This continues until the base rate is at or below a specified trigger rate on an interest fixing date or, in some cases, on two consecutive interest fixing dates. At that time the interest rate becomes fixed at a specified rate for the remaining lifetime of the bond.

Mismatch FRN

FRN with a coupon structure that is refixed more often and for different maturities than the interest periods (e.g., the interest rate is based on six months' LIBOR but adjusted every month).

Mini-Max (or Collared) FRN

FRN with a minimum and a maximum interest rate.

Capped FRN

FRN with a maximum interest rate.

Flip-Flop FRN

FRN that combines an FRN with a very long final maturity, or even a perpetual issue, and an investor option to convert after a specified period into a short-dated FRN that typically pays a lower margin over LIBOR than the original issue. The investor further has the option at a later date to convert back into the initial issue before redemption of the short-dated note.

Convertible Rate FRN

Issue that carries the option to convert either from an initial floating-rate note into a fixed-rate bond or from a fixed-rate bond into a floating-rate note. This provides ways in which investors and borrowers can speculate or hedge against the future course of interest rates.

Variable-Rate Note

FRN where the margin over the reference rate is fixed by the issuer and the remarketing agent several days before the following interest period. The holders, during a predetermined period of time, have the right to either bid for the new applicable margin over the reference rate or (under certain conditions) put the notes to the arranger (but not the issuer) on the following interest payment date.

Defined by Maturity

Bond with Call Option

The issuer has the right to redeem the bond at a specified earlier date than the one originally fixed as the final maturity.

Bond with Put Option

The investor has the right to require redemption of the principal at a specified date earlier than the one originally fixed as the final maturity.

Retractable Bond

Issue carrying the option (for both the issuer and the investor) for early redemption at one or several fixed dates.

Extendable Bond

The investor has the option at one or several fixed dates to extend the maturity.

Perpetual Bond

Bonds that are due for redemption only in the case of the borrower's liquidation. Usually the terms and conditions provide a call option at a premium. The interest rate can be fixed for the whole maturity or only for an initial period (e.g., 10 years). For each subsequent period the interest is reset as provided in the terms and conditions. (Issued in bearer form; entire bond should be reprinted after coupon sheet is used up.)

Bullet Bond

An issue with no call and no prepayments until maturity.

Sinking Fund

Payments made by the borrower on a regular basis to a special account to set aside the necessary funds for the redemption of its long-term debt. In the Euromarket, borrowers can meet their requirements through purchases in the open market or through drawings by lot.

Defined by Currency

Dual-Currency Bond

A dual-currency bond is a hybrid debt instrument with payment obligations over the life of the issue in two different currencies. The borrower makes coupon payments in one currency, but redeems the principal at maturity in another currency in an amount fixed at the time of the issue of the bonds. The price of the bonds in the secondary market is indicated as a percentage of the redemption amount.

The following are variants of dual-currency bonds:

Foreign Interest Payment Security (FIPS)

FIPS is an instrument in the Swiss capital market. Its features are similar to a reverse dual-currency bond that offers interest payments in a foreign currency but keeps the principal in Swiss francs.

Adjustable Long-Term Putable Security (ALPS)

The currency conditions are similar to a FIPS; however, the bonds have a floating interest rate and a put option.

Yen-Linked Bond

Bond expressed in U.S. dollars or Swiss francs, whose face value is also indicated in yen (parity fixed at issuance). Issuance and redemption are in yen, which are converted into the original currency at the parity of the payment date.

Multiple Currency Clause Bond

Issue with an investor's option to choose the currency for redemption and sometimes also for interest payments.

Special Drawing Right (SDR) Bond

The SDR bond is issued in the currency of the IMF. The SDR is a composite currency unit based on a standard basket system of valuation. SDR bonds are traded only in U.S. dollars.

Shogun or Geisha Bond

Non-yen-denominated issue in the Japanese domestic market by a non-Japanese borrower. (Issued in bearer or registered form; may be held as global certificate.)

Defined by Borrower

Brady Bonds

Eurobonds issued by the government of a developing country refinancing its debt to foreign commercial banks under a Brady-type agreement. The agreement is characterized by introduction of an IMF plan and the opportunity for the creditor to exchange its debt against a set of instruments aimed at satisfying both counterparts of the deal. The main features of Brady bonds are collateralization, debt reduction, debt-equity conversion, underwriting against new money, and options on oil revenues.

Guaranteed Bond

Guaranteed bonds have their interest, principal, or both guaranteed by another corporation. It is common for a parent company to guarantee bonds issued by subsidiaries. (Bearer or registered; may be held in book-entry form.)

Defined by Amount Issued

Deferred or Partial-Payment Issues

Instruments that consist of debt obligations where the investor pays only a portion of the issue price on the initial payment date and the balance several months later. The structure allows the borrower to achieve a lower all-in cost compared with straight issues by offering the investor a potential gain from a decline in rates and/or protection against depreciation of the currency between the time of the initial payment and that of the final payment. The appeal of these securities is a function of the interest rate and currency outlook at any given time.

Defined by Collateral

Mortgage-Backed Security (MBS)

A generic term that refers to securities backed by mortgages, including pass-through securities, mortgage-backed bonds, mortgage pay-through securities, and collateralized mortgage obligations (see below).

Pass-Through Mortgage-Backed Security

A security representing an ownership interest in an underlying pool of mortgages. The cash flow from the underlying mortgages is "passed through" to the security holder as monthly payments of principal, interest, and prepayments. Pass-through securities have been guaranteed and issued by the Government National Mortgage Association (GNMA), the Federal National Mortgage Association (FNMA or "Fannie Mae"), and the Federal Home Loan Mortgage Corporation (FHLMC or "Freddie Mac"), as well as private institutions. (Registered; usually in book-entry form.)

Private Pay-Through Security

These securities are secured by mortgage collateral and are issued by private financial entities (sometimes called "private conduits") with no guarantees by any government or government-sponsored agency. Some securities are issued by public offering (registered with the Securities and Exchange Commission, SEC), and others are marketed through private placement. (Registered.)

Collateralized Mortgage Obligation (CMO)

CMOs are debt obligations of an entity established by a financial institution or other sponsor. They are collateralized by whole mortgage loans or by mortgage-backed pass-through securities guaranteed by the Government National Mortgage

Association (GNMA), the Federal National Mortgage Association (FNMA), or the Federal Home Loan Mortgage Corporation (FHLMC). CMOs are sold in multimaturity classes called tranches. (Registered; usually in book-entry form.)

Asset-Backed Security

A security collateralized by loans, leases, unsecured receivables, or installment contracts on personal property, automobiles, or credit cards. The cash flows generated by the underlying obligations are used to pay principal and interest to the asset-backed security holders. (Registered; usually in book-entry form.)

Defined by Convertibility/Exchangeability

Convertible Issue

A bond or note that can be converted for newly issued shares or bonds at predetermined prices during specified periods of time.

Exchangeable Issue

A bond or note that can be exchanged for existing shares or bonds of a third party at predetermined prices during specified periods of time.

Straight Bond

Bond without clauses granting conversion or warrant privileges.

Reverse Convertible Bond Obligation

Convertible bond that may be redeemed at the issuer's discretion against existing shares of an underlying company that has no economic relation with the issuer or the guarantor of the bonds.

Defined by Subordination

Subordinated debt (sometimes called mezzanine finance) has many of the characteristics of both debt and equity. A subordinated creditor agrees to rank after senior creditors but before ordinary shareholders in a liquidation. For regulatory purposes certain forms of subordinated debt issued by financial institutions may be treated, like equity, as "primary capital."

Money Market Instruments

Euronote

A short-term, negotiable bearer promissory note usually issued at a discount with maturities of less than one year. (Issued in bearer form; may be held as a global certificate.)

Certificate of Deposit (CD)

A negotiable instrument issued by a bank, evidencing a deposit for a stated rate of interest (floating rate or fixed rate). Because the bulk of CDs in the international securities market are issued by a bank in London or a London branch of a foreign bank, these issues are termed "London CDs." However, CDs are also issued on the international securities market by banks from their country of origin. (Issued in bearer form; may be held as a global certificate.)

Revolving Underwriting Facility (RUF)

A medium- to long-term finance instrument that allows the borrower, by issuing short-term paper, to benefit from cheaper short-term funds. An RUF consists of the following:

- Euronotes;
- The borrower issues short-term paper for periods of less than one year through different mechanisms (CDs, in the case of banks);
- Underwriting banks' contingent liability (backup line);
- A group of underwriting banks, whose obligation consists of purchasing any of the above-mentioned unsold short-term notes at previously arranged rates or, alternatively, who provide funds through separate lending arrangements that offer the issuer the certainty that the requested amount will be available. The instruments that RUFs most closely resemble are floating-rate notes and syndicated loans. An RUF, however, includes the special feature of staggered maturities. (Issued in bearer form.)

Transferable Revolving Underwriting Facility (TRUF)

Similar to an RUF, but the underwriting banks' contingent liability (backup line) to purchase notes in the event of nonplacement by the borrower is fully transferable.

Note Issuance Facility (NIF)

Another name for an RUF.

Grantor Underwriting Notes (GUNs)

A floating-rate note facility is similar to an RUF in that a group of banks (grantors) undertake to purchase any notes put back to them by investors on any FRN interest rate fixing date. Put notes are then auctioned out to the market by the grantors.

Banker's Acceptance (B/A)

Bill of exchange accepted by large American banks. B/As bear interest for three to six months. B/As constitute an irrevocable primary obligation of the drawer and of any endorsers whose names appear on them. The minimum amount accepted is $10,000. B/As primarily serve to finance imports and exports. (Bearer or registered in book-entry form.)

London Eurodollar Banker's Acceptance (LEBA)

A short-term, negotiable, bearer money market instrument in the form of a "bill of exchange" drawn by a company on a prime bank and accepted by the bank. LEBAs are generally issued with maturities of three or six months, in either interest-bearing or discount-to-yield form. The rate of interest on a LEBA is usually set at a margin below the three- to six-month LIBOR rate to approximate a rate close to the three- or six-month prime bank CD rate. The interest is calculated on the basis of the actual days over a 360-day year. After a LEBA is accepted by the bank on which it is drawn, it becomes a primary obligation of that bank.

Euro Commercial Paper (ECP)

Euro Commercial Paper is an unsecured general obligation in the form of a promissory bearer note, issued on a discount or interest-bearing basis by large commercial and industrial organizations. Maturities of ECP range from a few days up to one year, with most being 182 days; the minimum amount is usually $500,000. ECP provides a flexible alternative to short-term finance credit lines with commercial banks, and the rate for prime issuers is usually set at a small margin above that offered by prime bank money market securities of comparable maturities.

Treasury Bill (T-bill)

Government obligation, issued for periods of three to 12 months. T-bills are traded on a discount basis. They are the most liquid form of short-term investment. (In book-entry form only.)

Municipal Note

Municipal notes are interest-bearing securities issued by state and local governments as interim financing for a period usually less than one year. (Registered; may be held in global or book-entry form.)

Appendix VII: International Securities Identification Number (ISIN) Code System

One initial point of contact for compilers could be the national numbering agency (NNA). As explained in Chapter 4, Section III, NNAs allocate a unique identifier to each security. In addition, they are linked into the Association of National Numbering Agencies' (ANNA's) Global ISIN Access Mechanism (GIAM) network. This allows them to make enquiries concerning any security worldwide that has an ISIN number, regardless of which NNA allocated the number.

Box A7.1 provides a list of NNAs. The ANNA Web site (http://www.anna-nna.com) contains the official directory of members and Internet links to NNA sites.

Background

In 1989 the Group of Thirty[1] recommended the adoption of ISIN codes as the international standard for the identification of securities. Although ISINs had been in existence since 1981, there is little evidence of their use before 1989. In 1990 ANNA was formed with the primary objective of maintaining and implementing the international standard. The International Standards Organization (ISO) designated ANNA as the registration authority to coordinate all aspects of the implementation of the ISIN numbering system.

In 1994, at the initiative of ANNA, GIAM (the Global ISIN Access Mechanism) was developed to link NNAs and GIAM participants electronically, allowing them to pass ISIN information to each other.

In 1995, ISO designated ANNA as maintenance agency and registration authority of the ISO 10962 (Classification of Financial Instruments [CFI]).

[1] A private sector group based in Washington, D.C., that reports on issues pertaining to the securities markets.

In the past several years, ANNA has been working out a new strategy to guarantee the full implementation of ISIN and CFI codes and the swift and general availability of the codes to users. The global financial industry has been rapidly moving toward the automated processing of securities transactions (Straight-Through Processing), and the ability to precisely identify the securities has become essential. In this context, ANNA has developed a new network for the exchange of information among participant members, called GIAM-2, based on the combination of CD-ROM and Internet technologies.

ISIN Codes

The standard provides a uniform structure for the ISIN, a number that uniquely identifies securities. It details NNAs that are responsible for issuing the ISIN in each country. In those countries where no NNA is in operation, three NNAs have agreed to act as a substitute agency on a regional basis.

ISINs consist of a total of 12 characters, as follows:

- The first two characters are the alpha-2 country code as issued in accordance with the international standard ISO 3166 of the country where the issuer of equity securities is legally registered or in which it has legal domicile. For debt securities, the first two digits represent the country of the lead underwriter of the security. In the case of depository receipts, such as American depository receipts (ADRs), the country code is that of the organization that issued the receipt instead of the one that issued the underlying security.
- The next nine characters are the local number of the security concerned. Where the national number consists of fewer than nine characters, zeros are inserted in front of the number so that the full nine spaces are used.
- The final character is a check digit computed according to the modulus 10 "Double-Add-Double" formula.

Box A7.1: National Numbering Agencies

Country	Numbering Agency
Argentina	Caja de Valores S.A.
Austria	Oesterreichische Kontrollbank AG
Australia	Australian Stock Exchange
Belgium	C.I.K.—Secretariat des Valeurs Mobilieres
Brazil	Bolsa de Valores de Sao Paulo
Bulgaria	Bulgarian National Bank
Canada	Canadian Depository for Securities Ltd.
Costa Rica	Central de Valores—Ceval
Croatia	Central Depository Agency, Inc.
Cyprus	Cyprus Stock Exchange
Czech Republic	Securities Commission
Denmark	Vaerdipapircentralen
Egypt	Capital Market Authority
Estonia	Estonian Central Depository For Securities
Finland	Finnish Central Securities Depository Ltd.
France	Sicovam S.A.
Germany	Wertpapier-Mitteilungen
Greece	Central Securities Depository S.A.
Hong Kong SAR	The Stock Exchange of Hong Kong Ltd.
Hungary	Central Clearing House and Depository (Budapest) Ltd.
Indonesia	Indonesian Central Securities Depository
India	Securities and Exchange Board of India
International	Euroclear Operations Centre
Iran, Islamic Republic of	Tehran Stock Exchange Services Company
Ireland	Irish Stock Exchange
Israel	Tel Aviv Stock Exchange
Italy	Ufficio Italiano dei Cambi
Japan	Tokyo Stock Exchange
Korea, Republic of	Korea Stock Exchange
Latvia	Latvian Central Depository
Luxembourg	Cedel Bank
Malaysia	Kuala Lumpur Stock Exchange
Mexico	S.D. Indeval, S.A. de C.V.
Netherlands	Aex—Clearing and Depository N.V.
Norway	Verdipapirsentralen
Pakistan	Central Depository Co. of Pakistan Ltd.
Panama, Republic of	Bolsa de Valores de Panama
Peru	Bolsa de Valores de Lima
Philippines	Philippine Stock Exchange, Inc.
Poland	National Depository for Securities
Portugal	Interbolsa
Romania	National Securities Clearing Settlement Depository Corporation
Russia	National Depository Center
Singapore	Stock Exchange of Singapore Ltd.
Slovakia	Stredisko Cennych Papierov, A.S.
Slovenia	Central Securities Clearing Corporation
South Africa	Johannesburg Stock Exchange
Spain	Comision Nacional del Mercado de Valores
Sri Lanka	Colombo Stock Exchange
Sweden	Vardepapperscentralen—VPC
Switzerland	Telekurs Financial Information Ltd.
Taiwan Province of China	Taiwan Stock Exchange Corporation
Thailand	Thailand Securities Depository Co., Ltd.
Tunisia	Sticodevam
Turkey	Takasbank
Ukraine	National Depository of Ukraine
United Kingdom	London Stock Exchange
United States	Cusip Service Bureau
Venezuela, Bol. Rep. de	Bolsa de Valores de Caracas, C.A
Yugoslavia, Fed. Rep. of	Federal Commission for Securities and Financial Market

In the case of securities (other than debt securities, where an NNA recognized by ANNA operates), this organization issues the ISINs for securities whose issuer is registered or domiciled in the country where the NNA operates. For debt securities, the NNA that issues the ISIN is either one of the international securities clearing organizations or the responsible NNA in accordance with ISO 6166. In the case of those countries where no NNA exists, a substitute agency allocates the number.

The standard ISO 6166 describes the structure of the ISIN codes and which organizations are allowed to allocate ISIN codes to which securities. The aim of the guidelines is to obtain a uniform process among the various NNAs for the allocation of ISIN codes.

CFI Code

The CFI code has been developed to address a number of problems that have concerned the financial community for the past several years. The following problems, among others, have affected the financial community:

- lack of consistent and uniform approach to grouping financial instruments,
- use of similar terminology for instruments having significantly different features in the different countries, and
- inability to group securities in a consistent manner, which leads to reports of holdings being categorized differently.

The benefits of the new code include the following:

- definition and description for an internationally valid system to classify financial instruments,
- provision of a set of codes to be used by all market participants in an electronic data-processing environment and easier electronic communication among participants, and
- improved understanding of the characteristics of financial instruments will lead to a better understanding by investors.

The CFI reflects characteristics that are defined when a financial instrument is issued and that remain unchanged during its lifetime. The CFI consists of six alphabetical characters.

The **first** character indicates the highest level of classification (category).

Categories:
Equities (E)
Debt instruments (D)
Entitlements (Rights) (R)
Options (O)
Futures (F)
Others/Miscellaneous (M)

The **second** character indicates specific groups within each category.

Groups (e.g., for equities):
Shares
Preferred shares
Convertible preferred shares
Units, for example, unit trusts/mutual funds
Others

The **third** to **sixth** character indicate the most important attributes to each group.

Attributes (e.g., for equities):
Voting right
Ownership/transfer restrictions
Payment status
Form

Global ISIN Access Mechanism (GIAM) Network

NNAs allocate ISIN codes in accordance with ISO 6166 and on behalf of their customers for the securities that those customers issue. In addition to the fundamental process of allocating numbers, the NNA's role also includes ensuring that the ISINs for those securities are published, disseminated, and used as widely as possible throughout the world.

The NNA may also provide information services to its own organizations and to its customers relating to ISINs issued by other Numbering Agencies in other countries. Therefore, NNAs have a basic need for agreed standards for defining and exchanging ISIN information among themselves and a networking vehicle to carry that information. GIAM was conceived by ANNA members in the early 1990s to help meet those needs.

The primary objective of the GIAM Project is to support NNAs by providing a networking vehicle to aid communication among the numbering agency members of ANNA and other authorized organizations in the securities industry. The aim is to achieve rapid dissemination of ISIN information and to provide standardized methods for entering, exchanging, and querying ISIN information.

GIAM-1

GIAM-1 started operation in 1994 but was superseded by GIAM-2 and was terminated in July 1999. The defined ISIN record and batch layouts originally established for GIAM-1 have been continued in GIAM-2.

GIAM-2

GIAM-2 is operational and has its own search engine to facilitate locating ISIN records registered in its own "ISIN keyword dictionary." It uses the Internet as its basic communications vehicle for distributing ISIN records among GIAM participants, but it is also available on CD-ROM. ISIN data relating to more than 500,000 ISIN records from 48 NNAs are now included in the GIAM search engine.